W0079674

Markt- und Unternehmensentwicklung
Markets and Organisations

Series Editors
Arnold Picot, München, Germany
Ralf Reichwald, Leipzig, Germany
Egon Franck, Zürich, Switzerland
Kathrin M. Möslein, Erlangen-Nürnberg, Germany

Change of institutions, technology and competition drives the interplay of markets and organisations. The scientific series 'Markets and Organisations' addresses a magnitude of related questions, presents theoretic and empirical findings and discusses related concepts and models.

Professor Dr. Dres. h. c. Arnold Picot
Ludwig-Maximilians-Universität
München, Germany

Professor Dr. Egon Franck
Universität Zürich, Switzerland

Professor Dr. Professor h. c. Dr. h. c.
Ralf Reichwald
HHL Leipzig Graduate School of
Management, Leipzig, Germany

Professorin Dr. Kathrin M. Möslein
Friedrich-Alexander-Universität
Erlangen-Nürnberg & HHL
Leipzig, Germany

More information about this series at http://www.springer.com/series/12561

Stefan Michael Genennig

Realizing Digitization-Enabled Innovation

A Service Systems Perspective for Management

With a foreword by Prof. Dr. Kathrin M. Möslein

Springer Gabler

Stefan Michael Genennig
Nürnberg, Germany

Dissertation Friedrich-Alexander-Universität Erlangen-Nürnberg/2019

Markt- und Unternehmensentwicklung Markets and Organisations
ISBN 978-3-658-28718-4   ISBN 978-3-658-28719-1   (eBook)
https://doi.org/10.1007/978-3-658-28719-1

This Springer Gabler imprint is published by the registered company Springer Fachmedien Wiesbaden GmbH part of Springer Nature.
The registered company address is: Abraham-Lincoln-Str. 46, 65189 Wiesbaden, Germany

Foreword

Digitization, and in particular the use of digital technologies, is an enabler of innovation in organizations. However, many organizations, and especially SMEs, are faced with the question of how to integrate new digital technologies into their offerings and how to realize innovation based on digitization. Enabling and realizing innovation based on digitization is still a challenge, not only for practitioners. There is also a lack of a deeper understanding and of pragmatic, but well-founded tools and methods for application in business practice.

Stefan Michael Genennig addresses this challenge. He sets the focus on digitization-enabled innovation as a complex and interdisciplinary effort in organizations and chooses a service systems perspective in order to derive valuable knowledge for managers in business organizations, especially SMEs.

The research at hand, thus, brings a fresh perspective on managing the integration of digital technology with a focus on innovation. Digitization-enabled innovation is analyzed, a method for a parallelized and integrated approach of technology management and service innovation is developed and a tool for the design of digitization-enabled value propositions is designed. In addition, first applications of the artefacts showcase examples of digitization in SMEs. The book invites the reader to stepwise explore four core topics:

- the digitization in MDAX-listed organizations and their service systems,
- the role of human agents as decision-makers in the integration of digital technologies in service systems,
- the integration of digital technologies in service systems, and
- the development of digitization-enabled value propositions for service systems.

The work appeals by its theoretical reach and empirical scope, the fresh methodological approach and the didactic approach by which the findings are presented. The developed artifacts are ready for use and offer immediate support in the realization of digitization-enabled innovation for organizations. It has been accepted as doctoral dissertation in 2019 by the School of Business, Economics and Society at the Friedrich-Alexander University Erlangen-Nürnberg (FAU). The book deserves broad dissemination both in the research community and in management practice. It is a must read for those with a deep interest in the realization of digitization-enabled innovation. They will enjoy the fresh perspective that the service systems approach brings to the field.

Prof. Dr. Kathrin M. Möslein

Preface

This book will help you understand the tremendous power of digitization in innovation. To draw a full picture of the current state and to respond to present challenges and opportunities, the research behind this book has always been geared towards a close exchange with companies and practitioners and a symbiosis of research and practice. This book is meant to both enrich service research on digitization-enabled innovation and help companies overcome existing challenges on the way to such innovation.

But before that, I would like to thank to all the people who have been at my side over the last three and a half years and made this book possible. Prof. Dr. Kathrin M. Möslein offered support, optimism and trust in me and consistently helped my research reach new levels through her inspiration and advice. The same applies to Prof. Dr. Angela Roth, who I would like to thank for the many small feedback loops and for secondary supervision.

Second, my parents and family were at least as decisive on this path. Just like in all the previous chapters of my life, they have unconditionally supported me during this project and had no doubts about its successful completion. Furthermore, over the years, Lisa has always stood by my side and assisted me with everything she has.

Third, I would like to express my thanks to my colleagues and friends at the chair of information systems, innovation & value creation. Through their backing, I was able to gain a lot of experience and develop my research freely. Sharing an office with Martin, Max, Natalie and Sascha made the start easy, kept the motivation high along the way and gave me stamina for the final spurt. Thanks to Julia for inspiration and support.

Finally, I would like to thank all the members and supporters of the "BigDieMo" and "SmartDiF" research projects. This book was only possible because of the close exchange of knowledge and insights with other researchers and practitioners.

Overview of Contents

References 123

Table of Contents

List of Figures

List of Tables

List of Abbreviations

A2A	Actor-to-Actor
DIGITALISS	Method for Digitization-Enabled Innovation in Service Systems
DSR	Design Science Research
ICT	Information and Communication Technology
IoT	Internet of Things
IT	Information Technology
IS	Information Systems
NSD	New Service Development
NSF	National Science Foundation
SaaS	Software-as-a-Service
SDL	Service-Dominant Logic
TM	Technology Management
$V^{di}P$	Digitization-Enabled Value Proposition

Part I

Introduction:

Research Objective

1   Research Motivation and Relevance

"Digitization — i.e. the networking of people and things and the convergence of the real and virtual worlds that is enabled by information and communication technology (ICT) — will be the most powerful driver of innovation over the next few decades" (Kagermann, 2015, p. 24).

Digitization offers enormous potential for companies and the economy in general, as this quote reveals. However, the use of this potential seems to be unevenly distributed. According to a recent Bitkom study[1], 74 percent of companies with 2000 or more employees see themselves as digital pioneers, whereas only 35 percent of small and medium-sized enterprises (SMEs) in Germany have this perception. This again reinforces an earlier study which examined the concrete form of digitization among SMEs and found that "only one fifth of medium-sized companies have started integration of digital products and services and can thus be counted as pioneers" (Saam, Viet, & Schiel, 2016). However, the difference between large and smaller enterprises is not due to different assessments of digitization. According to a recent Ernst & Young study[2], 74 percent of the SMEs surveyed see digitization as an opportunity, 60 percent of them even see an impact on their current business model. These current study results therefore suggest that SMEs are on the one hand currently undergoing a digital transformation process and will therefore have to make pivotal decisions for the future, and on the other hand that their characteristics often prevent

---

[1] Bitkom is Germany's digital association. Founded 1999 in Berlin through a merger of various industry associations, it represents more than 2,600 companies of the digital economy. It includes more than 1000 SMEs, over 400 startups and virtually all global players (https://www.bitkom.org). For the study Bitkom Research 2018 surveyed 604 companies. Received from:
https://www.bitkom.org/Presse/Presseinformation/Deutsche-Wirtschaft-kommt-bei-Digitalisierung-voran-aber-langsam.html

[2] For the study commissioned by Ernst & Young, 2,000 medium-sized companies in Germany were interviewed by telephone in November/December 2017 by an independent market research institute (Valid Research, Bielefeld). Received from: https://www.ey.com/Publication/vwLUAssets/ey-digitalisierung-im-deutschen-mittelstand-maerz-2018/$FILE/ey-digitalisierung-im-deutschen-mittelstand-maerz-2018.pdf

them from playing a pioneering role in digitization. The alterations brought about by digitization appear to be complex and companies need support on the way to new digitization-enabled value increase. In this sense the digitization brings both, new opportunities and challenges to companies, in particular SMEs, from which they cannot elude (Roth, Höckmayr, & Möslein, 2017). On the one hand, the use of new digital technologies promises additional revenues via new value propositions and forces the innovation of services and business models (Velu & Jacob, 2016). On the other hand, companies face novel needs for adoption through altering technologies and consequential altered value constellations (Kagermann, 2015; Kieliszewski, Maglio, & Cefkin, 2012; Oesterreich & Teuteberg, 2016).

The advancements of information and communication technology (ICT) and thus the progressive digitization of all parts of the value chain is therefore changing the business environment. But in addition to technologies, services have also gained enormous importance. Ever since Vargo and Lusch's (2004) explanations of a service-dominant logic (SDL) and since the efforts to establish an independent service science (Maglio & Spohrer, 2008; Spohrer & Maglio, 2008), the increase in significance has also arrived in research. According to the SDL, services constitute the core of all value creation (Akaka & Vargo, 2014) and goods are only equipment (tools, distribution mechanisms) that serve as an alternative to direct service provision, since service is the general and universal case of exchange (Lusch & Nambisan, 2015). This view of the service-based creation of value is also anchored in service science. The two developments, digitization and the orientation towards services, cannot be viewed in isolation from each other. Both are changing innovation in companies and digitization is acting as an enabler of innovation in the service sector (Roth et al., 2017). The service science takes this up and integrates other fields of research into service research (Spohrer, Maglio, Bailey, & Gruhl, 2007) to solve problems and exploit opportunities to create service innovations in this context (Maglio, Srinivasan, Kreulen, & Spohrer, 2006).

The increasing importance of both reinforced the awareness for digitization-enabled and service-oriented innovation (Akaka & Vargo 2014) and expanded the use of digital technologies in service development and execution (Barrett et al., 2015; Ostrom et al.,

2010). In *management*, approaches to dealing with the changes brought about by digitalization and the increasing service orientation are often characterized by a process mindset. This is depicted, for example, in general business process management which also deals in one of its aspects with the management of technology (Rosemann & vom Brocke, 2015), but can also be found in a more specific nature in a process-oriented approach to technology introduction in technology management (Cetindamar, Phaal, & Probert, 2016). And even though Eberhard Witte had already critically questioned whether a fixed phase scheme for innovation processes was suitable in his discussion on the falsification of the phase theorem in 1968 (Witte, 1968), innovation practices are also frequently mapped in process structures. Despite his critical appraisal of detailed process models in advance, this can also be exemplary seen in the six phase innovation process of Hauschildt (2004). Moreover, service research in some literature streams is also oriented towards process models for service innovation (Grove & Fisk, 1992; Skaalsvik & Johannessen, 2014).

The process models – and associated management methods and tools derived from them – often have a technology focus and a firm-specific perspective when it comes to digitization and innovation (Breidbach & Maglio, 2016; Makarem, Mudambi, & Podoshen, 2009). Integrating views of technology and service innovation which not only include the technical components but also the human actors in innovation are barely served. *Service science* meets this with a sociotechnical perspective and helps to study both, the technical alterations and the human agents (with knowledge and skills) in innovation (Böhmann, Leimeister, & Möslein, 2014; Breidbach, Kolb, & Srinivasan, 2013; Breidbach & Maglio, 2016; Breidbach, Smith, & Callagher, 2013). By its interdisciplinary approach, aspects of digitization were already depicted in service science at an early stage and continue to be an element of current service research (Breidbach & Maglio, 2015; Coreynen, Matthyssens, & Van Bockhaven, 2017; Daim, Jetter, Demirkan, & Maglio, 2010; Kocaoglu, Daim, & Jetter, 2008; Roth & Möslein, 2014).

In this sense, one aspect of service science is therefore the investigation of alterations within service innovation and delivery, for example triggered by digitization (Chang, 2010; Maglio & Spohrer, 2008). Services have shifted from a single company to systems for service offerings. These service systems are seen as configurations of actors (entities and stakeholders), technology, information (knowledge and skills), and other internal and external service systems (Maglio, Vargo, Caswell, & Spohrer, 2009; Spohrer et al., 2007; Spohrer, Vargo, Caswell, & Maglio, 2008). This requires also dispensing with the distinction between a producer (as a creator of value) and a consumer (as a receiver and destroyer of value) and adopting an actor-to-actor (A2A) perspective (Barrett et al., 2015; Vargo & Lusch, 2011). The service systems evolve, interact and reconfigure to (co-)create value and ultimately aim to enhance service innovation (Kieliszewski et al., 2012; Maglio and Spohrer, 2008). Value is created in service systems when its entities and stakeholders work together to improve common capabilities or act in specific situations or environments in a mutually beneficial way (Vargo et al., 2008). With this view many things can be viewed as service systems, "for example, people, corporations, foundations, non-governmental organizations, non-profits, government agencies, departments in an organization, cities, nations, and even families" (Maglio et al., 2009, p. 396). The boundaries of the service systems are defined by their resources and the respective value (co-)creation (Essén, 2009; Lyons & Tracy, 2013; Spohrer et al., 2008). Service systems offer an analytical perspective for an investigation range from individual actors to organizations integrated in complex value creation networks, which makes them also the basic abstraction of service science (Maglio et al., 2009).

The digitization, as the use of digital technology, can serve as enabler, promoter and improver of service systems (Fritzsche, Jonas, & Roth, 2018; Vargo & Lusch, 2017). But as digitization brings major changes through the orchestration of the mix of technology, actors and information, it complicates the service systems design and service innovation (Grenha Teixeira et al., 2017; Höckmayr & Roth, 2017). This also leads to new challenges in the management of the underlying approaches as both the service systems and the digital technologies have to be reconciled for the purpose of innovation (Daim et al., 2010; Kocaoglu et al., 2008). Simultaneously, the new technologies offer opportunities and can help service systems at the emergence of digitization-enabled innovation (Barrett, Davidson, Fayard, Vargo, & Yoo, 2012; Demirkan et al., 2015; Nambisan, 2013). Consequently, service science has already come up with the first replies to the digitalization and the increasing importance of service and can therefore inspire and enrich the management-oriented literature and the often still predominant process view in companies with new perspectives and adapt them to the changes made possible by digitalization. The integration of the service systems perspective and management approaches therefore offers promising avenues (Kocaoglu et al., 2008), but research is suffering from the "absence of a deep understanding of major concepts" and a "lack of frameworks and methods" to advance the integration of management and service science (Daim et al., 2010, p. 15). Small and medium-sized enterprises (SMEs) would benefit from these methods and tools because of challenges regarding resource accessibility, affordability and competence of technology adoption. The gap between SMEs and big players described at the beginning of this chapter increases, as small companies often have no experience with integrating new digital technologies and generally tend to act risk averse (Falkner & Hiebl, 2015; Kowalkowski, Witell, & Gustafsson, 2013; Radziwon & Bogers, 2018). Research activities in this direction will, through support and guidance, provide SMEs with an opportunity to use digitization for their own purposes and for structured digitization-enabled innovation activities in service systems.

However, in order to enrich management approaches with a service systems perspective, a number of research paths should be taken. Especially in the context of service innovation, the building and management of service systems remain a prevailing research topic (Benkenstein et al., 2017) and there are various tracks for future research. As Böhmann et al. (2014) outline, evidence-based knowledge on real-world service systems is still non-existent. Current literature lacks a general understanding of value creation and innovation in service systems (Ostrom et al., 2015). A predominant question for service systems in this context is how technology influences the ways in which value can be created (Vargo et al., 2008) and innovation is enabled (Breidbach & Maglio, 2016). Frost and Lyons (2017) have identified research directions that should inspire research on service systems. On the one hand, they recommend to focus more on the roles of service systems components and the effects of their interactions, on the other hand they also emphasize research to generate a better understanding of the role of innovation in service systems (Frost & Lyons, 2017).

By taking a service systems perspective in the management of digitization-enabled innovation, this research aims to alter the rigid management process structures and infuses an even stronger service and sociotechnical system perspective in digitization-enabled innovation. To this end, it continues the interdisciplinary approach of service science and brings together management-oriented and service research. It uses the theoretical perspective of service systems and therefore makes use of the abstraction of service science. This research thus operationalizes the service systems perspective for the purpose of realizing digitization-enabled innovation. At the same time, it aims to support management and its established processes in the targeted use of the digitization for the purposes of the respective company and thus serves a need that has been identified in practice. To this end, this research explores the following question:

How can organizations manage the use of new digital technologies for digitization-enabled innovation in service systems?

Four sub-research questions are formulated in order to explore this research subject comprehensively and rich in perspectives. For this purpose, a two-stage approach is carried out, which first looks at the status quo of digitization with a service systems perspective and resulting digitization-enabled alterations and explores the underlying drivers and challenges within service systems. Subsequently, a design-oriented approach for the development of management methods and the design of management tools with a service systems perspective is applied. Each of the two stages is examined by two studies, resulting in a total of four sub-research questions. The first study puts a service systems perspective on organizations and takes an external look at the alterations in these service systems brought about by digitization. It show how these lead to a reconfiguration of the service systems and to new value propositions:

Research question 1: What is the current state of digitization-enabled alterations in service systems and what are the expressions of the innovation enabling characteristics of digitization in this context?

In the following, the drivers and challenges of integrating a digital technology within service systems are investigated:

Research question 2: Which factors drive and challenge human agents in the integration of new digital technologies in service systems?

Subsequently, a method to support management in the integration of digital technologies in service systems and to transform the concomitant innovation in value increase and service innovation is developed:

Research question 3: How does a structured method for supporting the management of digital technology for the purpose of service innovation in service systems look like?

Finally, a way to develop digitization-enabled value propositions is designed and evaluated:

Research question 4: How can digitization-enabled value propositions in service systems be systematically developed?

The method and the tool are based on the first two studies and use their findings for inspiration, orientation and foundation, i.e. the exploration of digitization-enabled innovation in service systems and the factors driving and challenging the integration of digital technologies in service systems. Altogether, a management approach to guide the process of digitization-enabled innovation is developed under the consideration and with the integration of a service systems perspective. Figure 1 gives an overview of the research questions in this research.

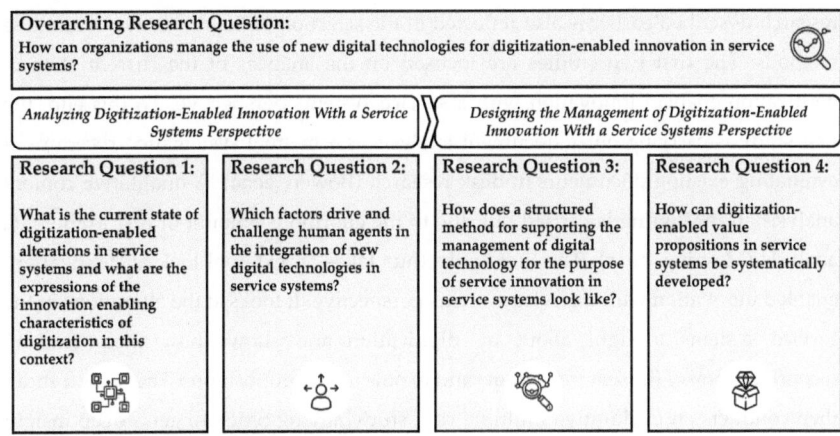

Figure 1: The research questions of this research

2   Research Design

Different approaches to qualitative research are used in this research to explore the overarching research question and the four research questions arranged below it. The general research goal is the examination of how organizations can manage the use of new digital technologies for digitization-enabled innovation in service systems. The nature of a how question requires the use of rich-data and prefers words rather than numbers what makes qualitative research methods, for example interviews, the preferred choice for data generation and analysis (Bryman, 2012). Miles and Huberman (1994) describe the advantages of qualitative methods as the "focus on naturally occurring, ordinary events in natural settings, so that we have a strong handle on what 'real life' is like" (p. 10). Furthermore, the authors argue that the fact that such data are typically collected over a sustained period makes them powerful for studying any process and assess causality as it actually plays out in a particular setting (Miles & Huberman, 1994).

In order to look at the research question with a methodological diversity, four different forms of qualitative research methods are applied, each expected the most suitable for the respective research sub-question. The two-stage approach in this research described earlier is also reflected in the selection of the respective qualitative methods. The first two studies are focused on the analysis of the current state of digitization-enabled innovation with a service systems perspective. To this end, the first study is carrying out a document analysis as a manual systematic procedure of evaluating existing documents in desk research (Bowen, 2009). A qualitative content analysis after Mayring is carried out due to the enormous amount of text in the data analysis (Mayring, 2015). The first study thus takes an external look at digitization-enabled innovation with a service systems perspective. It looks at the alterations in the service systems brought about by digitization and shows how these lead to reconfiguration of the service systems and to new value propositions. The second study then conducts an explorative multiple case study among SMEs to get a deep insight into digitization-enabled innovation at first hand (Miles, Huberman, & Saldaña, 2013;

Yin, 2018). With interviews and group discussions in each case of the multiple case study (Bryman, 2012), study 2 centers on the human agents in the digitization-enabled innovation. The drivers and challenges of integrating a digital technology are examined with a service systems perspective and get investigated with qualitative data analysis (Miles et al., 2013).

In the second step with the studies 3 and 4, a design-oriented approach is chosen which aims to develop and design methods and tools that include a service systems perspective. In this course artefacts are created following the understanding of Peffers et al. (2007), according to which "artefacts may include constructs, models, methods, and instantiations. They might also include social innovations or new properties of technical, social, and/or informational resources; in short, this definition includes any designed object with an embedded solution to an understood research problem" (p. 49). For the method development in study 3, an explorative holistic multiple case study is used under the research approach of systematic combining of theory and empirical reasoning (Dubois & Gadde, 2002; Miles et al., 2013). Four cases are examined in different contexts and get used for method development and refinement (Yin, 2009). The developed method aims then to support management in digitization-enabled innovation and to integrate technology management and service innovation. Study 4 is using a field-based Design Science Research approach with qualitative iterations to design a tool which is composed of existing and empirically derived new elements (Peffers, Tuunanen, Rothenberger, & Chatterjee, 2007). A physical and digital tool to support management in the development of digitization-enabled value propositions is designed.

Figure 2 illustrates the empirical part of this research with the two steps as consecutive blocks and organizes the four qualitative studies into the overall research. These are placed on a theoretical foundation by the introduction and the research context and are finally summarized and concluded by synthesis and implications.

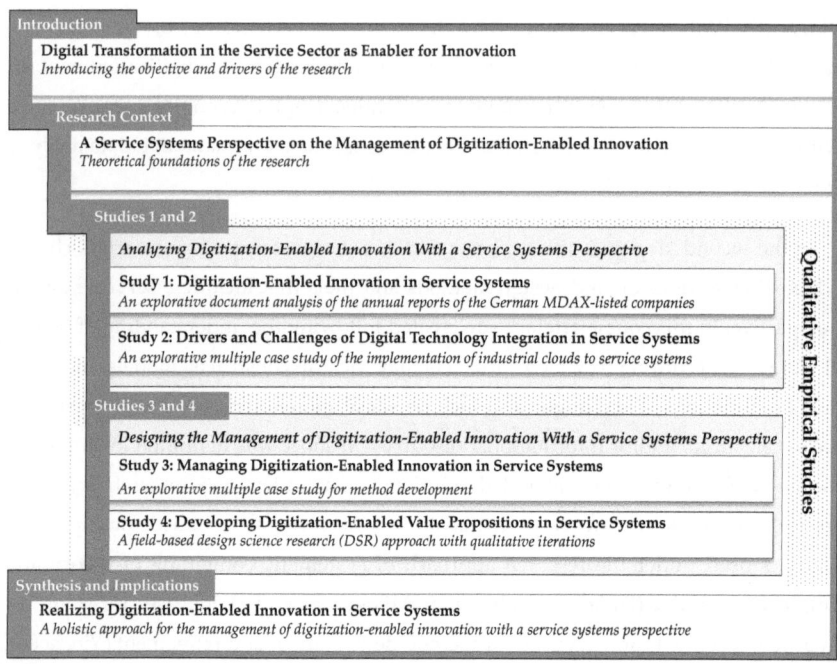

Figure 2: Design of the research

3   Structure of the Research Project

The service systems perspective is chosen to analyze digitization-enabled innovation in this research and is used to advance methods and tools for digitization-enabled innovation. The studies are therefore oriented towards the core elements of service systems: technology, actors and information, as well as the value propositions that form the service systems and define their boundaries (Maglio & Spohrer, 2008; Maglio et al., 2009). The different parts of this research are located around and within the service systems core elements to analyze the digitization-enabled alterations on and in service systems and to integrate the service systems perspective in management methods and tools by design-oriented research.

Part II initially provides the theoretical foundation for the research project. The part forms the structure for the following studies and covers service systems and their location in the research landscape. Part II also deals with innovation within service systems. Thus, a comprehensive state of research on the research fields contained in this research is given.

The following Part III then analyzes digitization-enabled innovation with a service systems perspective and outlines the changes that occur in the service systems core elements and the value propositions enabled by them. It will be shown how digitization influences the reconfiguration process between the service systems' core elements and how digitization-enabled value propositions result from it. This part of the research aims to explore the concrete changes within the core elements and the value proposition.

Part IV also deals with digitization-enabled alterations and examines the drivers and challenges for change in service systems. In particular, the drivers behind the integration of a digital technology and the challenges involved in its integration are identified. The aim of Part IV is to explore the motives of management to integrate a new digital technology and the respective challenges that arise in the integration. These drivers and challenges are then assigned to the service systems' core elements.

Part V then focuses on the processes of digitization-enabled innovation and in particular on the reconfiguration process of service systems and the resulting innovations. The part aims at managing the reconfiguration process of service systems in a target-oriented and structured way and to map this in a management method. It thus aims to integrate the service systems perspective into management. To this end, Part V develops and applies a management method which parallelizes technology management and service innovation for innovation in service systems in an integrating way.

Part VI continues to deal with processes of digitization-enabled innovation. Using the service systems perspective, this part focuses in particular on value propositions as the common alignment of each service system and the basis for its boundaries. In the context of digitization-enabled innovation and the changes elaborated in the previous parts, a tool for the development of new and adapted digitization-enabled value propositions is designed. Part VI thus aims at management support in this process.

The concluding Part VII presents the results of the individual studies in the overall context of the research activities in the field of digitization-enabled innovation and a service systems perspective on it and its management in a comprehensive discussion. It also outlines the limitations of the research and points out avenues for future research.

Figure 3 presents the overall research approach. The three core elements of a service system - technology, actors and information - are arranged exemplarily as a triangle in the middle of the figure. The following six parts of this research are arranged around these elements and the value proposition of the service system to illustrate their approach to service systems. Part II (Research Context) and Part VII (Synthesis and Implications) lay the foundation stone and conclude the research comprehensively. They are illustrated in the figure as upstream and downstream part.

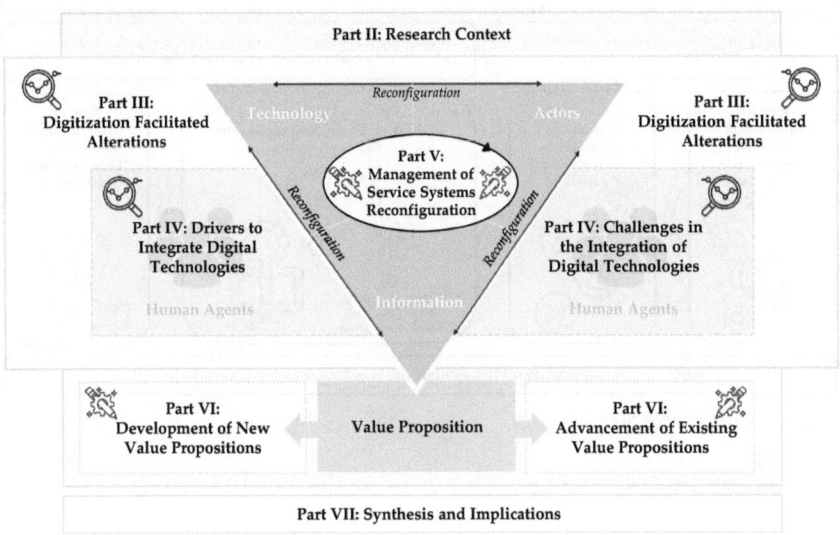

Figure 3: The overall research approach

After Figure 3 shows the overall research approach of this research in detail, the following figure (Figure 4) now breaks down the research approach and provides a clean overview of the structure of this research and helps with the classification of the respective parts´ contents and the orientation later on. It also shows the already elaborated two-step approach, which first focuses on the analysis and then on the design of digitization-enabled innovation with a service systems perspective. The first two studies (Part III and Part IV) deal mainly with the analysis of digitization-enabled innovation with a service systems perspective. Study 3 and 4 (Part V and Part VI) then focus on design-oriented research for managing the digitization for innovation and service innovation in service systems and take up the results of the analysis in order to transfer them into methodical procedures and application tools. In the following, this overview graphic is used to locate the respective chapters at the beginning of each part.

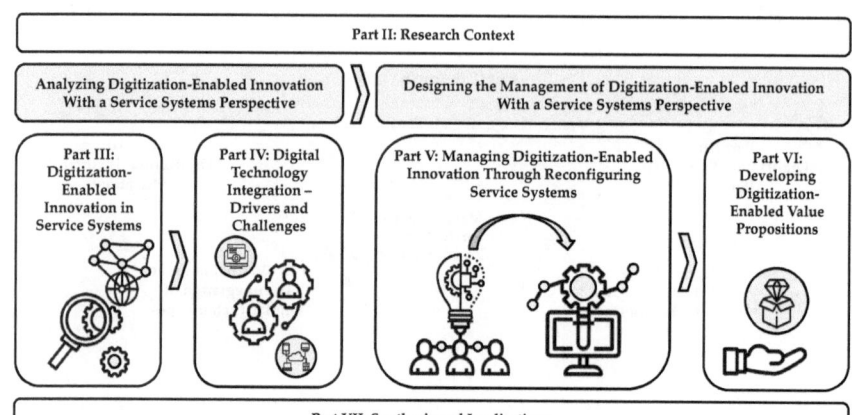

Figure 4: Structure of the research

Part II

Research Context:

Foundations of the Research

© Springer Fachmedien Wiesbaden GmbH, part of Springer Nature 2020
S. M. Genennig, *Realizing Digitization-Enabled Innovation*, Markt- und
Unternehmensentwicklung Markets and Organisations,
https://doi.org/10.1007/978-3-658-28719-1_2

1 Introducing Words About the Research Context

A study[3] on digitization in medium-sized companies has shown that the vast majority of the companies interviewed do not carry out digitization projects alone but in development networks. The network partners include spin-offs, external service providers (especially software companies), start-ups, consultants, research institutions, competitors or companies offering complementary products, and customers. Multiple companies are part of a complex development network (Saam et al., 2016). In order to respond to the challenges associated with digitization, many companies are no longer acting alone but are forming networks and participating in alliances to build up technical know-how and to systematically develop and implement offers.

This change in mindset can also be observed in the service sector (Chesbrough & Spohrer, 2006). Digitization has made the business environment more multifaceted and global and is forcing service providers to construct networks of partners and contractors to fulfill the service obligations as promised by its value propositions (Kwan & Hottum, 2014). Service recipients are also intensively involved in the systematic provision of services and in some cases even in their innovation (Jonas, Roth, & Möslein, 2016). Driven by the general increased importance of services already described above (Part I) and by the alterations in service through the digitization and the creation of service in systems, service research has also developed further. With service science, a new discipline has emerged in service research that uses interdisciplinary and system-oriented approaches to find solutions to the challenges of current developments in service (Spohrer & Maglio, 2008). For example, service science forces the interdisciplinary nature of service research and sheds light on the challenge of becoming more systematic about innovating in service (Lusch, Vargo, & Gustafsson, 2016; Sampson & Froehle, 2009; Spohrer et al., 2007). To this end, it uses the abstraction

---

[3] Conducted by the Zentrum für Europäische Wirtschaftsforschung GmbH as a research project on behalf of KfW Bankengruppe, Mannheim, 2016. Received from: https://www.kfw.de/PDF/Download-Center/Konzernthemen/Research/PDF-Dokumente-Studien-und-Materialien/Digitalisierung-im-Mittelstand.pdf

instrument of service systems, which take up and reflect the increasing formation of networks in the service lifecycle (Maglio & Spohrer, 2008; Vargo & Akaka, 2009).

Service systems vary in scope from individuals to organizations, governments, nations, and the world economy (Maglio et al., 2009). This shows that the theoretical lens of service systems can be used very variably, but it also means that the perspective must be elucidated for traceability. As mentioned before, the boundaries of service systems are defined by their resources and the respective value (co-)creation, but for the selection of the analysis unit, the chosen level of analysis is relevant. Depending on a micro, meso or macro level, the focus of analysis moves from individuals to entire organizations up to markets and the economy (Frow et al., 2014). Properly applied, however, the abstraction instrument of service systems offers a varied analysis basis. It can be used to break down the origins of services to identify its elements and to analyze the path to new innovations. In this sense, the service systems perspective also offers a promising approach to analysis and design of digitization-enabled innovation. Thus, the focus in the consideration of digitization is shifted away from a purely technical view to an additional consideration of the actors involved as well as the shared information. The aim is therefore to better identify and understand the links between digital technologies, actors and information in digitization-enabled innovation and to use this knowledge for design-oriented research. The service systems perspective thus provides a sociotechnical perspective for the analysis of digitization (Breidbach, Kolb, et al., 2013).

Part II therefore lays the foundations for the following parts and introduces the service systems perspective and its background. Hence, service systems are first introduced as the abstraction instrument of service science and their applicability is explained in the underlying research context. In this course, innovation in service systems will also be addressed. Chapter 3 then brings together the service systems perspective with digitization-enabled innovation. Part II thus provides the theoretical foundation of the research context and perspective of the following analyses. The following figure (Figure 5) illustrates this Part II in the overall research structure.

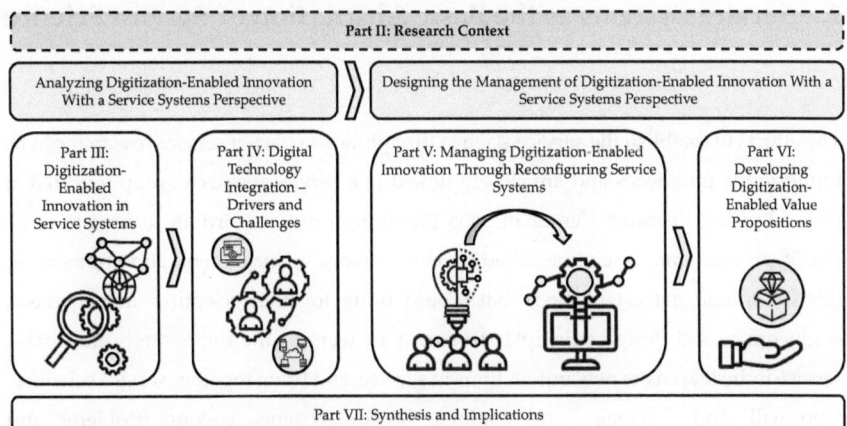

Figure 5: Part II within the overall research structure

2   Service Systems as the Basic Abstraction of Service Science

The efforts to establish the service science discipline as a part of service research can be found in the mid-2000s and are closely linked to a service research group founded at IBM Almaden Research Center in 2002 (Spohrer, 2017). According to Maglio et al. (2006), an academic discipline called services science, management, and engineering (SSME) should get established, that would bring together scientific, management, engineering, and design principles to create answers to the increasingly important service industry, create new innovations in service, and bring together service scientists who will study, manage, and engineer service systems, solving problems and exploiting opportunities to create service innovations. For example, with service engineering, a research direction that transfers the approaches of product and software development to service innovation (Bullinger, Fähnrich, & Meiren, 2003), and with servitization, a research direction that targets the increasing service orientation in manufacturing companies (Vandermerwe & Rada, 1988), various existing directions of service research have inspired the development of service science and have been brought together in it. But also research directions outside of service, such as the perspective of system science, are integrated in service science (Voss & Hsuan, 2009). The first scientific presentation on a "service science" and thus also more or less its starting signal took place on a service conference 2005 in Norway (Spohrer & Maglio, 2005). Since then, the focus on research and innovation in this field, which is on its way to an autonomous discipline, has developed and grown (Frost & Lyons, 2017).

This is also a result of the perspective of service-dominant logic (SDL), which pervades the service science as well (Vargo & Lusch, 2004). According to this, services constitute the core of all value creation (Akaka & Vargo, 2014). The resources of those involved are applied in the service process for the benefit of others or oneself. From this point of view, goods are only equipment (tools, distribution mechanisms) that serve as an alternative to direct service provision, since service is the general and universal case of the exchange process; service is what is always exchanged, and goods – when used – are only tools for the service process (Lusch & Nambisan, 2015). This view presents all value (co-)creation across disciplines as service-based. In addition, there are other core concepts within the service science which are important for this research. In the following these will be discussed individually.

2.1 Definitions of Selected Core Concepts of the Service Science Discipline

Before the following chapter explicitly deals with the service systems perspective and the service systems definition applied in this research (2.2 The Service Systems Perspective), relevant core concepts of service science are first discussed and worked out in this chapter. Service science combines organizational and human understanding with business and technological understanding to categorize and explain the types of service systems that exist as well as how these systems interact and evolve to co-create value (Spohrer & Maglio, 2008).

Following Vargo and Lusch (2008b), service is the application of particular competencies through deeds, processes, and performances for the benefit of another entity or the entity itself. Since the SDL places resources in the foreground in service innovation and in the SDL view, the recombining of new or existing resources can be understood as innovation, the analyses of services therefore often focus on the resources brought into service systems (Lusch & Nambisan, 2015). Resource integration in service systems is therefore defined by Siltaloppi and Vargo (2014) as the "broad range of interactive behaviors in which an actor or a service system applies knowledge and skills, in conjunction with other available operant and operand resources, to improve the state of others, and reciprocally, the state of oneself" (p. 1279). In this context, resources are divided into operant and operand resources. Operant resources are all those who have the capability of acting on other resources in the value creation process (e.g., people, knowledge, and skills) and therefore usually represent the core competencies and processes of an organization (Vargo & Lusch, 2004, 2017). Operand resources are defined as resources on which an operation or act is performed to produce an effect (e.g., materials and natural resources) and are often tangible or static (Vargo & Lusch, 2004). In digitization, this separation seems to dilute, as Barett et al. (2015) conceptualize digital technology as a resource with characteristics of both, operant and operand resources. Paragraph 3 of this chapter (3. The Extraordinary Importance of Technology in Service Systems) is devoted to the context of digital technologies in service systems in detail.

The resources of the individual actors in the service process are thus combined in such a way that the state of others, and reciprocally, the state of oneself gets improved. The way the resources are combined is guided by the jointly defined value proposition, which consequently also connects the respective actors and resources to a specific service system (Maglio & Spohrer, 2013). Therefore, these value propositions are formed through invitations from actors to each other to mutually engage in service (Amit & Han, 2017; Chandler & Lusch, 2015). In the realization of value propositions, service providers and service recipients access and combine their resources in the respective service system to co-create value (Beverungen, Lüttenberg, & Wolf, 2018). Especially the views of Chandler and Lush (2015) and Beverungen et al. (2018) emphasize the importance of human agents as active actors in the formation of value propositions.

Value can be defined as "an improvement in system well-being" and can be measured in "terms of a system's adaptiveness or ability to fit in its environment" (Vargo, Maglio, & Akaka, 2008, p. 149). In this context, there are two different views of value, value-in-use and value-in-exchange. Value-in-exchange can be understood as the nominal value through the exchange of resources and is determined, for example, by the market price (Spohrer et al., 2008). The value-in-use perspective can be understood as a contrast to this and is more appropriate for the view of service science. In the value-in-use perspective, value is always co-created, jointly and reciprocally, in interactions among providers and beneficiaries through the integration of resources and application of competences (Vargo & Lusch, 2008b; Vargo et al., 2008). As a partial aspect the term value-in-context can be seen, which describes the general ability of the service systems to access, adapt and integrate resources (Vargo et al., 2008).

To sum up, this research follows the view that value leads to an improvement for one or more actors of the service system. Value propositions are invitations from actors to each other to mutually engage in service and involve human agents as active actors in their formation. The following table (Table 1) summarizes the definitions of selected core concepts of the service science discipline. In the further course, service systems in particular will be discussed.

Table 1: Definitions of selected core concepts of the service science discipline (own illustration inspired by Beverungen et al., 2018)

Concept	Definition
Service	Service has four distinctive characteristics: intangibility, heterogeneity, inseparability and perishability (Moeller, 2010). Service is the application of particular competencies through deeds, processes, and performances for the benefit of another entity or the entity itself (Vargo & Lusch, 2008b).
Service science	Service science is the study of service systems and to this end combines organizational and human understanding with business and technological understanding to categorize and explain the many types of service systems that exist as well as how these systems interact and evolve to co-create value (Spohrer & Maglio, 2008).
(Operand and operant) Resources	Operand resources are often tangible and static (e.g., natural resources). They are resources that an actor acts on to obtain support (i.e., they enable or facilitate). Operant resources are often intangible and dynamic (e.g., a human skill, both physical and mental). They are resources that act on other resources to produce effects and act or operate on other things rather than being operated on (Lusch & Nambisan, 2015). Digital technology can be conceptualized as both, an operand and operant resource—one that is capable of acting on other resources and being acted on to create value and, thus, becomes a critical resource for value co-creation, service innovation and service systems (re)formation (Akaka & Vargo, 2014; Barrett et al., 2015).

Value proposition	Service Systems are formed by mutually beneficial value propositions (Maglio & Spohrer, 2013). They are formed through invitations from actors to each other to mutually engage in service (Chandler & Lusch, 2015). In the realization of value propositions, service providers and recipients access and combine their resources to co-create value (Beverungen, Lüttenberg, & Wolf, 2018).
Value-in-use	In the value-in-use meaning of value, the roles of producers and consumers are not distinct, meaning that value is always co-created, jointly and reciprocally, in interactions among providers and beneficiaries through the integration of resources and application of competences (Vargo et al., 2008). As the opposite of value-in-exchange, value-in-use implies that value creation is based on the integration of the actors' operand and operant resources (Vargo & Lusch, 2008a).

2.2   The Service Systems Perspective

In the following, service systems will be discussed and different definitions will be collected in order to derive a uniform definition for this research. Following Lyons and Tracy (2013), through an encompassing view, the abstraction of service systems can provide researchers with the analytical tools needed to better understand the behaviors and patterns that exist in service interactions and enables researchers to view a given phenomenon with focus on its characteristics to compare these. According to this argumentation, service systems provide an analysis perspective that enables comparisons and the mapping of characteristics.

One of the first definitions of service systems in the context of service science comes from Spohrer et al. (2007), outlining a service system as "a value-coproduction configuration of people, technology, other internal and external service systems, and shared information (such as language, processes, metrics, prices, policies, and laws)" (p. 72). This definition set the core elements of service systems and later publications in the service systems context usually refer to this basic definition. The core elements were later adjusted, but still form the basis for the definition of service systems. An essential adjustment to this definition is made by Maglio and Spohrer (2008), where the value aspect was included in the definition: "we define service systems as value co-creation configurations of people, technology, value propositions connecting internal and external service systems, and shared information" (p. 18). Accordingly, the core elements can be set as people, technology and information, all connected by value propositions.

Frow et al. (2014) replace the term "people" by the term "actors" to emphasize the meaning of this service systems´ core element and to highlight that this element directs the service systems but also in order to be able to highlight the parts to be understood under it. Thus, the term actor is used to encompass stakeholders and entities under it. The two terms of entities and stakeholders are not used uniformly and without overlap in the literature (Frost & Lyons, 2017). This research is following a broad research consensus outlined by Frost and Lyons (2017) and defines stakeholders as individuals and entities as departments and organizations, e.g. firms, customers, suppliers, and distributors (cf. Frow, Nenonen, Payne, & Storbacka, 2015). Maglio and Spohrer (2013) provide a description of entities as having "information-processing and communication capabilities as well as district resource-based capabilities" (p. 666). Both, entities and stakeholders can have a targeted influence on service systems. Frost and Lyons (2017) summarize these findings as follows: "Entities and stakeholders are both intentional actors with unique functions and capabilities within the service system" (p. 225).

Due to the co-creative nature of interactive value creation, the roles of service providers and recipients are becoming increasingly blurred (Lusch, Vargo, & O'Brien, 2007). The interactions that are taking place between the actors of the service systems are defined by the processes involved in the mobilization, exchange, and integration of resources through their competence (Lyons & Tracy, 2013). The actors of a service system are connected with other actors and other resources, and these connections provide the context for the actors to experience value (Lusch & Nambisan, 2015).

Resources are the information and technology of the service system. Information is primarily understood to mean the elements of the service systems shared by all actors, such as language, laws, values and standards, but also methods and practices (Maglio et al., 2009). Information is therefore defined as the knowledge and skills of the actors that are introduced into a service system by them along with other resources (Siltaloppi & Vargo, 2014). This research aims to analyze and design digitization-enabled innovation and therefore considers technology from the point of view of digitization. As digitization refers to the increasing use of digital technologies for connecting people, systems, companies, products and services (Coreynen et al., 2017) and digital technology can serve as enabler, promoter and improver of service systems (Fritzsche et al., 2018; Vargo & Lusch, 2017), in this research the service systems' core element technology reflects the use of digital technology. The following table (Table 2) summarizes the relevant foundational service systems definitions.

Table 2: Summary of relevant foundational service systems definitions

Author(s)	Definition
Spohrer, Maglio, Bailey and Gruhl (2007)	Service systems as value-coproduction configurations of **people**, **technology**, other internal and external service and shared **information** (such language, processes, metrics, prices, policies, and laws).
Maglio and Spohrer (2008)	Value co-creation configuration of **people**, **technology**, **value propositions** connecting internal and external service systems, and shared **information**.
Spohrer, Vargo, Caswell and Maglio (2008)	Service systems as a dynamic value co-creation configuration of resources, including **people**, organizations, shared **information** (language, laws, measures, methods), and **technology**, all connected internally and externally to other service systems by **value propositions**.
Vargo, Maglio and Akaka (2008)	Every service system as both, a provider and client of service that is connected by **value propositions** in value chains, value networks, or value co-creation systems.
Polese, Russo and Carrubbo (2009)	Service systems as networks, in which the same **entities** combine their **resources** towards enduring competitiveness.

In summary, this research defines a *service system* as system of actors (entities and stakeholders), technology (centered on digital technologies) and shared information (knowledge and skills), all connected by value propositions for mutual value co-creation. Service systems are connected to other internal and external service systems and are both, a provider and recipient of service.

The more elements, i.e. actors, technologies and information are integrated into a service system, the more complex it becomes. This also allows the complexity of the analysis of the service systems to be varied, since the selected analysis perspective determines the size of the service systems under investigation. "The smallest service system centers on an individual as he or she interacts with others, and the largest service system comprises the global economy. Cities, city departments, businesses, business departments, nations, and government agencies are all service systems" (Maglio & Spohrer, 2008, p 18). The increase in complexity is related to the fact that the more elements are involved in a service system, the more complex challenges are introduced into the system by the actors involved (Kieliszewski et al., 2012). For example, service recipients can co-create value by combining service offerings from multiple companies and create a system of service systems (Patrício, Fisk, e Cunha, & Constantine, 2011). Therefore, it is crucial to define the analysis level of the service systems in advance and to indicate whether an analysis is carried out on a micro, meso or macro level (Chandler & Vargo, 2011). Consequently, the level of analysis moves from individuals to entire organizations up to markets and the economy (Frow et al., 2014). This research is analyzing service systems on a meso level of analysis and targets the digitization-enabled aspects in the innovation in organizations with a service systems perspective examining the involved entities and stakeholders within an organization and the external actors connected to the organization (Akaka & Vargo, 2014; Lyons & Tracy, 2013).

A distinct perspective in service science are service ecosystems. These can be defined as relatively "self-contained self-adjusting systems of resource integrating actors connected by shared institutional logics and mutual value creation through service exchange" (Akaka & Vargo, 2014, p. 368). The focus here is therefore on self-improving processes for increasing value. This is why digital service systems are often considered as service ecosystems with boundaries in flux and open interfaces that allow for a more dynamic form of orchestrating services (Böhmann, Leimeister, & Möslein, 2018). Nevertheless, this research uses the wording of the service systems to distance itself from the self-adjusting views of ecosystems and to strengthen more the focus on actors as human agents with knowledge and skills that initiate and drive service systems' reconfiguration (Böhmann et al., 2014; Maglio, Kwan, & Spohrer, 2015).

2.3   The Facets of Innovation in Service Systems

To better adapt to changing environmental conditions, service systems are in an ongoing reconfiguration process, which involves accessing, adapting and integrating resources to create value for themselves and others (Vargo et al., 2008). This service system reconfiguration is defined as innovation (Breidbach & Maglio, 2015, p. 2). This argument, rooted in Arthur's (2009) view of technology evolution, is that reconfiguration of individual operand and operant resources is the driver of innovation and is particularly suitable for the analysis of digital technologies by broadening the output-oriented lens on innovation, and focusing on the actual innovation process (Breidbach & Maglio, 2015). In this research, the use of digital technology for digitization-enabled innovation is analyzed and designed under this definition of innovation.

The resource integration within the reconfiguration can be defined as a process that "captures the broad range of interactive behaviors in which an actor or a service system applies knowledge and skills, in conjunction with other available operant and operand resources, to improve the state of others, and reciprocally, the state of oneself" (Siltaloppi & Vargo, 2014, p. 1279). This resource integration then leads to a reconfiguration of the service systems in a way that increases the value for the involved actors and ultimately aims at innovation (Kleinschmidt, Peters, & Leimeister, 2016). Following Lusch and Nambisan (2015), human agents integrate resources for two reasons. First, the resources an actor obtains can never be used in isolation but need to be combined or bundled with other resources for value increase. Second, innovation is always the result of resource recombination (Lusch & Nambisan, 2015).

To conclude, the human actors (human agents), who hold the driver's seat when integrating new resources, allow the reconfiguration process to be initiated in a target-oriented manner (Demirkan, Spohrer, & Welser, 2016). In order to emphasize the importance of the human aspect in service systems, Maglio et al. (2015) therefore focused on human agents in service systems (Maglio, Kwan, & Spohrer, 2015). The actors, as human agents, initiate the reconfiguration of service systems and thus the innovation in service systems. In the analysis of digitization-enabled innovation in this research, study 2 (Part IV) therefore focuses in particular on the human agents as decision maker in service systems´ reconfiguration. The later design-oriented studies 3 and 4 (Part V and Part VI) consider the decisional power of human agents in innovation with a design-oriented approach. The following figure (Figure 6) summarizes the service systems view in the context of this research.

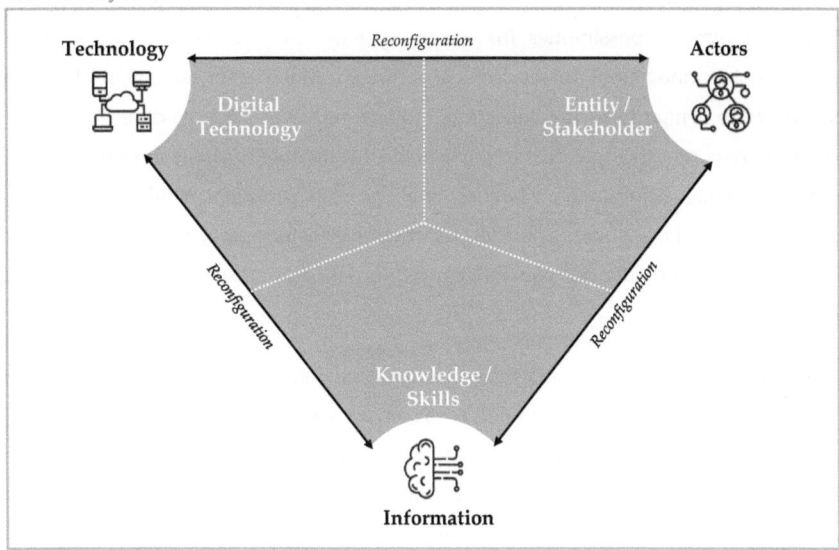

Figure 6: The elements of a service system and their reconfiguration in the context of this research

2.4   Smart Service Systems

Within the service systems perspective, the field of smart service systems represents a specification for a particular type of service system. This still very new field takes up the latest developments in digitization and incorporates them into the service systems literature. One definition of smart service systems is formulated by Barille and Polese and refers to them as "service systems designed for a wise and interacting management of their assets and goals" (Barile & Polese, 2010, pp. 32-33). In addition, the authors highlight the outstanding importance of digital technologies for smart service systems (Barile & Polese, 2010). Later publications on smart service systems frequently refer to this definition, which underlines their anchoring in research activities in this field (i.a. Beverungen, Matzner, & Janiesch, 2017; Beverungen, Müller, Matzner, Mendling, & vom Brocke, 2017; Calza et al., 2015; Demirkan et al., 2015; Polese, Tommasetti, Vesci, Carrubbo, & Troisi, 2016; Spohrer, Siddike, & Kohda, 2017).

However, smart service systems are primarily the result of the planned combination of service systems and smartness. Accordingly, the progressive digitization creates new configuration possibilities for service systems and creates so-called smart X scenarios for innovations in services (Beverungen, Matzner, et al., 2017). The term smart refers primarily to the collection, storage and evaluation of data. Numerous recent papers on this topic deal in particular with the role of smart devices in smart service systems (Beverungen, Matzner, et al., 2017; Beverungen, Müller, et al., 2017; Paluch, 2017). Those papers consider smart devices as necessary boundary object to connect service provider and consumer and thus define smart service systems on basis of smart products.

Recent publications on smart service systems define them as human-centered service systems (Beverungen, Müller, et al., 2017; Demirkan et al., 2015; Maglio, 2014, 2015; Maglio & Lim, 2016; Spohrer et al., 2017). In line with the definition of service systems in this research presented above, human agents are put in the center of analysis in this view and are seen as important determining factor of value.

The presented definitions of smart service systems show how these fall under the definition of service systems in this research. But due to their specialization in smart technologies, their scope is much narrower than that of general service systems. Moreover, the focus on digital technologies in this research does not exclusively imply smart technology. Nevertheless, the different parts constantly return to the views of smart service systems in the classification of the results of the individual studies and represents points of contact to the smart service systems literature. In this way, the findings gained are also examined for their significance for smart service systems.

3   A Service Systems Perspective on Digitization-Enabled Innovation

This research takes the service systems perspective to analyze and design digitization-enabled innovation. Digitization is defined as the networking of people and things and the convergence of the real and virtual worlds that is enabled by information and communication technology and by the increasing use of digital technologies for connecting people, systems, companies, products and services (Coreynen et al., 2017; Kagermann, 2015). Through the use of digital technologies, digitization is acting as an enabler of innovation in the service sector (Roth et al., 2017).

With the service systems perspective, innovation is defined as service systems' reconfiguration (Breidbach & Maglio, 2015). The introduction of new operant or operand resources can be one initiator of the reconfiguration process (Vargo & Lusch, 2017). According to Barett et al. (2015), the separation between operant and operant resources is less evident under digitization, as digital technology can take on both characteristics. On the one hand it can act as an operant resource – one that is capable of acting on other resources to create value – on the other hand it can also represent an operand resource and enables the effect of other resources for reconfiguration (Akaka & Vargo, 2014; Barrett et al., 2015; Breidbach & Maglio, 2015). Thus, digital technologies offer a promising resource for management to accelerate innovation with their integration and are at the same time an attractive analysis object for service research.

3.1   Technology as Enabler in Service Systems Reconfiguration

Technology, and particularly digital technology, is often considered as a main enabler of innovation in service contexts (Bitner, Zeithaml, & Gremler, 2010). Digitization can change the technologies in service systems and thus also the innovation. These changes were perceived by academia and their exploration was incorporated into the research activities. Technology has enabling characteristics for innovation in service systems (Breidbach, Kolb, et al., 2013) and the digitization is retrospectively being called one of the foundations of services science (Coreynen et al., 2017). Technology-enablement refers to the usage of digital technology to connect actors within the service systems (Breidbach, Kolb, et al., 2013). It connotes in this context as technology mediated interactions between human agents, that often take place in knowledge-intensive business services (Breidbach & Maglio, 2016). It is this aspect of human agents that represents the key differentiating factor as compared to other technology-generated services that do not include this element (Glückler & Hammer, 2011). The publications on this topic mainly contain analyses of how technology enables value co-creation (i.a. Breidbach, Kolb, et al., 2013; Breidbach & Maglio, 2016).

This research introduces and subsequently uses the term *digitization-enablement*. This stands for digital-technology-enabled innovation and is both used as a distinction to the previous terms to signal the clear orientation towards digital technologies and also to incorporate the human-centered aspect known from technology-enablement. The perspective of technology-enablement, namely that technology brings together the actors and the knowledge of a service system and thus leads to co-created value, continues to be in the focus. Value is therefore the innovation achieved by reconfiguring the service system, which has led to value increase for one or more of the actors involved.

3.2 Digitization-Enabled Service Innovation

The digitization-enabled innovations in service systems can ultimately lead to new service innovation. In this context, digitization as the use of digital technology enables service processes to become more efficient and effective and also allows the exploitation of new areas of business and fosters the development toward a digital economy (Kleinschmidt et al., 2016). But the simple reconfiguration of service systems and the associated innovation does not automatically mean a subsequent increase in value or service innovation. The transformation of innovations into value increase and possibly into service innovation in order to strengthen the competitiveness of the service systems is a following step (Breidbach & Maglio, 2014; Kleinschmidt et al., 2016; Spohrer & Maglio, 2008). The figure (Figure 7) visualizes this viewpoint on which this research is based.

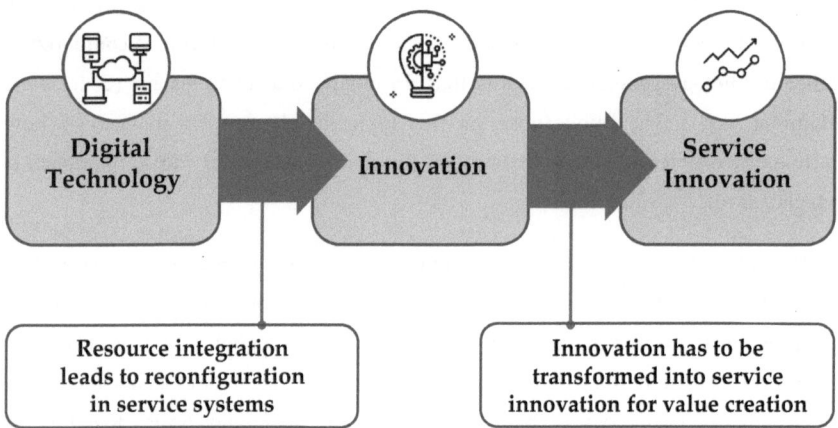

Figure 7: The relation of innovation and service innovation in the context of this research

According to the phase model of service innovation developed by Barras already in 1986, technology can lead to three types of service innovation. First, he suggests that companies integrate a technology (such as a new digital technology) for service improvement, as to increase the efficiency of existing services. In the second type, the technology integration is conducted for improving the quality and effectiveness of the services. The third type describes wholly transformed or new services in the companies through technology integration (Barras, 1986). In this sense, the reconfiguration of service systems enabled by digital technology integration and the associated innovation can be transferred into new service offerings or also help to improve current service offerings. In both cases, however, this is not an inevitable consequence of digital technology integration. New and improved service offerings and the associated value increase are obtained through service innovation (Breidbach & Maglio, 2015; Den Hertog, Van Der Aa, & De Jong, 2010; Kowalkowski et al., 2013).

3.3   A Service Systems Perspective for the Management of Digitization-Enabled Innovation

As outlined before, approaches to dealing with the changes brought about by digitization and the increasing service orientation are often characterized by a process mindset in contributions from management-oriented disciplines (Grenha Teixeira et al., 2017). In the case of the management of digitization-enabled innovation, this concerns primarily the concepts of innovation management and technology management (TM). On the one hand, in the course of innovation through digital technology integration, the management of the technology integration process is the distinct task of TM (Cetindamar et al., 2016), on the other hand, the development of innovations involves innovation management, for example to convert innovations into service innovation (Daim et al., 2010).

In this setting, service systems provide a new perspective on the management of digitization-enabled innovation and at the same time deal with questions in current research. According to Grenha Teixeira et al. (2017), in a digitization context, "models from a management perspective do not address in detail the [...] interaction between actors and technologies" (Grenha Teixeira et al., 2017, p. 241). The consideration of all core elements of service systems, i.e. technology, actors and information, as well as the analysis of their interplay in digitization-enabled innovation therefore offers a new perspective for management. Furthermore, Benkenstein et al. (2017) outline a need in service related management research for new process tools and techniques that are facing digitization. The design-oriented approach of this research (Part V and Part VI) subsequently includes the service systems perspective in the development of management methods and tools aimed at the management of digitization-enabled innovation. With the reconfiguration of service systems, the perspective also brings a service systems' specific view of innovation to management and attaches importance to reconfiguration processes (Breidbach & Maglio, 2015). As a result, two paradigms are brought together in a calculated manner.

4 Concluding Words About the Research Context

Part II lays the theoretical foundation for this research and introduces the relevant terms and definitions for the analysis and design of digitization-enabled innovation. This part is initiated by observed digitization enabled developments in business practice – such as an increasing network orientation and a general intensification in the importance of service – as well as by outlined fields of future research in current service literature. The theoretical foundations are mainly anchored in service science, an emerging discipline within service research (Maglio et al., 2006). Service science aims at solutions in an increasingly complex world of service and also addresses the fact that services are created on the basis of systemic value creation. One focus of service science is the interdisciplinary response to an existing set of problems and the development of systematic approaches to service innovation (Chesbrough & Spohrer, 2006). Service systems are the basic abstraction of service science and constitute its analysis perspective. This perspective is chosen for the analysis and design of digitization-enabled innovation in this research and is therefore introduced in Part II. For this purpose, the service systems perspective is also merged with a management perspective.

From a research point of view, this part is crucial out of three reasons. First, it brings together and links existing concepts of service science in the context of digitization-enabled innovation. Second, with the service systems perspective, it provides the underlying theoretical perspective for the entire investigation of this research. An integrated definition of service systems is provided. In this regard, also the three core elements of service systems – actors, technology and information – are defined. The role of human agents is made explicit as being an active influencer of innovation. In addition, the concepts of innovation in service systems (as reconfiguration of service systems) and service innovation are distinguished from one another. Third, in this overall construct, the implications of digitization are presented and the role of digital technologies for innovation is examined from a service systems perspective.

From a management point of view, this part with service systems provides a new perspective on the management of digitization-enabled innovation. Thus, views of service science are integrated into management-oriented perspectives. Moreover, a definition of digitization-enablement is presented, which reflects the importance of digital technology. The review of literature has also revealed perspectives that allow the targeted management of the integration of new resources and thus the reconfiguration process for innovation in service systems. In the further course of this research, these will be taken up again and pursued further by design-oriented approaches.

In conclusion, Part II sets the foundation to take a service systems perspective on the field of digitization-enabled innovation. Thus the views of service science are reflected in this perspective, such as the importance of human agents or the consideration of resource integration for innovation. By taking up aspects of management, design-oriented approaches result, which are pursued through the development of methods and tools for digitization-enabled innovation in this research.

Part III

Digitization-Enabled Innovation in Service

Systems:

Analysis of MDAX-listed Companies

© Springer Fachmedien Wiesbaden GmbH, part of Springer Nature 2020
S. M. Genennig, *Realizing Digitization-Enabled Innovation*, Markt- und
Unternehmensentwicklung Markets and Organisations,
https://doi.org/10.1007/978-3-658-28719-1_3

1 Needs and Objectives

The first two parts of this research dealt with the research context and laid the foundations of a service systems perspective for the analysis of digitization-enabled innovation. Part III[4] now covers in detail the digitization with a service systems perspective and examines the alterations with this perspective. It is the first empirical study and at the same time also the first step in the analysis of digitization-enabled innovation in this research. This study thus takes an external look at digitization-enabled innovation with a service systems perspective on the digitization activities of organizations. With the service systems perspective, the study looks at the alterations in service systems brought about by digitization and shows how these lead to reconfiguration of the service systems and to new value propositions.

The digitization and in particular the use of digital technology leads to change in organizations (Kagermann, 2015). The aim of the present study is to take up this change and to identify the characteristics of it for the respective service systems. As digital change is also associated with concrete innovation potentials by the integration of new resources, the study identifies the innovation resulting from digital change. This is done by identifying the alterations within the service systems and also by detecting the emergence of value propositions that have arisen through digitization-enabled alterations within the service systems. Hence, this study aims to explore the first sub-research question of this research:

RQ1: What is the current state of digitization-enabled alterations in service systems and what are the expressions of the innovation enabling characteristics of digitization in this context?

---

[4] An earlier version of this research has been presented at the annual conference of the *European Academy of Management (EURAM)* 2018 in Reykjavik, Iceland, (Genennig, Pauli, Roth & Möslein, 2018). See Annex A for more information.

The motivation for this study originates in the absence of concrete fact-based knowledge about the digitization-enabled innovations in service systems. Although service science often deals with the innovation potentials for services and business models inherent in digitization (e.g. Baden-Fuller & Haefliger, 2013; Barrett, Davidson, Prabhu, & Vargo, 2015a; Yoo, Henfridsson, & Lyytinen, 2010), there is a lack of insights from its application, i.e. the use of digital technologies. Broken down to service systems, this means showing the alterations within the three core elements of the systems and additionally identifying the enablement of value increase by digital technology. This increase can best be derived from new formed value propositions or the improvement of existing value propositions, as these not only form the respective service systems, but also make changes visible (Barile & Polese, 2010).

The objectives of the study are to explore the digitization-enabled alterations in service systems and to identify the resulting new and altered value propositions. The study also answers the question whether digitization leads only to alterations at the technology level of service systems, or whether it also affects the other two core elements of service systems and thus leads to digitization-enabled alterations concerning actors and information.

The explorative study is performed through document analysis by a desk research and uses a qualitative content analysis approach for manual coding of findings (Mayring, 2015). The data basis for the analysis are the annual reports of the companies listed in the German MDAX. A stock index comprising 50 companies from different sectors. These are German companies or companies operating predominantly in Germany. The size of the companies is under the 30 largest German companies listed in the DAX. The companies listed in the MDAX are nevertheless large companies which, according to the Bitkom study presented in Part I, can be regarded as digital pioneers. Due to its cross-industry composition, the MDAX index provides a reflection of the German corporate diversity. The analysis of the companies listed in the MDAX thus also allows comparisons to be made between sectors and provides an overall overview of digitization activities. Other companies, such as SMEs, can then benefit from the results of this study and use them to derive current trends and as a starting point for their own digitization activities.

The study forms Part III of the research and consists of seven chapters. Following the introduction in chapter 1, chapter 2 and chapter 3 present the literature background and theoretical underpinning of the study. The research design and research process is explained in chapter 4. The results are then presented in chapter 5 and discussed in chapter 6. Chapter 7 concludes this part with concluding remarks. Figure 8 below illustrates how this study can be integrated into the overall structure of this research.

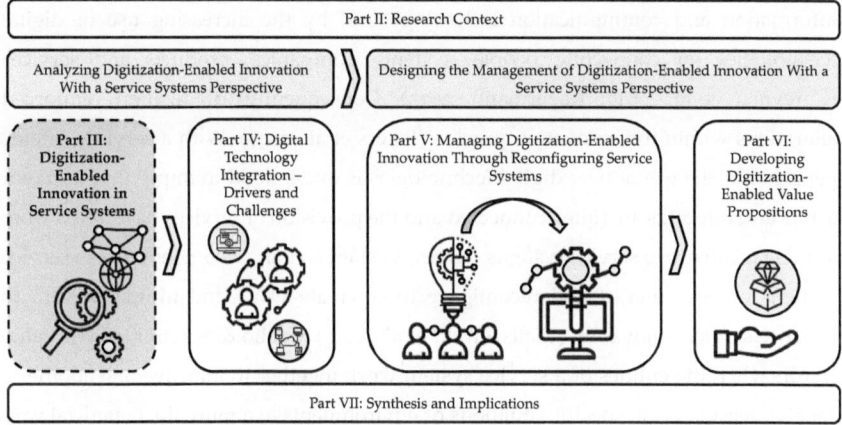

Figure 8: Part III within the overall research structure

2   Understanding the Context: Innovation in Service Systems through Digital Technology

The progressive digitization of all parts of the value chain is changing the business environment. Digitization is defined in this research as the networking of people and things and the convergence of the real and virtual worlds that is enabled by information and communication technology and by the increasing use of digital technologies for connecting people, systems, companies, products and services (Coreynen et al., 2017; Kagermann, 2015). Consequently, digitization reinforced alterations within the innovation process (Peters et al., 2016). With a service systems perspective, the use of new digital technologies is understood to imply that different actors and offerings are (inter)connected and the provision of services has shifted from a single company to service systems offerings (Maglio et al., 2006, 2009). These service systems evolve, interact and reconfigure to co-create value and ultimately aim to enhance service innovation (Kieliszewski et al., 2012; Maglio & Spohrer, 2008). Value results when the entities of a service system work together to improve one another's capabilities and act in specific situations or environments in a mutually beneficial way (Vargo et al., 2008). The use of new digital technologies can serve as enabler, promoter and improver of service systems (Fritzsche et al., 2018; Vargo & Lusch, 2017). In this sense, the use of digital technologies empowers actors to improve or enhance current service systems and therefore leads to innovation and creates new value potentials (Barrett et al., 2015; Chandler & Lusch, 2015).

To lead to value increase, digital technologies must be understood and used purposefully. Although the influence factors of digitization on service systems are already discussed in service science (Coreynen et al., 2017), current research in this field is suffering from the absence of real-world findings (Böhmann et al., 2014) and "a deep understanding" (Daim et al., 2010, p. 15).

Common value propositions connect the different entities of a service system on a content-related basis (Vargo et al., 2008). Changes in the value propositions of a service system have significant impact on the service systems architecture and can modify the configuration of actors and resources (Böhmann et al., 2014). But current literature lacks a general understanding of value increase and innovation in service systems (Chandler & Lusch, 2015; Ostrom, Parasuraman, Bowen, Patricio, & Voss, 2015). In this context, a general understanding of mechanisms and reconfiguration patterns within service systems is required as source for further work.

Building on these observations, this study is exploring the digitization related alterations and digitization-enabled innovation in service systems and therefore contributes to a better understanding. The changes within the service systems under investigation are identified on the basis of the three core elements technology, actors and information and the service systems' value propositions. The focus of analysis lies on the enabling characteristics of digital technologies for both, the reconfiguration of service systems and the development of new and altered value propositions for the service system as a whole. In this way, the effect of digital technologies on the innovation in service systems is examined. The results deliver real-world insights for the management of digital technologies in service systems. These can form examples for possible approaches in SMEs.

3   Theoretical Underpinning

The core elements of a service system are the analysis object of this study. To this end, the changes facilitated by digitization within these three core elements – technology, actors and information – are collected and the new value propositions made possible by these changes are identified.

The theoretical foundations for the service systems perspective were laid earlier in this research. In the following, the possible characteristics of the changes within the core elements of service systems will be discussed in more detail and a framework will be derived from the theory which will later provide the theoretical basis for the empirical analysis.

3.1   Digitization Facilitated Alterations in Service Systems

Through the use of digital technology, the exchange of actors and resources is possible anytime and anywhere today (Ostrom et al. 2010). Digitization is therefore leading to alterations in service systems (Barrett et al., 2012). These alterations in the service systems aim at an effective and efficient allocation of resources and actors (Lusch & Nambisan, 2015). Lusch and Nambisan (2015) describe this as resource density, with the maximum density occurring when the best combination of resources is mobilized for a given situation, naming four possible changes: "time, space, actor and constellation" (p. 160). To identify and classify the alterations triggered by digitization in the service systems element *information*, i.e. the resources of knowledge and skills, these four change options are used as categorization. Only alterations that affected all four changes are included. The actor in this case constitutes the source or recipient of the information.

As a difference to this, the alterations in the service systems element *actor* are affecting the changes in the entities and stakeholders of the service systems (Frost &

Lyons, 2017). Human agents, who hold the driver's seat when integrating new resources, allow the reconfiguration process to be initiated in a target-oriented manner (Demirkan et al., 2016). In this study, the human agents and thus the decision makers are located in the organization which is being analyzed. The alterations within the service systems element *actor* are then broken down into internal and external changes. Internal alterations are changed constellations of actors within the organization. External alterations involve adding or changing stakeholders and entities outside the organization.

In addition, the changes in the service systems element *technology* will be recorded in the following analysis. For this purpose, the digital technologies within the service systems are recorded. According to Legner et al. (2017), digital technologies such as social media, big data, the Internet of Things, mobile computing, and cloud computing significantly influence processes and services, for instance by connecting machines, things, and individuals, as well as by enabling new work, collaboration, and automation models (p. 306). According to this, digital technologies have numerous characteristics and areas of application. The classification in the following analysis is made on the basis of the use of digital technology in the service process, thus distinguishing between service development (i.e. bringing a service system to usage and generating the service) and service delivery (i.e. bringing value increase to the service system and distributing the service) (Design Council, 2013; Kleinschmidt et al., 2016; Ostrom et al., 2015).

3.2 Digitization-Enablement of Value Propositions

In that respect, digital technology leads to innovation in service systems and enables the (co-)creation of value and the facilitation of new value propositions (Breidbach & Maglio, 2015; Skålén, Gummerus, von Koskull, & Magnusson, 2015). The technology-enablement refers to the usage of digital technology in order to connect actors (i.e. entities and stakeholders) within the service systems (Breidbach, Kolb, et al., 2013). In this context digitization-enabled connotes digital-technology mediated interactions between human actors, which are often taking place in knowledge-intensive business services (Breidbach and Maglio 2016; Glückler and Hammer 2011). In this sense, digitization not only enables the exchange between the actors of the service systems, but also forces the reconfiguration process and ultimately leads to new and altered value propositions (Kindström, Kowalkowski, & Sandberg, 2013; Peters et al., 2016).

Enabled by digitization, value propositions can change their "form, time, place and possession" (Lusch & Nambisan, 2015, p. 159). These four change characteristics serve to subdivide the digitization-enabled value propositions in the following analysis. In addition, the enabling nature of digitization for the emergence of new value propositions is explored. The framework below (Figure 9) summarizes the theoretical construct of this study and will be used for the following empirical analysis.

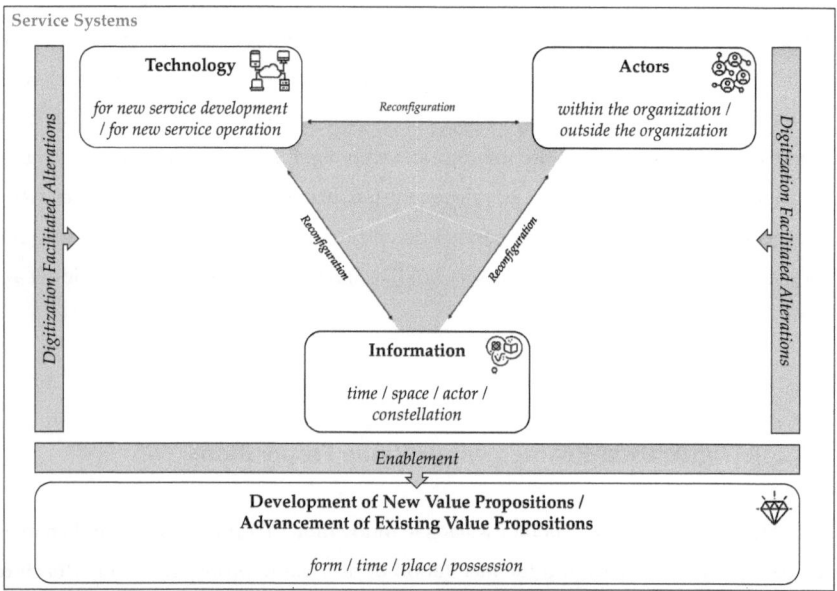

Figure 9: Core elements of a service system and their location in this study (own illustration based on Lusch & Nambisan, 2015; Maglio et al., 2006; Vargo & Akaka, 2009)

4 Research Design

To analyze digitization-enabled innovation in service systems, this study explores digitization facilitated change in the German MDAX-listed companies and examines how these alterations lead to value propositions. For this purpose the annual reports of all 50 companies listed under the MDAX index are chosen as the source of analysis. A document analysis as a manual systematic procedure of evaluating existing documents in desk research is conducted (Bowen, 2009). For this purpose, the study is using a qualitative content analysis approach for analyzing the data (Mayring, 2015). Through this method, the analysis material was evaluated systematically, rule-governed, and theory-driven.

The application of the content analysis approach is also following the quality criteria of qualitative research after Wrona (2006), ensuring validity, reliability, and objectivity of the research project. Following, the research design is described in detail by outlining the empirical field, explaining the approach in the data collection and describing the data analysis practice.

4.1 Data Collection

Data was collected through the publicly accessible annual reports of the 50 companies listed in the German MDAX. The MDAX was chosen because it is Germany's second most important stock index after the DAX and represents middle sized German or predominantly in Germany operating companies (Mid-Caps). The German economy is mainly based on medium sized industrial enterprises. This company type represents over one third of the MDAX and makes this index therefore more representative for the German economy than the DAX. In terms of size and turnover, the companies of the MDAX are thus placed between SMEs and large multinational enterprises. However, they see themselves as large but still medium sized companies and can be counted as such due to the management structures, the manageability of the business segment and the frequent reliance on individual core competencies and niches. For example, the management forecasts of MDAX-listed companies are more precise and accurate than those of DAX-listed companies (Nölte, 2009). The undertaken digitization-enabled adaptions of the MDAX-listed companies are expected to be illustrative examples for other organizations, especially SMEs. A list of all MDAX-listed companies and the field of their business operations can be found in the annex (Annex B).

The annual reports were chosen as material for analysis, as they also express the general attitude towards the digitization of the publishing companies. The companies mainly use the sections about the general business situation, the information about company related topics and the section of the management's beliefs to explain how they are dealing with digitization. In these sections, the annual reports outline the self-perception of the companies and provide a sound picture of how they see themselves handling digitization-related topics.

The sample was limited to the years 2014, 2015 and 2016 to ensure both, a manageable amount of text for analysis and a holistic picture of the adaptations in the companies during the last years. In this sense, changing processes could be accompanied over a period of time to also perceive the pace of alteration. In total, approximately 28,000 pages of text were manually viewed and evaluated for analysis.

4.2   Data Analysis and Interpretation

The data analysis followed the principles of Mayring's (2015) qualitative content analysis approach. This structured method is particularly suitable when large amounts of text need to be analyzed. As in this research project the source material exists in a fixed format and is not changing over time or through its analysis, content analysis is seen as a suitable method (Brosius, Haas, & Koschel, 2016).

Mayring (2015) defines a sequential model following ten steps during the analysis. First, the data for analysis is defined. In this case, the annual reports of the German

MDAX-listed companies in the years 2014, 2015, and 2016 are evaluated. Afterwards an analysis of the data source and its formal characteristics follows. In this research project, the data is not self-generated and therefore the author has no influence on its creation. Although there are no concrete legal provisions for editing annual reports in Germany, their functions to be fulfilled predefined a structure that is similar in all reports. Additionally, the German "Corporate Governance Kodex" gives companies orientation for the construction of their annual reports on an annual basis (dcgk, 2017). Since the structure is similar across all annual reports, the analysis is facilitated and the reports become comparable. In the following step, the direction of analysis is defined through the data's classification within the communication model. In this research project, the MDAX-listed companies are the source of information and the origin of communication. These first steps help to structure and systemize the analysis material.

The definition of the analysis units and the definition of the category system are the last steps before the first material run. The analysis units determine the size of the text elements entered. The encoding unit designates the smallest text element that can be captured, for example a single word. The context unit is the largest text element that is captured, for example an entire page (Mayring, 2015, p. 61). In this analysis, sentences and short sections are used as context units.

The structuring content analysis serves to extract and summarize elements from the text on specific topics (Mayring, 2015, p. 99). For this purpose, a category system is developed after the definition of the analysis units, into which the respective codes are classified. The categories and sub-categories are first theory-based and deductively determined on the basis of the research question. Herein, the core elements of service systems – technology, actors, and information as well as value propositions - provide the first order categories for coding. In addition, the specific characteristics of the changes in the three core elements of service systems are consulted as second order categories. Technology is accordingly subdivided into technology for service development and service delivery. Actors are subdivided into internal and external. Information is subdivided into time, space, actor, and constellation. In addition, the new value propositions are subdivided into form, time, place, and constellation.

With the help of this preliminary category system, 30% of the material is then analyzed in order to determine to what extent all sites can be adequately classified by the categories defined. In this case, the annual reports of 2014 are analyzed. If many text elements are identified that cannot be assigned to a category or if it turns out that the categories have not been formulated with sufficient selectivity, the category system is revised after the test run. The revised category system will then be applied to all annual reports in the final material run. In this text application, the third order categories for coding are generated. In addition, for many entries under a third order category, further sub-categories are formed to structure the results. This is applied to the enabled value propositions. For this purpose, categories are formed inductively from the material. Thus, the third order categories are formed on the basis of the findings from the whole data – all annual reports. The annual reports were coded using MAXQDA, a software for qualitative data analysis. In the last step, the results of the analysis are processed and interpreted in the direction of the research question in order to be able to answer them. The figure below (Figure 10) gives an overview of the data analysis procedure. Exemplary screenshots of the data analysis with MAXQDA can be found in the annex (Annex C).

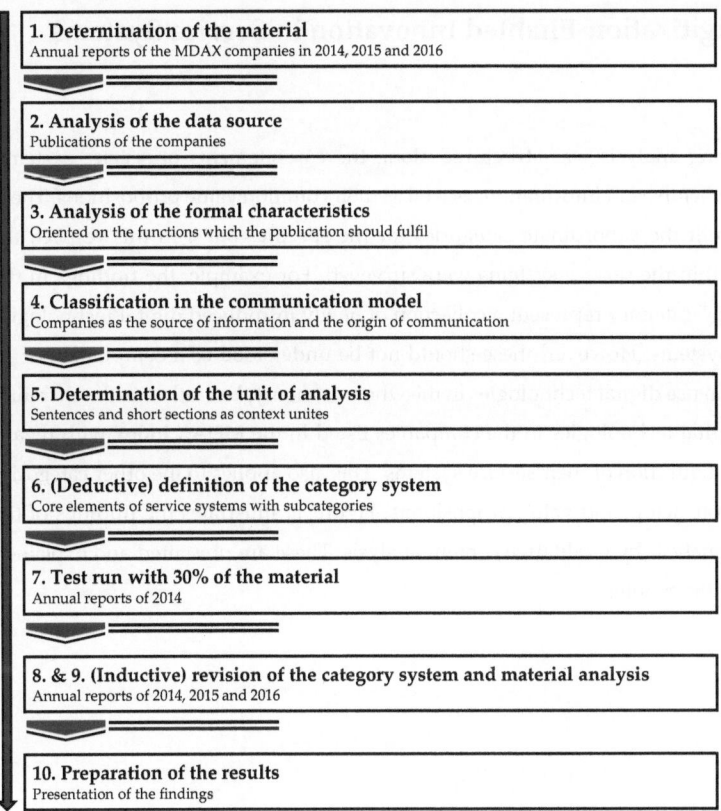

1. Determination of the material
Annual reports of the MDAX companies in 2014, 2015 and 2016

2. Analysis of the data source
Publications of the companies

3. Analysis of the formal characteristics
Oriented on the functions which the publication should fulfil

4. Classification in the communication model
Companies as the source of information and the origin of communication

5. Determination of the unit of analysis
Sentences and short sections as context unites

6. (Deductive) definition of the category system
Core elements of service systems with subcategories

7. Test run with 30% of the material
Annual reports of 2014

8. & 9. (Inductive) revision of the category system and material analysis
Annual reports of 2014, 2015 and 2016

10. Preparation of the results
Presentation of the findings

Figure 10: Content analytical process model based on Mayring (2015, p. 62; p. 98)

In doing so, qualitative content analysis combines both, a deductive and an inductive analysis approach. In the evaluation of findings, the qualitative content analysis approach also allowed quantitative elements, like the deduction of some categories´ importance over others by their number of mentions. In the annex (Annex D) an overview of the number of mentions per third order category can be found, which is the basis for the sorting of the following findings. The annual reports are partly in German and partly in English. For the purpose of preparing the results below, direct quotations from German are literally translated into English.

5   Digitization-Enabled Innovation in Service Systems

The following analysis was structured along the core elements of service systems, technology, actors, and information, as well as their common value propositions. These elements built the subordinate categories for the specific codes. In this respect, the changes within the service systems were surveyed. For example, the findings in the "Technology" category represent a collection of newly introduced digital technologies in service systems. However, these should not be understood as a compilation of all existing or in use digital technologies in the whole economy, but rather as the currently relevant digital technologies in the companies listed in the MDAX index with regard to the reconfiguration of their service systems. This also applies to the other categories – information, actors and value propositions. Figure 11 illustrates the findings of the document analysis by qualitative content analysis. These are presented and explained in detail in this chapter.

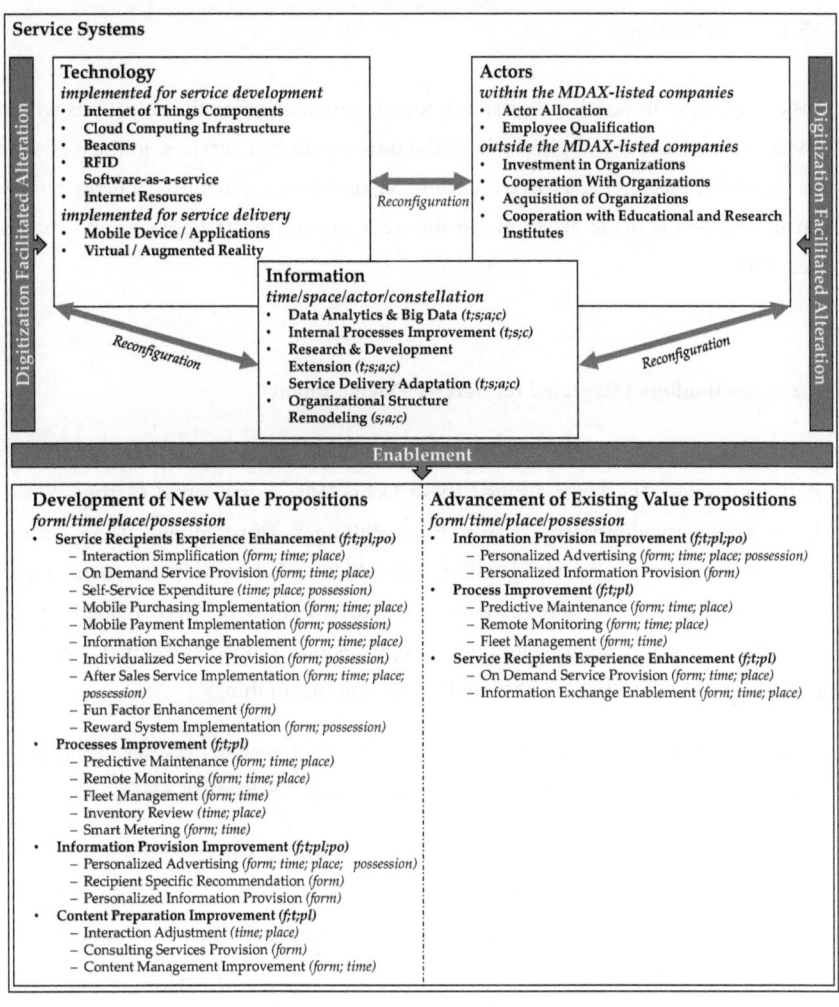

Figure 11: Digitization related alterations and digitization-enabled value propositions in the service systems of MDAX-listed companies

5.1 Technology

This category points out that digital technologies are facilitating the alterations within service systems and are applied within the development of services. In the course of this process, the technologies used are compiled under their general technology names. The subdivision is made according to the steps of service development and service operation.

5.1.1 Technology Integrated for Service Development

Technologies related to the "internet of things" were frequently used by the MDAX-listed companies. The latter applied these technologies for internal (Airbus, Stroer Media) or external purposes (Aareal Bank, Bilfinger, Dürr, Innogy, Kion Group, Krones, Metro Group, Osram, Schaeffler, Stroer Media). Solutions in use, for example, concerned logistic equipment in assembly lines (Airbus) or were related to the deployment of smart home solutions (Innogy). Some companies aligned emerging business fields with technologies linked to the "internet of things":

"We are about to build up a digital ecosystem to integrate components, systems and machines to the continuously growing world of the "internet of things" (Schaeffler, 2016).

Ten out of the 50 MDAX-listed companies integrated cloud computing in their organization. In this case, the companies mainly integrated external solutions. The drawn use cases varied from manufacturing related solutions like maintenance (Schaeffler) and energy efficiency solutions (Bilfinger) to broader usage like fleet management solutions (Jungheinrich, Kion) and cloud-based data analysis (Leoni). Only few companies operated their own cloud platforms. Schaeffler ran its services on the Schaeffler-Cloud through which the organization offered automated data analysis tools (Schaeffler, 2016). The Aareal Bank developed its individual cloud platform called Aareon cloud on which the organization provided software-as-a-service solution (Aareal Bank 2015, 2016). With its software-as-a-service offer, the Aareal Bank was the dominant organization in the MDAX using this digital technology.

Stoer Media is the dominant user of the Beacon technology among MDAX-listed companies. Although Euroshop and the Metro Group also use this technology, Stoer Media is carrying out the comparatively largest projects and plans. For example, it plans to install 50,000 iBeacons nationwide in cooperation with Deutsche Bahn (Stoer Media, 2015).

In addition, RFID technology was used in the development of services and was applied in B2B (Metro) and B2C (Eventim, Hugo Boss, Euroshop, Stoer Media). A concrete example of this is the parking service of Euroshop:

"RFID parking will greatly simplify the parking process for shopping center visitors in the future. Instead of rolling down the window and purchasing a parking card every time a center car park is entered in all weathers, users of the new service will in future be able to enter the car park comfortably and without drawing a ticket" (Euroshop, 2014).

Finally, the internet was mentioned for general use in several annual reports. In the described cases, the internet was employed as an information transmitting technology (Aareal Bank, Hella).

5.1.2 Technology Integrated for Service Delivery

Mobile devices and the applications running on them were suggested to play a dominant role within the operation of services. 23 of the 50 companies were providing own applications within their service systems. Mentioned in 167 codes, "mobile devices" was the most frequently used topic concerning digitization-enabled alterations in the service systems element *technology*. The content of the applications varied, e.g. online shopping (CTS Eventim, Fielmann, Fraport, Hugo Boss, Metro Group, Zalando), media provision (RTL Group, Stoer Media, Axel Springer) and maintenance (Bilfinger, Fuchs Petrolub, Schaeffler). The applications were closely related to the main products of the companies, like the "Lightify" app of the illuminant producer Osram, *enabling intelligent, wireless control of the lights via smartphone and tablet* (Osram Licht, 2016).

Further digital technologies named in the annual reports were virtual and augmented reality. Dürr has integrated virtual commissioning and virtual plant models which could be visited in the virtual reality (Dürr, 2015). Airbus used *"augmented reality and virtual reality devices for employees to improve their methods of working"* (Airbus, 2016). Other companies employing virtual reality were Axel Springer (*virtual reality coverage*, 2015), Hochtief (*augmented reality in construction*, 2014), Metro Group (*virtual reality for shopping*, 2015), and Zalando (*virtual reality magazine*, 2014). These two technologies, mobile devices and virtual / augmented reality, were the point of contact with the service recipient, while the technologies used for service development were downstream technologies and required additional processing.

5.2   Actors

The findings of the analysis of the service systems core element *actors* are divided into alterations within the organization and outside the organization. The alterations are all located within the respective service systems of the companies listed in the MDAX index.

5.2.1   Alterations Within the MDAX-listed Companies

The second most named point on the actor side are codes referring to the altered allocation of actors within the MDAX-listed companies. In most cases, these alterations related to digitization topics targeted the transfer of knowledge between business unites and know-how sharing inside the company. To target challenges posed by digitization, the companies set up "competence teams" (Hochtief, 2014) and "CTO organizations" (Kion, 2015). Some companies even founded new independently working business units, like Evonic stated: *"we grouped a team of digital experts und put them into a separate unit that can act like a start-up"* (Evonic, 2016). These newly founded entities are then in charge for all digitization related touch points, for example:

"Corporate F&E management, corporate innovation, F&E processes, methods & tools, F&E competences & services, legal protection and information technology" (Schaeffler, 2016).

The digitization-enabled alterations in the actor allocation could also be geographical. To proceed their technology expansion, for the first time ever Zalando opened two technology sites outside Germany in 2015 and built two *"Fashion Insights Centers"* in Dublin and Helsinki (Zalando, 2015).

The improvement of the qualification of their employees was another digitization-enabled alteration within the actor category and within the organization. Specific training programs were integrated to prepare the employees for challenges related to the digitization. Hugo Boss was an example for a targeted employee qualification program.

"We found our IT Excellence Program to accompany the digital transition and to teach our employees the professional skill required in the IT sector" (Hugo Boss, 2016).

This process was extended to upstream activities. As the recruitment of knowledge workers has been increasingly difficult, Aurubis has been educating its required knowledge workers in the IT sector through their own efforts. Therefore, they launched a dual curriculum in co-operation with the Hamburg School of Business Administration (Aurubis, 2014).

5.2.2 Alterations Outside the MDAX-listed Companies

Examining the actor side, the investment in other organizations was the most commonly named and undertaken digitization-enabled alteration to the service systems. Those activities were aimed to build connections with other organizations, but leaving both parties independent. Fourteen companies reported their investments in other organizations, most commonly made by the Metro Group and the RTL Group. The investments were often closely linked to the original business, for example "Orderbird" and "Shore" (Metro Group, 2015) or *"SpotX (...), the leading global players in programmatic video advertising"* (RTL Group, 2015). By investing in the start-up

"Shore", the Metro Group intended to build competences in the field of cloud computing to be able to provide services concerning the management and control of its customers´ business processes (Metro Group, 2015).

The analysis of the annual reports uncovered that the MDAX-listed companies were most active in segments already covered through their portfolio. The intention behind the investments was often to generate digital technology know-how.

"To generate know-how in the sense of our strategic orientation, we started an investment in the Swiss start-up Adaotricity AG in the end of 2016 which was integrated in February 2017. Leoni holds two thirds of the software-based consulting specialist. With this investment, we secure us access to competences in software, simulation and cloud-based data analysis" (Leoni, 2016).

Digital technology related co-operation with other organizations was set up by twenty MDAX-listed companies. This covered a wide range, from licensing (Eventim, 2015) to Joint Ventures (Fraport, 2015). Most co-operations were established to serve a specific project and time, as the example of Jungheinrich showed.

"Jungheinrich developed a machine-to-machine platform for ISM online together with Device Insight, one of the leading providers of remote service platforms for machines, plants and vehicles" (Jungheinrich, 2014).

In some cases, the co-operations also tended to conduct business with the new partner. Airbus for example explained how they built a new digitization-enabled service offering with their allied partner One Web.

"Under a pioneering business model, Airbus Group has teamed up with OneWeb to provide an affordable Internet connection for everyone by developing a constellation of hundreds of small telecommunications satellites" (Airbus, 2015).

Taking a step further, some companies undertook a complete acquisition. This procedure integrated the former independent actor into the companies listed in the MDAX index through their takeover. The relevant coding category was included under "outside the organization", as the acquisition of previously independent organizations not represented in the service systems is primarily of importance here. Besides merging independent actors, generating competences in digital technologies constituted a motivating factor for the integration. As Dürr stated, *"through the acquisition of iTAC and DUALIS we enlarged our software offerings in the course of Industry 4.0 platforms"* (Dürr, 2016).

Some companies forced the identification and integration of new interesting start-ups by setting up their own accelerators. Examples in this context were Airbus and Hella, both hold own start-up accelerators and incubators.

"Airbus operates a global network of accelerator facilities – called Airbus BizLabs – to speed up the transformation of ground-breaking ideas into valuable business propositions. In developing its BizLab concept, Airbus leveraged the experience of start-up support programs from other sectors – having forged collaborations with such companies as Microsoft Ventures, Orange Fab and Google. Airbus Group has established sourcing offices in China, India, the United States and Brazil (Airbus 2015).

"For being able to anticipate technological trends and to generate new business models from them, HELLA found a technology incubator in Berlin and opened a branch office in Silicon Valley" (Hella, 2015).

Finally, fifteen MDAX-listed companies sustained co-operations with educational and research institutes to extend their digital technology portfolio. These co-operations were formed with both, research institutes and universities (Bilfinger, 2016). The co-operations of the MDAX-listed companies were aiming to improve competence and enable innovation through targeted research activities which were, in most cases, related to their core business.

"We cooperate with prestigious research institutes to develop algorithms that derive a great advantage to our customers. So far, these services are not integrated, but we see a great potential in Industry 4.0 solutions" (Krones, 2014).

To drive digitization-enabled innovations, some companies opened up their R&D processes to external know-how during the development of new service offerings.

Airbus set an example for this approach. The aviation company was promoting open innovation, especially the integration of external technical and scientific experts.

"The CTO is also in charge of developing the Airbus-wide R&T Roadmaps and executing Demonstrator projects together with the divisions. This organization applies a lean, project-based approach, will encourage collaboration with external research communities and develop partnerships, especially through open innovation with technical and scientific experts" (Airbus, 2016).

5.3   Information

The analysis of the annual reports has shown that the second order categories must allow multiple answers for the service systems' core element *information*. A separation of the alterations in time, space, actor and constellation cannot be represented, since their limits are fluid. Accordingly, multiple mentions are subsequently permitted.

The analysis of data and the use of big data was the most relevant digitization-enabled alteration concerning information involved matters. Out of the MDAX sample, 21 companies explained their data simulation and analysis approach in the annual reports of the last three years. The digital technologies, like cloud platforms, supported a *"more effective processing of data"* (Evonik, 2016). In this sense, Aurubis was using mathematical methods and computer systems for *"advanced analytics"* and *"big data"* to evaluate the existing amount of data (Aurubis, 2015). The companies especially used big data for *"data management"* (Leoni, 2016) and the *"connection and application of large data volumes to support connected business"* (Innogy, 2015). Moreover, the importance of big data for the purpose of acquiring information was stated in the annual reports. The alterations affected the time, space, actor and constellation of information.

"In the age of digitization, the role of 'big data' – in the form of cookies, clusters or cross-device analytics – is becoming ever-more prominent" (RTL, 2016).

"Big data has an increasing importance in the supply chains of the chemical industry" (Brenntag, 2016).

While the first point is dealing with the information generation, the second point in this category is addressing information processing within the companies and thus the internal processes improvement through the use of digital technology. This refers to processes behind the service development. LEG (2016) was using digital technologies for internal process improvement in accounting, human resources management and customer relationship management.

"We use the digitization for improvements in all our functional areas to save expenses and to actively shape the future. (...) We can only constantly grow our business if we timely recognize challenges of our time and drive change actively" (LEG, 2016).

In some cases, these improvements could be measured. Uniper was integrating data analytics to improve the production process of its plants. Additionally, the company used digital twins for simulations. In this regard, the digital technologies were used to improve the internal process of service creation and changed the time, space and constellation of information.

"The performance of our plants could be improved by system services. In this regard, we were able to increase the secondary power of an 820-megawatt plant over 50%. Expensive test beforehand were avoided through the use of a digital twin" (Uniper, 2016).

In this context, digital technologies were also applied for research and development extension and in many cases also constituted the center of current R&D activities. As Innogy outlined their objectives, employing technologies for innovation remained the overall focus.

"The focus lies on the use of technology for innovation. During the last year, we conducted 150 research and development (R&D) projects in which we aimed to improve existing products and procedures and addressed the technologies of the future" (Innogy, 2016).

In this sense, the use of digital technologies was granting access to new information for innovation to the MDAX-listed companies. These innovation potentials were expected to lead to new services. The alterations in this context affected all four changes of information, as the research and development activities targeted the generation of new information and ultimately aimed new services.

"Today, Bilfinger has positioned numerous mobile applications for maintenance for industrial plants already. Additional digital services are in current development" (Bilfinger, 2015).

Additionally, digitization was leading to alteration in the exchange of information with the service recipients and consequently altered the service delivery. The digitization related alterations could be incremental, as companies improved the security of the information exchange (Airbus, 2016), or could be radical, as more and more companies switched to e-business processes in their sales procedure (Lanxess, 2016; Zalando, 2016) and therefore fundamentally changed their interactions with the recipients. In this regard, all four information changes were present.

Finally, for an altered information allocation, some MDAX-listed companies forced an organizational structure remodeling. They integrated a *"technology and innovation committee"* (Aareal Bank, 2015), an independent *"technology committee"* (Aurubis, 2015) or reformed their *"innovation management"* (Hannover Rückversicherung, 2016). Exercising these actions, the digitization topics were prioritized within the MDAX-listed companies. In this sense, the time of information was unattached by this alteration.

5.4   Value Propositions for Digitization-Enabled Innovation

The altered allocations of the three elements of service systems were assumed to enable new digitization-enabled *value propositions*. During the analysis it was distinguished between two different forms, the development of new value propositions and the advancement of existing value propositions. These value propositions were then categorized according to the improvement potentials: form, time, place, and possession. In this case, too, as with the service systems core element information, multiple answers were possible in the allocation to the predefined improvement potentials. Figure 12 illustrates the digitization-enabled value propositions in the service systems of MDAX-listed companies. The categories represent the sections for their presentation below.

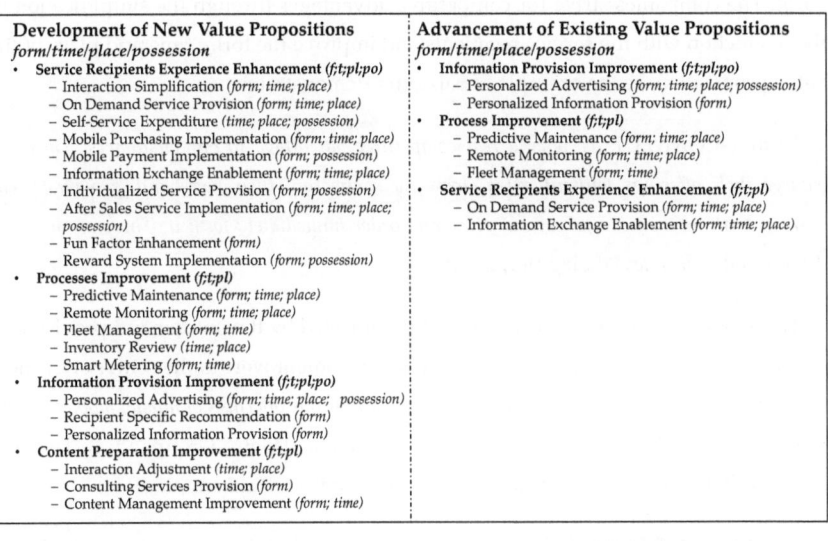

Development of New Value Propositions *form/time/place/possession*	Advancement of Existing Value Propositions *form/time/place/possession*
• **Service Recipients Experience Enhancement** *(f;t;pl;po)* – Interaction Simplification *(form; time; place)* – On Demand Service Provision *(form; time; place)* – Self-Service Expenditure *(time; place; possession)* – Mobile Purchasing Implementation *(form; time; place)* – Mobile Payment Implementation *(form; possession)* – Information Exchange Enablement *(form; time; place)* – Individualized Service Provision *(form; possession)* – After Sales Service Implementation *(form; time; place; possession)* – Fun Factor Enhancement *(form)* – Reward System Implementation *(form; possession)* • **Processes Improvement** *(f;t;pl)* – Predictive Maintenance *(form; time; place)* – Remote Monitoring *(form; time; place)* – Fleet Management *(form; time)* – Inventory Review *(time; place)* – Smart Metering *(form; time)* • **Information Provision Improvement** *(f;t;pl;po)* – Personalized Advertising *(form; time; place; possession)* – Recipient Specific Recommendation *(form)* – Personalized Information Provision *(form)* • **Content Preparation Improvement** *(f;t;pl)* – Interaction Adjustment *(time; place)* – Consulting Services Provision *(form)* – Content Management Improvement *(form; time)*	• **Information Provision Improvement** *(f;t;pl;po)* – Personalized Advertising *(form; time; place; possession)* – Personalized Information Provision *(form)* • **Process Improvement** *(f;t;pl)* – Predictive Maintenance *(form; time; place)* – Remote Monitoring *(form; time; place)* – Fleet Management *(form; time)* • **Service Recipients Experience Enhancement** *(f;t;pl)* – On Demand Service Provision *(form; time; place)* – Information Exchange Enablement *(form; time; place)*

Figure 12: Digitization-enabled value propositions in the service systems of the analyzed MDAX-listed companies

5.4.1 Value Propositions Targeting the Service Recipients´ Experience

Most new digitization-enabled value propositions targeted the service recipients´ experience. All new value propositions with a focus on the wellbeing of the recipient were collected under this premise. Altogether, ten sub-categories under the third order category were identified and allocated to the improvement potentials. The categories mainly served the potential for improvements in form, time and place. Some categories also include improvements in possession.

The first and most frequently named sub-category was the digitization-enabled simplification of the interaction between the recipient and the MDAX-listed companies. For example, this was addressed by new digital *"booking services"* (Airbus, 2016), an *"interactive 360 degree preview feature"* during the purchase of event tickets (Eventim, 2016) or smartphone applications for instore navigation (Euroshop, 2016; Fraport, 2016). The companies strive for competitive advantages through the simplification of the interaction with the service recipients and improve the form, time and place of the value proposition, as the example of Salzgitter demonstrates.

"With e-CONNECT we offer a real competitive advantage to our customers. They can enlarge their offerings without extra stock. By connecting their merchandise management systems with us they can access our stock and order immediately form it. There are no more detours and wait times" (Salzgitter, 2015).

The experience of the recipients was also improved by the on-demand provision of services. In this field, especially music and video content were at the center of the new digitization-enabled value propositions. *"We bundle our offerings of music, movies, series, e-books, games and software on a new streaming platform"* (Metro Group, 2014). The new services enable the recipient to access the service anytime and anyplace.

"In May 2016, RTL II launched its digital video offering RTL II You, which is available 24/7 for linear and on-demand viewing on PC, smart TV and mobile devices" (RTL, 2016).

Self-service expenditure was also one way to optimize the experience of the service recipients. Using digital technologies to involve the service recipients in the service creation, the companies were meeting the specific customer needs. For example, this was ensured by *"a unique booking service that allows passengers to book with all A380 operators"* (Airbus, 2016). In this case, the possession within the value proposition also changes, as Airbus does not operate the flights to be booked itself but merely acts as an intermediary.

Additionally, new digitization-enabled value propositions emerged in the purchase process of the services, as companies offered new solutions for mobile purchasing und mobile payment. In this field, digital technologies enabled a better pricing through digital price tags (Metro Group, 2015), "click & collect" solutions that help finding and purchasing service (Euroshop, 2014; Hugo Boss, 2016) and contactless payment by the use of smartphones and NFC (Near Field Communication) to transfer money at the point of sale (Metro Group, 2014).

Using digital technologies, some MDAX-listed companies provided new ways for information exchange with their service recipients. This was realized by own applications (Hugo Boss, 2016) or through social media like Instagram (Metro Group, 2014; Rational, 2016). Giving the recipients the opportunity to formulate their specific needs was the determining factor in the provision of new information

These needs could then be addressed by new digitization-enabled services. In this regard, new value propositions were emerging in the field of individualized service provision. In the example of Fraport, the possession within the value proposition also changes, as these then act as agents for other service providers.

"By personalizing our services, we accompany our passengers more individually. By this, we respond to changing customer needs with regard to information, orientation, service and shopping – especially in the combination of the usage of mobile devices" (Fraport, 2015).

Additionally, the process after the actual service purchase was targeted by new digitization-enabled value propositions. Specific after sales services were developed to ensure customer loyalty. In most cases, these services were closely linked to the actual service provision. For example, Rational launched a mobile application and utilized social media to *"use efficient ways to help our customers after the service provision and to foster our relationship with the customer"* (Rational, 2016).

Finally, the MDAX-listed companies developed new digitization-enabled value propositions to increase the recipients' experience through services which entertain and increase the *"fun factor"* during the interaction (Zalando, 2014). Additionally, there were solutions which aimed at the recipients' loyalty. Therefore, reward systems were put in place which made every interaction worthwhile (Fraport, 2016; Metro Group, 2014).

5.4.2   Value Propositions Targeting Process Improvement

Value propositions enabled by digital technologies were not only targeting the specific service recipients' experiences. New digitization-enabled value propositions aiming for process improvements were also developed frequently by the MDAX-listed companies. These value propositions focused more on joint processes and promised advantages for both, the service recipient and the MDAX-listed companies. Five sub-categories were identified which mainly aimed improvements in form, time and place.

Predictive maintenance referred to the use of digital technologies for *"monitoring"* plants and machines to realize an *"efficiency enhancement through advanced knowledge"* (MTU, 2016). Especially manufacturing companies (e.g. Bilfinger; Dürr, Schaeffler) integrated these solutions. Value propositions in this field target the provision of advantages for both the service recipients, as they increase their machine availability, and the MDAX-listed companies, as they save resources in the machine *"analysis and maintenance processes"* (Düll, 2016).

In the same vein, MDAX-listed companies developed new value propositions for remote monitoring. In this case, the digital technologies were applied for a troubleshooting via remote systems. The companies integrated *"control centers"* from which they operate the systems (Schaeffler, 2016).

"With our remote service we directly connect with the defective machine for data transmission and can thus provide a troubleshooting and debugging over distance" (Krones, 2016).

The digitization-enabled value propositions for fleet management supported the service recipients in overviewing their machines or vehicles. In return, the MDAX-listed companies attached their services and received an overview of their customers' fleets.

"The KION premium brands also continued to enhance their fleet management solutions. STILL introduced the new 'neXXt fleet' software, which intelligently merges data sets from different applications and areas so that customers can analyze their fleets accurately and

comprehensively. The tool comprises a variety of web applications (apps) that can be accessed easily and conveniently from anywhere" (Kion, 2016).

Value propositions for the inventory review were developed to generate *"efficiency and quality advantages"* (Bilfinger, 2015). By applying digital technologies the process was shortened and human error could be eliminated. Again, in return the MDAX-listed companies received an overview of their customers´ stock.

Furthermore, the development of new value propositions took place in the field of smart metering. In this case, the MDAX-listed companies ensured an energy efficient operation of their machines or *"analyzed the energy consumption in real time and provide solutions building on the observation"* (Bilfinger, 2015).

5.4.3   Value Propositions Targeting the Improvement of Information Provision

Additionally, several new digitization-enabled value propositions were developed in the field of information provision. Three sub-categories were identified which show that this third order category also affects all four improvement potentials of value propositions.

The employment of digital technologies provided personalized advertising by connecting recipients with the service provider. In this process, media companies acted as intermediary (Axel Springer, Eventim, RTL Group, Stoer). The new services which realized this value proposition were offered to advertisers and targeted the service recipients. The innovation potential possession has therefore been assigned to this sub-category, as the MDAX-listed companies deliberately act as intermediaries and thus seek to involve the advertiser in the advertising process through its technological improvement.

"With our new self-developed solutions Bonial Connect, from now on, we directly put digital advertising brochures to the internet presence of the brand manufacturers and connect the consumers to their favorite brands. By this, Bonial Connect is answering specific customer needs" (Axel Springer, 2016).

Through the use of data analysis and big data, the MDAX-listed companies were able to provide recipient specific recommendations of the services required (EuroShop, Metro Group, RTL, Zalando). This new value proposition analyzed the recipients and recommended the most suitable solution. Afterwards, the solutions were communicated to the recipient and got offered for sale.

"Thanks to our data based recommendations in our `Mein Zalando´ function, the customer is finding his most suitable item of closing faster and more efficient" (Zalando, 2015).

5.4.4   Value Propositions Targeting the Improvement of Content Preparation

Digitization also enabled the MDAX-listed companies to personalize their information provision, for example through *"search & match algorithms"* (Axel Springer, 2016). This value proposition helped the recipients to a more effective information search and to make better informed purchases.

Interaction adjustment refers to new digitization-enabled value propositions in the connection between the MDAX-listed companies and their service recipients. In many cases, the companies used mobile devices to improve the interactions. But also cloud platforms were used to improve interactions mainly within the companies. For example, Schaeffler provided an own cloud solution to *"enable automated data transfer and analysis"* (Schaeffler, 2016). In these cases, the use of digital technologies enabled improvements in time and place of the value propositions.

Furthermore, new value propositions emerged as data analysis provided new information to the MDAX-listed companies which they used for consulting services. One example is Leoni, who broadened its service portfolio by "Industry 4.0 related data-based consulting services" (Leoni, 2016). In this case technology was both, enabler and content of the consultancy service and led to a new form of value proposition.

Finally, new digitization-enabled value propositions were developed in the field of content management. The companies used individual-related data to improve their offerings and to learn more about their customers (e.g. Axel Springer; Eventim;

Zalando). The improvements were located in the form and time of the new value propositions.

5.4.5 Advancement of Existing Value Propositions

In addition to the development of completely new value propositions, digitization-enabled advancements to existing value propositions could also be identified. These were far less pronounced in the annual reports than the communication of new value propositions and therefore play only a marginal role in the results of this study. Nevertheless, the changes identified in existing value propositions are presented in the following section.

In this instance, the companies used digital technologies to adapt existing value propositions, often to better respond to their existing recipients and to improve the form, time, place and possession of the existing value propositions. For example, the companies improved their information provision by bringing new functions to already existing mobile applications (e.g. Metro Group, 2015). An example of this is the continuous improvement of recommendation systems for personalized advertising, which have been in constant evolution since their creation and are being improved in order to make more specific recommendations to recipients (Zalando, 2015). For example, new features are continuously incorporated into existing applications:

"The latest feature [...] gives customers product recommendations that are tailored to individual needs and a real benefit for online shoppers" (Zalando, 2014).

In addition, technical improvements often have an impact on the improvement of existing value propositions. This shows the example of Stoer Media (2014), which have improved their personalized information provision:

"An improved retargeting mechanism, which is able to identify the new customer potential of a user, will also contribute to the attractiveness of our offer" (Stoer Media, 2014)

Another field in which the MDAX-listed companies advanced their existing value propositions was the improvement of processes. Fuchs Petrolub was one example, as they used digital technologies to improve their maintenance process by digitizing the maintenance reports (Fuchs Petrolub, 2016). A similar example was provided by Bilfinger:

"Dynamic maintenance is the key word. All information about power plants, customers and our own resources is available in digital form. [...] This enables us to react quickly and networked at any time" (Bilfinger 2014).

Fleet management has also been incrementally improved through the use of digital technology in some areas. Driven by legal changes, Kion (2016) introduced new procedures for entry and exit controls:

"A smartphone or tablet can now be very easily used to carry out the check that is required each time before a truck is used, as stipulated by the rules of the DGUV (German Social Accident Insurance organization)" (Kion, 2016).

Moreover, the improvement of the recipients´ experience was also the focus of advanced value propositions in this category. For example, on-demand services were further expanded. A concrete example of this is Jungheinrich's Call4Service application, which was rolled out to further countries:

"With the Call4Service app, we are making it possible for our customers in currently 25 countries very easy to request the Jungheinrich service - for regular maintenance as well as in case of repair. Vehicle type and faults can thus be transmitted quickly, the customer can view the processing status at any time" (Jungheinrich, 2016).

As a final point, companies used the digitization to implement incremental improvements to their existing value proposition in information exchange. For example, mobile end devices were used to record and process information in order to digitize it faster and thus process it faster:

"We used the digitization to future develop our mobile tablet application for new apartment inspection" (Aareal Bank, 2014).

5.5 Industry Specifics

Finally, the analysis revealed industry-specific findings. The companies with the highest number of codes are located in three different sectors. The industries were mechanical engineering (Schaeffler), media (Axel Springer), and e-commerce (Zalando). Especially in the analyzed manufacturing companies the number of codes increased throughout the years (concerning the companies: Airbus, Dürr, Hella, Jungheinrich, Leoni, MTU, Schaeffler). In contrast, the number of codes remained on a high level in the analyzed reports of the MDAX's media companies (Axel Springer, RTL Group, Stöer). In other industries, e.g. mining (K+S), food processing (Südzucker) or real estate (Alstria office REIT, TAG Immobilien), the number of codes stayed on a low level throughout the three years of analysis. In this context, the chemical industry stood out as an exception and presented an uneven picture. While some companies communicated various digitization-enabled innovations in their annual reports (Evonic; Lanxess; Wacker) others presented only a few or none (Brenntag, Covestro, Fuchs Petrolub).

In conclusion, across all industries, companies who started their activities in the field of digitization-enabled innovations before 2014 kept them on the same level. Only some companies could catch up between 2014 and 2016 and started activities in the field of digital-enabled innovation. However, a large number of MDAX-listed companies is still lacking activities in this field.

6   Discussion and Implications

The content analysis of the annual reports outlined the impulse of the digitization for both, the facilitation of alterations within the service systems and the consequent enablement of new and altered digitization-enabled value propositions for the service systems (Breidbach, Kolb, et al., 2013). This reflects the significance of new digital technologies for the innovation processes and the value increase in service systems (Demirkan et al., 2011). The digitization of elements of the service systems affect the service system as a whole (Breidbach & Maglio, 2014). Moreover, the integration of new digital technologies constitutes an enabler for new value propositions and thus also for value increase in the service systems (Demirkan et al., 2011; Vargo & Lusch, 2016).

6.1   Discussion

The integration of a new digital technology fosters innovation efforts, as the service systems attune to the digitization changes (Spohrer & Maglio, 2008). Adding a new digital technology, like a cloud platform (Schaeffler, 2016), initiates alteration to all three service systems´ core elements and focuses on value (co-)creation (Breidbach & Maglio, 2016). For example, new actors could be introduced into the service systems through the cloud platform, which in turn evaluated data and turned them into knowledge and thus made changes on the information side possible. According to earlier publications, the reconfigurations of actors and resources enable new digitization-enabled value propositions (Breidbach & Maglio, 2016; Peters et al., 2016), like process improvements through predictive maintenance. In this sense, the integration of digital technologies leads to the reconfiguration of the service systems and therefore to digitization-enabled innovation in service systems (Maglio et al., 2006). The findings in this context also indicated that digital technology can act as both, operand and operant resource in the reconfiguration of service systems and and consequently support Barrett's propositions with real-world findings (Barrett et al.,

2015). For example on the one hand as an operant resource in the form of software-as-a-service and on the other hand as an operand resource in the form of a cloud platform or mobile device.

Moreover, the findings have also revealed the importance of platforms, i.e. clouds. This is in line with publications in information systems research, highlighting digital platforms as instrument upon which many companies are able to innovate and as a foundation upon which companies can develop digital capabilities throughout their service systems (Yoo, Boland, Lyytinen, & Majchrzak, 2012; Yoo et al., 2010). Like a large part of the identified technologies, cloud computing was used in the step of service development. Accordingly, the innovations made possible still require an intermediate step towards the final value increase in service innovation (Kleinschmidt et al., 2016; Ostrom et al., 2015).

Numerous new digitization-enabled innovations were data-driven services, e.g. the predictive maintenance services "Predictive Maintenance 4.0" (Schaeffler), the personalized advert "Bonial Connect" (Axel Springer), the after sales service "ChefLine" (Rational, 2015), or the online table reservation portal "Dinnersite" (RTL Group, 2015). As a consequence, this study is adding fact-based knowledge to the field of data-driven value creation and is targeting the avenue of future research according to an exploration of "established organizations" (Schüritz, Seebacher, & Dorner, 2017). The content analysis offered insights into the practices of the MDAX-listed companies that generate value with data-driven services. With the associated focus on independent data evaluation and knowledge generation, the results also contribute to the literature on smart service systems (Beverungen, Matzner, et al., 2017; Maglio, 2015). The analysis revealed the dominant role of smart technologies for innovation in service systems by a high number of codes. Several MDAX-listed companies used digital technologies to enhance the level of information within their service systems by collecting and analyzing data (i.e. mobile devices and the "internet of things"). This supports the smart service systems view of Beverungen et al. (2017), outlining the transformational impact of smart products on service systems. In many cases, the digitization-enabled value propositions arise from smart product integration to the service system.

On the side of the actors, most of the alterations concerned activities outside the companies. These changes were primarily aimed at expanding the knowledge and skills of the service systems and represented a conscious and systematic extension of the service systems (Beverungen et al., 2018; Vargo et al., 2008).

The changes proposed by Lusch and Nambisan (2015) on the information side (time, space, actor and constellation) and the potential for improvement of value propositions (form, time, place and possession) were identified in the data. The findings show how these can be used for subdivision and also reflect their characteristics in real-world settings. Form and time were the most frequently identified innovation potentials in value propositions.

6.2   Implications for Practice

Looking at how the companies listed in the MDAX index used the digitization for alterations and digitization-enabled innovation in their service systems may suggest immediate implications for managers. Although the MDAX-listed companies named numerous integrated digital technologies in their annual reports, the analysis revealed two dominant technologies for alteration in the service systems and for the development of new value propositions: Mobile devices and cloud platforms. Both were integrated to connect (better) with (new) actors and to improve the information retrieval, exchange and memory. For example, mobile applications were used for service delivery adaptation while cloud computing enabled data analytics, internal processes improvement and research and development extension. The analysis showed user patterns of the most frequently used technologies. Cloud computing was supporting the MDAX-listed companies in backend processes, whereas mobile devices and applications were mainly used in the frontend and the interaction with the service recipients.

The most commonly named alterations on the actor side were investments in companies. Numerous companies used this as a way of perspective competence development. Even though the advantages sought by the company could often not immediately be realized, building the targeted know-how was perceived to be easier with a supporting partner. Additionally, this approach was assumed to be less risky and more cost efficient. In most cases the investments were related to technology and aimed at providers of specific technologies and specialists for data analytics. For example, cloud platform was identified to be the main driver of a lot of investment activities, as the MDAX-listed companies considered cloud solutions as an essential future technology (e.g. Aareal Bank, Dürr, Leoni, Metro Group). Almost all digitization-enabled alterations on the actor side referred to the generation of new competences. Digital technologies are used for connecting new entities and stakeholders as well as allocating information within the MDAX-listed companies. Altered actor allocations refer to organizational restructuring and remodeling, as some companies were opening up new divisions entrusted with digitization related topics (e.g. Airbus, Evonic, Hochtief, Kion, Schaeffler).

Consequently, the alterations in the service systems enabled digitization-enabled value propositions. Especially the improved information processing within the service systems and the incorporation of new actors facilitated the development of value propositions. Again, the use of digital technologies was leading to enhancements on both, the service recipients´ side and in the MDAX-listed companies. In the value provision, the use of mobile applications primarily focused on optimization of the service recipients´ experience and improvements in the information provision. The use of cloud computing was prevalent in enabling process improvements. The companies put more effort into the development of new value propositions than into the advancement of existing ones.

Altogether, the digital innovations realized by the MDAX-listed companies were generated by a reconfiguration of the service systems as whole. Digital technologies facilitated alterations at the information and actor side and enabled value propositions that lead to innovation. But the cross-sectoral comparison of all MDAX industries revealed specifics in this process. Especially manufacturing companies (Airbus, Dürr, Hella, Jungheinrich, Leoni, MTU, Schaeffler) have been active in the years of analysis. This sector is situated in a decision stage when it comes to the use of digital technologies for innovation.

7   Concluding Words on the Analysis of Digitization-Enabled Innovation in Service Systems

Part III of the research is a desk research project to analyze the annual reports of the companies listed in the German MDAX index with a document analysis by applying a qualitative content analysis approach. The annual reports of all MDAX-listed companies from the years 2014, 2015, and 2016 were manually evaluated to identify alterations in their service systems in connection with the digitization and to detect the resulting digitization-enabled innovation in service systems. By doing so, the specific alterations on the three elements of service systems – technology, actors and information – were identified and the resulting digitization-enabled value propositions were determined. In this way, the effect of digital technologies on the innovation in service systems was examined. The study thus represents the first step in the analysis of digitization-enabled innovation with a service systems perspective.

Using the service systems perspective (Maglio et al., 2009), Part III contributes to the emerging discipline of service science by real-world findings. Additionally, the connections between digitization triggered alterations in service systems and resulting value increase by digitization-enabled value propositions are established. Moreover, the findings outline the development of digitization-enabled innovations in service systems.

The results of this study are relevant for management as they reveal the characteristics of digitization and look at it from an application-oriented perspective, in detail the use of digital technology. Part III thus provides real-world insights into the field of digitization in service systems. It offers possible orientations and best practices for companies dealing with alterations of digitization. In addition, a first industry comparison shows the differences in the approach of different companies to digitization. It is particularly evident here that companies that have already started with digitization activities before 2014 keep them at a high level and that companies that did not (or only rarely) deal with digitization topics before 2014 did not undertake any increased activities during the period under study.

The data source and the method of sampling expose this study to a set of limitations. As the annual reports of the 50 companies listed in the German MDAX were used as the basis of data analysis, the current composition of the MDAX determined the selection of companies. The MDAX was chosen because of its interdisciplinary nature and its focus on same sized industrial enterprises. The MDAX is representative of the German economy. The presented findings provide a summary of the digitization related alterations in the companies of the MDAX and their service systems. Nevertheless, future research should analyze separate industry fields for more specific findings and should primarily focus on small and medium sized companies. Nevertheless, SMEs can benefit from the findings of this study and use them as comparative cases.

Additionally, the analysis is limited through the information provided by the MDAX-listed companies in their annual reports. The information is chosen by the companies because of their representative character and to demonstrate the innovative strength. In this sense, the publications represent the companies in the way they like to be perceived in public. The reports lack in a documentation of failure. With that in mind, the analysis was able to identify patterns and priorities in the digitization activities of the MDAX-listed companies on the basis of their prechosen topics to share and give a sound overview of the digitization topics currently affecting all companies. It can be assumed that MDAX-listed companies are conducting more activities which they have not shared (yet). In depth longitudinal case studies with single companies can shed light on the wide-ranging processes within the companies.

Part III presents the current state of digitization-enabled alterations in service systems and shows expressions of the enabling characteristics of digitization. It has also demonstrated that mainly companies have carried out digitization activities that already addressed digitization issues before 2014. The entry into this field therefore seems challenging. In the following, the drivers and challenges will be identified first, before supporting methods and tools for this process will be developed.

Part IV

Digital Technology Integration in Service

Systems:

Identification of Drivers and Challenges in SMEs

© Springer Fachmedien Wiesbaden GmbH, part of Springer Nature 2020
S. M. Genennig, *Realizing Digitization-Enabled Innovation*, Markt- und
Unternehmensentwicklung Markets and Organisations,
https://doi.org/10.1007/978-3-658-28719-1_4

1   Needs and Objectives

"More than four fifths of medium-sized companies carried out digitization projects between 2013 and 2015" (Saam et al., 2016, p. 2).

Even if the quote states that a large number of SMEs are already carrying out digitization projects, the studies presented earlier have also shown that the SMEs do not perceive themselves as digital pioneers at all. The previous study has also demonstrated that the field of companies is subdivided into active users of digital technologies and actors who are still in a waiting position or at least do not communicate their efforts in the use of digital technology. Accordingly, many organizations are in a decision-making stage regarding the use of new digital technologies. On the one hand, there are the opportunities already mentioned above which can be achieved through the introduction of digital technologies, but on the other hand, companies still seem to be hindering integration. Part IV[5] addresses the integration of digital technologies and focuses on small and medium-sized enterprises.

These form the backbone of the German economy and are the most important form of business. According to current BMWi (Federal Ministry of Economics and Energy) figures, SMEs are the dominant form of enterprise in Germany making up 99.6% of all companies (BMWi, 2018). In addition, SMEs have special characteristics that make them particularly valuable as an object of analysis. They usually have specific expertise on which their entrepreneurial activity is based. In addition, they do not have large financial and human resources to try things out and accept failures (Vajjhala & Ramollari, 2016). Nevertheless, SMEs are currently in technology integration processes or have recently integrated new digital technologies.

---

[5] An earlier version of this research has been presented at the *9th Service Operations Management Forum* 2017 in Copenhagen, Denmark (Genennig, Jonas & Möslein, 2017) as well as in a further developed version at the annual *R&D Management Conference (RADMA)* 2017 in Leuven, Belgium (Genennig, Roth & Möslein, 2017). See Annex A for more information.

The service systems perspective chosen in this research places special emphasis on the human agents in the decision-making process of resource integration (Breidbach & Maglio, 2016). They evaluate the advantages and disadvantages and then make the decision to integrate their and other resources into the service systems. Within digitization-enabled innovation, human agents are thus also responsible for the integration of digital technologies. In view of this crucial role, this study explores the drivers and challenges in technology integration from the perspective of human agents in service systems. The drivers therefore lead to a technology integration while the challenges tend to inhibit and prevent it. The following study aims to explore the sub-research question:

RQ2: Which factors drive and challenge human agents in the integration of new digital technologies in service systems?

Part IV thus takes the second step in the analysis of digitization-enabled innovation with a service systems perspective, taking into account the human agents who are crucial to the decision-making process within service systems. The results are collected in SMEs because of their great importance for the German economy and their current state of decision-making. The objectives of the study are to identify the specific drivers and challenges of SMEs in the integration of new digital technologies. As already identified and presented in Part III, digital platforms, and industrial clouds in particular, represent a technology of great importance in this context (Barrett et al., 2015; Roth et al., 2017; Yoo et al., 2010). The following analysis therefore deals with the integration of an industrial cloud. It explores the concrete drivers for the integration of a cloud and the obstacles to its integration. Another sharpening of the following study is the focus on manufacturing companies. As already shown in Part III, the changes and the associated innovations are currently most evident in the service systems of manufacturing companies. Thus, these service systems are currently undergoing a digitization-enabled change what makes them an interesting object of analysis and can provide insights that can also be used as examples for other industries. As a last point, the study is also identifying fields of action in which the human agents of manufacturing SMEs need additional support, which consequently also provides approaches for management-oriented research. These approaches will then be taken up and pursued in the following design-oriented studies (Part V and Part VI) of this research.

To explore the research question, a qualitative multiple case study is chosen in the following analysis. For this purpose, 22 different companies are surveyed in 46 interviews. The empirical context are the service systems of SMEs in the manufacturing industry whilst their integration of an industry cloud. The SME definition is following the IfM Bonn (IfM, 2016), classifying SMEs as companies with less than 500 employees and an annual turnover below 50 million Euro.

The study forms Part IV of the research and consists of seven chapters. Chapter 2 presents a classification into the research context before Chapter 3 prepares the theoretical basis. Chapter 4 then deals with the research design and explains the course of the empirical study. Chapter 5 presents the findings and lays the foundation for the discussion in Chapter 6. Chapter 7 provides the concluding words to close the study. The figure below (Figure 13) shows the study in the overall picture of this research.

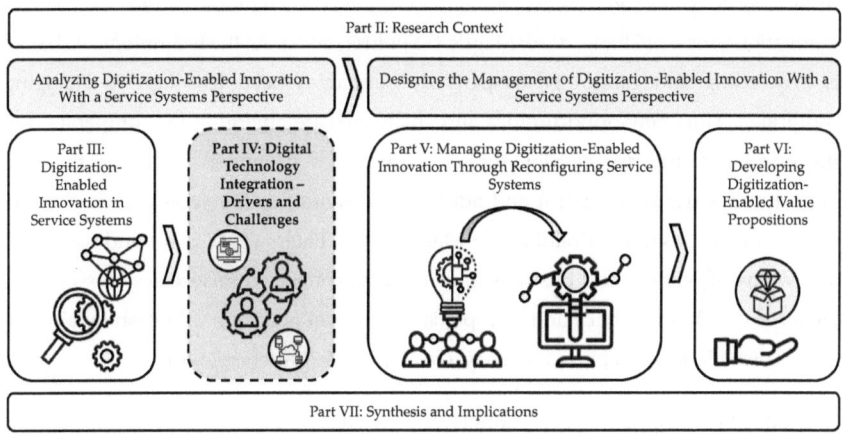

Figure 13: Part VI within the overall research structure

2   Understanding the Context: Technology Integration in Service Systems

The increased use of digital technologies is changing more and more parts of the value chains and the value flows between the actors involved (Böhm, Müller, Krcmar, & Welpe, 2018; Coreynen et al., 2017). These modified value flows lead to completely new actor constellations and shift service provision from a single company to service systems offerings, whereby service systems are seen as configurations of actors, technology, information, and other internal and external service systems (Maglio et al., 2009; Vargo & Lusch, 2017). Innovation is defined as the service systems' reconfiguration (Breidbach & Maglio, 2015). For this purpose, the elements of a service system work together to improve common capabilities to act in specific situations or environments in a mutually beneficial way (Vargo et al., 2008).

The use of digital technologies can serve as enabler, promoter and improver of service systems (Vargo et al., 2008) and reinforces changes within the service innovation process (Chang, 2010; Maglio & Spohrer, 2008). As the technological change is proceeding and cannot be suspended, companies need to adapt to changing conditions. Thus new opportunities and challenges are emerging for companies. On the one hand, the use of new digital technologies promises enormous financial opportunities (Hammer, 2019) and additional revenues in the service provision via new value propositions (Breidbach & Maglio, 2016; Peters et al., 2016) and forces the innovation of services and business models in the connected service systems (Velu & Jacob, 2016). On the other hand, companies face novel needs for adoption by altering value constellations (Kagermann, 2015; Oesterreich & Teuteberg, 2016)

Digitization triggers this technological change within service systems and particularly challenges inexperienced organizations in the management of new digital technologies. As a consequence, predominantly SMEs struggle to keep abreast because of challenges regarding resource accessibility, affordability and competence of technology adoption (Vajjhala & Ramollari, 2016). The gap between SMEs and big players increases, as small companies often have less experience with integrating new digital technologies, are mindful of their resources and generally tend to act risk averse (Falkner & Hiebl, 2015). Consequently, challenges to adapt to digitization are perceived greater in SMEs then the potential opportunities to the integrating SMEs (Leyh & Bley, 2016).

In this study, the digital technology under investigation are industrial clouds. This technology is chosen, as it connects unified data standards and common ontologies with open and shared architecture in order to facilitate data exchange and service composition. In the vein of the argumentation outlined before, industrial clouds are not only a digital technology within service systems, but also connect different entities and amplify innovation in service systems (Le, Dong, Hussain, Hussain, & Chang, 2014; Wlodarczyk, Rong, & Thorsen, 2009). Digital platforms, for example cloud computing, are becoming increasingly important through their support of service innovation (Barrett et al., 2015). With access to scalable technologies, SMEs can offer services that in the past only large enterprises could deliver, flattening the competitive arena (Alshamaila, Papagiannidis, & Li, 2013). But alongside the increasing importance of industrial clouds for SMEs, the technology brings along complexity, high cost and security efforts (Trigueros-Preciado, Pérez-González, & Solana-González, 2013). These joint characteristics make this technology a worthwhile field of analysis.

Summarizing, this study is about analyzing digitization-enabled innovation with a service systems perspective by the exploration of the integration of a digital technology into service systems in particular. This study aims to reveal the specific drivers and challenges pertaining manufacturing SMEs when integrating a new digital technology, in this case an industrial cloud.

3   Theoretical Underpinning: Drivers and Challenges for Reconfiguring Service Systems

New digital technologies serve to improve services and to create innovation as well as value potentials for the service systems as a whole (Agarwal & Selen, 2011; Demirkan et al., 2011). As a consequence, digital technology can serve as enabler, promoter and improver of service systems (Fritzsche et al., 2018; Vargo & Lusch, 2017). With a service systems perspective on a meso and organizational level (Lyons & Tracy, 2013), in this study SMEs and their service systems are under investigation.

Industrial clouds, together with the associated reconfiguration of the respective service systems, are ascribed a supporting role in overcoming challenges and realizing the potential of digitization (Roth et al., 2017). In this context, the extent to which industrial clouds occupy characteristics as an operand and operant resource is explored (Akaka & Vargo, 2014; Breidbach & Maglio, 2016).

As the service systems core element "technology" is inevitably extended by the cloud technology, drivers and challenges are identified within the framework of the core elements of a service system. The study focuses on the core elements "actors", "information" and "value propositions" (Maglio et al., 2006). Within the service systems perspective, human agents are the decision-makers and thus set the starting point for the integration of a new resource, in this case for the use of a digital technology, and thus trigger the reconfiguration within the service systems (Peters et al., 2016). Within the scope of digitization-enabled innovation, human agents are exposed to both drivers (Ordanini & Parasuraman, 2011) and challenges (Demirkan & Delen, 2013). The identification of drivers and challenges relevant for digital technology integration is the focus of this study. The human agents are used as sources of information.

As the integration of digital technology includes expected challenges in processes, organizational structures and general management (Legner et al., 2017; Matt, Hess, & Benlian, 2015), in addition to the service systems perspective, this study also takes a management perspective to explore the resulting areas where extra management support for affected organizations is needed. Consequently, the results will also be viewed and classified from this perspective in the discussion, which lays the foundation for subsequent design-oriented studies and answers the need of Demirkan et al. (2015) to "understand [the] system" and "manage [the] complexity" (p. 35). The following figure (Figure 14) illustrates the framework of the study.

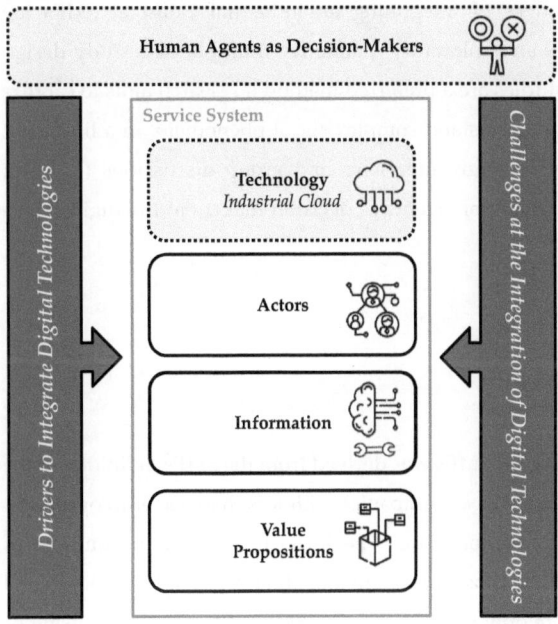

Figure 14: The framework for the empirical study in Part IV of this research

4   Research Design

To take a further step in the analysis of digitization for innovation in service systems
and to explore backgrounds of digitization-enabled innovation, this study examines
the drivers and challenges of integrating digital technologies into service systems. To
this end, drivers and challenges of integrating an industrial cloud at SMEs are
examined. The study chooses an exploratory qualitative multiple case study design
(Yin, 2018), as multiple case studies are a preferred method if research aims to capture
a holistic view and intends to understand complex social phenomena in a linear but
iterative manner (Yin, 2014). Through interviews and group discussions (Bryman,
2012), this study centers on the human agents as decision-makers in the digitization-
enabled innovation.

4.1   Data Collection

The theoretical underpinning for SMEs was derived from the SMEs definition of the
IfM Bonn[6], classifying German SMEs as companies with less than 500 employees and
an annual turnover below 50 million Euro. The focus here is on the number of
employees, since companies of this size are usually not obliged to publish their annual
turnover and this can therefore only be assumed. The SMEs of the study are using or
are about to use industrial clouds in their organizations. The reasons for the
introduction of the industrial clouds and points that prevented an earlier introduction
are raised in the SMEs.

The primary data for analysis was collected by semi-structured individual
interviews and small group discussions with four participants maximum. The

---

[6] The IfM (Institut für Mittelstandsforschung) Bonn last adapted its definition for small and medium-
sized enterprises on 01.01.2016. The SME definition can be found on the following website:
https://www.ifm-bonn.org/definitionen/kmu-definition-des-ifm-bonn/ (01.10.2018).

intention was to generate in-depth knowledge and to get rich, detailed answers (Bryman, 2012). The companies were selected on the basis of size and their activities in the mechanical engineering context and a request was made to the respective management. This study aims to explore the motivations of human agents for resource integration, why interviews were conducted with the decision-makers of the respective companies, i.e. the executive directors or general management. The organizations were each treated as a single case of the multiple case study.

Altogether, 46 participants of 22 different organizations (cases) contributed to the case study in interviews and group discussions in the springtime 2016. In certain cases (c05, c06, c10, c17, c18), the executive directors were interviewed together with selected executives at the request of the organizations. In the case of large medium-sized organizations (c20-c22), group discussions for the development of the results through consensus building were requested from the researcher and conducted in three companies. In these cases, the aim was to reach a mixed audience of employees from different backgrounds. The aim of the data collection was always to talk to the human agents responsible for the industrial cloud integration in the respective organization in order to understand their drivers and the challenges associated with the integration.

The interviews were taken to provide insights about the drivers and challenges behind the technology integration while the group discussions were used to validate the drivers and gather additional challenges during the realization and integration of digital technologies. This approach is chosen as the different perspectives of the participants in the group discussions helped to contextualize the drivers found in the interviews. Additionally, specific challenges during the integration of an industrial cloud are identified. This triangulation of data sources and data collection verifies and confirms propositions in the interviews and enhances the validity of the case study (King & Horrocks, 2010; Yin, 2014). An overview about the 22 cases and the interview partners of each case as well as the participants of the group discussions of case 20, 21 and 22 can be found in the following table (Table 3).

Table 3: Companies and participants of the interviews

Case Acronym	Company	Participant(s)
c01	Component manufacturer	Managing director
c02	Power generator manufacturer	Managing director
c03	Switch manufacturer	Executive director
c04	Machine optimizer	CEO
c05	Component manufacturer	CEO (E1)
		Technical director (E2)
c06	Machine optimizer	CEO (E1)
		Technical director (E2)
c07	Machine manufacturer	CEO
c08	Steering component manufacturer	CEO
c09	Forklift manufacturer	Service director
c10	Component manufacturer	CEO (E1)
		Technical director (E2)
c11	Component manufacturer	Managing director
c12	Component manufacturer	Managing director
c13	Cigarette-machine manufacturer	Service director
c14	Granulating-machine manufacturer	Service director
c15	Component manufacturer	Managing director
c16	Automotive press manufacturer	Service director
c17	Baking-oven manufacturer	CEO (E1)
		Technical director (E2)
		Service director (E3)
		Production manager (E4)
c18	Machine optimizer	Managing director (E1)
		Marketing director (E2)
		Technical director (E3)
c19	Wind turbine manufacturer	CEO

c20	Component manufacturer	Staff innovation dept. (E1-G1)
		Service portfolio mgmt. (E2-G1)
		Internal IT (E3-G2)
		Research & Development (E4-G2)
		Product Management (E5-G2)
		Business Development (E6-G3)
		Research & Development (E7-G3)
		IT (E8-G3)
c21	CHP manufacturer	Product manager (E1-G1)
		Product manager (E2-G1)
		Product manager (E3-G1)
		Internal IT (E4-G1)
		Product manager(E5-G2)
		Customer service (E6-G2)
		Product manager (E7-G2)
c22	Plant-manufacturer	Product manager (E1-G1)
	German section	Engineer (E2-G1)
		Domestic service (E3-G2)
		International service (E4-G2)

4.2   Data Analysis and Interpretation

To track the interviews, an audio recording device was used. Afterwards, the interviews have been transcribed and analyzed following the general principles of data analysis brought forward by Miles et al. (2013). The transcripts of the interviews and group discussions were put together and notes were scanned. Subsequently, the data were conscientiously studied and structured several times. The categories "Actors", "Information" and "Value Proposition" and the framework of Chapter 3 taken from the literature served as deductively derived first-order categories. Among these, the subcategories were formed inductively. First, the drivers and challenges were assigned to the three first-order categories and then grouped and headed within them. The statements were grouped by thematic fields derived from the interviews. Through this procedure, seven drivers and seven challenges were formed as second-order categories by in-vivo coding. This coding approach is used to ensure proximity to everyday life and content validity (Wrona, 2006). The units of analysis were sentences and short paragraphs. To support this process, it was decided to use MAXQDA as a computer aided qualitative data analysis software (CAQDAS) to ensure a systematic approach and increase both transparency and methodological rigor (Miles et al., 2013). Subsequently, the drivers and challenges raised by the human agents in the integration of an industrial cloud will be presented and explained in detail.

5   Drivers and Challenges of Industrial Cloud Integration in Service Systems of SMEs

The objective of this study is the identification of factors that drive and challenge the integration of new digital technologies in organizations with a service systems perspective. To this end, the drivers and challenges to integrate an industrial cloud into service systems are surveyed at the executive directors and general management as human agents of the service systems and as the decision-makers in SMEs of the manufacturing sector in a multiple case study. The findings are presented in two steps: First, the drivers for integrating a specific digital technology are investigated. In a second step, the internal challenges are identified. The figure below (Figure 15) provides a summary of all findings and thus an overview of the factors to be presented and explained in detail in this chapter.

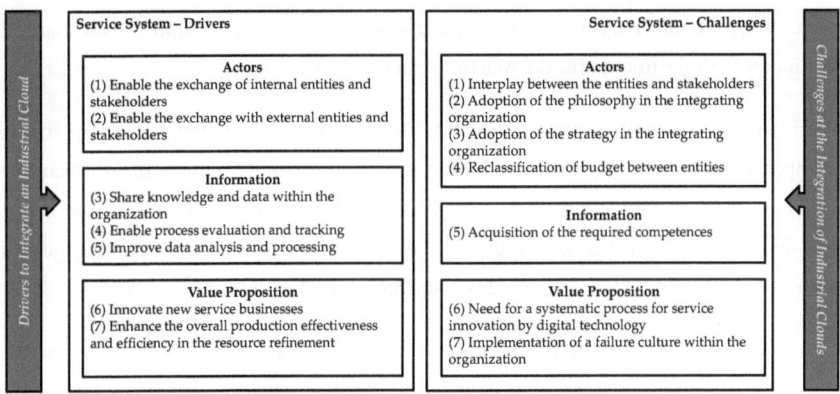

Figure 15: Drivers and challenges of industrial cloud integration in service systems

5.1   Drivers to Integrate an Industrial Cloud

To understand the motives behind the integration of industrial clouds as an example for digital technologies, the drivers behind human agents' decision for its integration are evaluated. Collected data at the participating SMEs revealed seven drivers.

5.1.1   Actors

(1) Actors: Enable the exchange of internal entities and stakeholders. Industrial clouds can provide *"a central platform to integrate every authorized to gain access to information like tools, confirmations and workflows"* (c05). In this sense SMEs have used the cloud technology to improve the data flows within the organization between the entities and stakeholders and, for example, to process, store and make data available digitally at any time to connect the actors better with each other (c18).

In addition, the exchange between departments was addressed in particular. Cloud technology was used to connect one department to another, for example the mechanical engineering department and the machine operator (c06).

However, this also requires *"new structures"*, which must first be set up in the companies (c13). This requires a lot of resources, as the forklift manufacturer's example shows. *"At the beginning it was a team of five people, now we are maybe twenty, but that is still far too little"* (c09). This is also due to the fact that the tasks of the team change and new ones are added. Data exchange is a starting point for further assignments:

"At first, this department was only concerned with producing a data transfer, but we currently have no one at all to really analyze and enhance the data in a second step. We don't have any data specialists or anyone that could evaluate anything" (c09).

(2) Actors: Enable the exchange with external entities and stakeholders. SMEs are increasingly using industrial clouds to integrate partners along the value chain

stronger into processes and communication. These external entities and stakeholders can be start-ups and suppliers (c10), but also customers of the organization:

"Of course this is an interesting approach: I have this data somewhere and the customer, with whom I work very trustfully anyway, also has the possibility to access it" (c18, E1).

The exchange platforms made possible by cloud technology then allow, for example, for internal and external exchange between *"sales and service (internal) and customers"* (c16). At an automotive press manufacturer, for example, an accessory catalogue was developed in which the customer can select his own accessories in an online catalogue in the customer portal. This in turn is also communicated to sales and distribution (c16). In this case the exchange between internal and external actors was changed in such a way that direct communication was no longer necessary.

There is a strategic, innovative and operational intention to integrate new actors and to improve the exchange with already connected actors:

„[…] involve technologies for some sort of customer connectivity for communication reasons but also for a better customer retention. Additionally, we also consider the technology side and make them more integrated in our production" (c05).

5.1.2 Information

(3) Information: Share knowledge and data within the organization. The use of technology for production capacity visualization is one example for this point. In this way, the industrial cloud can be used to *"offer free capacities and overcome machine standstills"* (c08). In this view, the technology can be used to share knowledge within the organization and its connected service systems to advance the operative dealings:

"By using the platforms on which data is stored permanently, we have a thing comparable to Wikipedia. That is a fact. Thereby we can react faster and better on things to support our customers" (c10).

A concrete example was shared by a component manufacturer. In this case *"the corresponding mechanical engineering department can easily access the required data in order to make better predictions when maintenance cycles are to be carried out" (co5)*.

Data from external actors can then also be integrated into this information exchange, which in turn means an information advantage for the respective company and its activities, as the example of the cigarette-machine manufacturer outlines:

"My plea was: Let's build the structure in such a way that we can incorporate expertise from third parties. So if we now have axle bearings from Schaeffler or similar, and they have the ability to determine the fatigue strength and residual life of their bearings, we should use their models in the background. Like this it would be smart to see incorporate this information: I enter input, let the result come out and use this result in my maintenance strategy or in my software" (c13).

(4) Information: Enable process evaluation and tracking. Cart tracking and evaluation is an exemplary usage scenario for the enabling capacity of industrial clouds in the service systems key component information (*"digital tracking of the processes within the company"*, c17). This driver also targets the general processes within the organizations:

"We aim to integrate systems into our machines for a superordinate process steering where we then are able to use algorithms wherever additional information is needed" (co5).

A future scenario is the decoupling from specific suppliers and other stakeholders of the production process through industrial clouds. This leads to interchangeability of distributors and parts of information about the requirements, as they are shared to multiple suppliers and acceptance is given to the best offer (*"our goal is to make us independent and flexible of suppliers though digital operations"*, c17).

This also implies that there is a *"return flow of information"* from external actors to the company (co6). Through the permanent exchange with customers, for example, added values can be generated:

"One added value is, that both supplier and customer are always on stock. This means that a lot of additional communication is not necessary, then the whole thing is simply effective" *(c15).*

(5) Information: Improve data analysis and processing. Central storage capacities and specific applications for visualization support this driver (*"by log-time tracking and analysis we can predict machine deterioration"*, co4). This topic was summarized by a machine optimizer under the term "data grid":

"This means making information from the different systems or even from distributed locations transparently available in real time at one location and immediately seeing where I have to act, where dependencies arise and where I can improve" (co6).

One concrete example in this context is the analysis of the production bottleneck (*"we can give these bottleneck analysis to the engineers for a better expertise"*, c10). In this case, the driver behind the integration of an industrial cloud is to improve operations within the organization and to establish a basis for innovation:

"[...] we need consistent quality. If I can analyze my machine – through sensors and data that are stored in an industrial cloud and get analyses constantly – about this quality over days and month, several derivatives are possible" (c12).

In the field of entities outside the organization, the purchaser often drives the integration of new technologies, as they want to improve their knowledge about them and as a result enhance their own production:

"[The customers] are the driving forces, particularly if a customer has many plants in action. They want to review the production process" (c17).

5.1.3   Value Proposition

(6) Value Proposition: Innovate new service businesses. The industrial clouds are also used by the SMEs to conceptualize, develop and offer new services. This leads to new and altered value propositions. Existing services can be enriched by the support of an industrial cloud. Some examples addressed in the interviews were remote maintenance (*"sending a video to the mechanics' iPhone"*, c02), predictive maintenance (*"telling our customers that one spare part has to be replaced in three month from now"*, c03) or condition monitoring (*"constantly informing the customer about his plant condition"*, c10). Often these services are data-based or data-driven. Ultimately, this can lead to new business models like performance-as-a-service (*"at the end, I'm not selling the machine, but the performance"*, c01). There are diverse opportunities for further services in this field and companies push the ideas:

"We want to improve our service processes because a great part of our business is achieved throughout service contracts. This is why we seek to optimize our service offerings" (c09).

In some cases, the pressure to improve value propositions also comes from entities and stakeholders outside the organization. The new services have to deliver a perceived value to at least one entity or stakeholder, often the customers. This shows the strategic status of this motivation to integrate new digital technologies:

"There are services we have to deliver to our customers, otherwise we are not able to sell hardware. There are also additional services which could be interesting to our customers and which hold a real value for them. But this value hast to be constituted to make our customers buying these services" (c17).

The enrichment of existing products and services often plays a major role and thus leads to an expansion of value propositions. The *"innovation of service products"* and in particular *"teleservices such as condition monitoring"* are the focus in many companies in which the new digital technology is used (c14). This can lead to radical changes within organizations:

"Digital technology is a great supporter for us to undertake big steps in our company. We integrate a complete new e-commerce strategy" (c13).

(7) Value Proposition: Enhance the overall production effectiveness and efficiency in the resource refinement. The use of industrial clouds to enable intuitive machine learning during the start-up process is one specific example where new digital technologies can help for improvement of value propositions (*"increasing the process stability during the critical start-up period"*, co1). In addition, the raw material is one part with potential for refinement in the course of productivity (*"the moisture and condition of our raw material is tracked and the machine takes these into account"*, c13). The driver targets all entities and stakeholders and intends to improve the resource allocation even outside the organization:

"[…] this is a huge topic for the production. The capacity forecast and planning is one field we are currently working on and where we identified a long-term effect" (co8).

Nevertheless, the organizations who integrate a new technology have an intention to enhance the production of their purchasers. With a better overview through data analysis on the industrial cloud, they can *"tell their customers if their equipment becomes insufficient because of size or performance"* (co5). So this can finally lead to follow-up business.

The particular significance of this point was summarized by a component manufacturer in his final statement:

"The networking of the entire production system is crucial. In the end, it is always a question of whether the customer needs something like this. It's not just a question of integrating something because it's nice-to-have and the iPhone shows something nice, but in the end it's just a question of increasing efficiency" (co1).

Altogether, the seven drivers show the potential for innovation in the service systems and the development of new value propositions in organizations, triggered by the integration of a new technology. The human agents as decision-makers of the service systems perceived the digital technology under investigation – industrial clouds – as enabler for innovation and for new and altered value propositions.

5.2   Challenges in the Integration of an Industrial Cloud

Yet, to integrate new digital technologies and bring new value propositions to life brings along some challenges within organizations. In the setting of integrating an industrial cloud into service systems of German manufacturing SMEs, seven challenges are identified and presented in detail below.

5.2.1   Actors

(1) Actors: Interplay between the entities and stakeholders. This challenge targets the need of change in the interplay of actors and the required adaptability of processes when integrating technology:

"Some entities do not communicate with each other. Sometimes one does not know that the other entity even exists but through a combination of data, the generated information would be worth a mint" (c22, E4-G2).

The main challenge named in this context is the collection and sharing of data within the organization. In many organizations, the data is currently stored in *"turrets"* (c21, E2-G1) or *"silos"* (c20, E2-G1) closely connected to only some departments. The challenge is to overcome the barriers in the interplay:

"It is important to overcome the silo mind-set. Although this will always exist and people will always belong to a specific functional unit of the organization, it is a central skill to break out of the existing entity and the former way of thinking" (c20, E3-G2).

In addition, the interaction between the actors at headquarters and from the regional representations is also decisive in this respect. Here, the structures for the development direction of the industrial cloud are often ambiguous, as the example of the CHP manufacturer outlines:

"It is often headquarters against locals and if the headquarters says nothing the locals decide and vice versa" (c21, E2-G1).

Moreover, the interviews have shown that the application situation for the industry cloud is often complex and that the interplay of a large number of relevant actors is therefore challenging. This is particularly relevant when external know-how carriers are involved, too. An example here is the use case of a component manufacturer where the internal IT and mechanical engineering department had to work together with external *"machine operators"* and *"maintenance staff"* to *"set up the algorithms for maintenance predictions"* (c05).

(2) Actors: Adoption of the philosophy in the integrating organization. This challenge refers to the need for a fundamental change in the general alignment of the organization, as the digitization requires a different dealing with technology throughout all entities and stakeholders: *"The task is also to bring this whole organization into a mental state that is open to it"* (c22, E2-G1).

One challenge in this context, for example, is the attitude towards the industrial cloud itself:

"With all the information leaving our organization, we have one internal barrier – the cloud itself. We do not know why, but in some leaderships the industrial cloud is put on a level with the devil. In this way we have to missionize and tell people that there is no alternative to industrial clouds (c20, E3-G2).

This challenge also includes the change in the general mindset of the organization. This was mentioned in the group discussions, particularly in connection with the required changes, and highlighted as an obstacle:

"We are a very conservative company, just like the equipment business in general. In some areas we are world leaders, (...) but overall the whole business is still quite old-fashioned. From the structures to the mindset" (c21, E2-G1).

(3) Actors: Adoption of the strategy in the integrating organization. Industrial clouds require adjusted handlings before, during and after its integration. In this sense, an

"analytical approach is required to identify the internal potentials" (c22, E2-G1). The innovation potential is often blocked, as the strategy for new digital technology usage is made by decision makers of the top level:

"Once you get to the point of fundamental decisions – like the adoption of an industrial cloud – our hands are tied. This is a present challenge to name" (c20; E4-G2).

Convincing the management board to introduce an industrial cloud was in the group discussion at a component manufacturer therefore described as a challenging task:

"We need hybrid cloud models to connect all entities, especially if customers and partners are currently using different clouds. To convince the internal leaders to do so is one challenge right now" (c20, E3-G2).

In this sense, the integration of an industrial cloud requires specific adaptation of the strategy of the organization what all relevant entities and stakeholders can then orient themselves to. Among other facets, the strategy needs to consider local, legal and data privacy aspects since industrial clouds allow worldwide data sharing and storage:

"One has to consider some aspects. Data in the cloud could be exposed to political arbitrariness or other aspects if it gets stored abroad" (c21, E1-G1).

One point to consider is variation in the status of the use of digital technologies between organizations – even in the same industry sector. The different entities find themselves in different stages with different goals in their digitization strategies. Some companies formed a digitization strategy over a decade ago, others are about it right now:

"In general, there is a great variety in the level of knowledge between different industries. One extreme example is the iron and steel industry where today almost everything is digitized and atomized through digital technologies. An industry you would probably not expect this from" (c04).

This variation of the status of current digitization strategies is closely connected to the time exposure for its elaboration. The detailed development of a strategy to integrate a new technology and scheduling of its use for innovation can be perceived as an obstacle for the fast launch of new solutions:

"We think the solution is ready now and we want to start with it. We do not want to elaborate a detailed strategy over the next two years. Otherwise we might find out that in the meantime someone else is providing our solution on the market already" (c20, E2-G1).

(4) Actors: Reclassification of budget between entities. As new digital technologies change business processes, different entities become more important and others dwindle in importance. Consequently, budget needs to be allocated differently:

"A big breaking factor are the different capacities at the various entities - resulting from different budgets" (c22, E2-G1).

In the group discussions, it was also criticized that too little budget is still being made available for service topics, since product innovation dominates. *"In people's minds, there is only one thought: Product, product, product"* (c22, E1-G1). This in turn presents the innovators for service innovation at the industrial clouds with challenges in their daily work and requires improvisation:

"We lack the support for the innovation department which means budget. I do not want to call us a hobby group but it is instantiated like this" (c20, E6-G3).

5.2.2   Information

(5) Information: Acquisition of the required competences. This challenge considers the attainment of altered competences geared to the new digital technologies. New knowledge and new skills are needed to use a new digital technology in organizations. It targets single entities and stakeholders but also the organization as a whole. The organizations need to create the new required competences, which are triggered by the digitization and are required to make use of the new technologies:

"Finally, there are completely different competences required. The requirements develop more into the direction of a cross section of many competences like product development, software engineering and service engineering" (c20, E3-G2).

This also means that industry-specific know-how is already taken into account when setting up an industrial cloud. Consequently, this also requires the acquisition of industry-specific competencies in the application-specific individualization of cloud solutions. The cigarette machine manufacturer has formulated this as follows:

"The cloud is supposed to provide an infrastructure, but it has to be individually customized and enriched with industry-specific know-how, so that in the end we get the results we want" (c13).

The example of the CHP manufacturer has shown that the exact certainty about the competences required can be found in the data collected and evaluated. This knowledge can then be used to make decisions about the development and acquisition of competencies:

"We have to conclude from the data which competences we will need in the future. What do we need and where do we involve suppliers? Here is also the question: What can we buy economically" (c21, E1-G1).

5.2.3   Value Proposition

(6) Value Proposition: Need for a systematic process for service innovation by digital technology. The request for adjustments in the service innovation process is found to be triggered trough the change of technology properties:

"There has to be a structured process for the development and engineering of digital and data-based services. So far, nothing in this sense is existing in our organization" (c20, E2-G1).

To transfer the new technologies into new value propositions and to use digital technology to innovate service in this sector remains a challenge for the organizations. The innovation triggered by technology is perceived to be more complex through its *"technical substructure"* and the increased *"need of explanation"* of the innovated services (c22, E1-G1).

However, the need for further developments in this field has been recognized in the companies but as the interview with the machine optimizer has revealed, it still takes time:

"We are a bit at the beginning as far as the development of services is concerned. We have to develop further at this point. But we also see ourselves as an extended workbench for service in the future" (c06).

Nevertheless, there are visions for new services, such as the emergence of service ecosystems on the industry cloud, as the interview with the cigarette machine manufacturer has shown:

"One of my visions is to shape something like Apple has already done. An ecosystem around the machine. To set an industry standard that in turn keeps the customer in the product family" (c13).

(7) Value Proposition: Implementation of a failure culture within the organization. Deciding for or against digital technologies requires faster decisions and entails risks. A culture that condenses failure is required in the development of new and altered value propositions and innovations. With this culture, the organizations hope to develop new digital solutions faster:

"I miss the chance to prototype and test new digital solutions. Having the ability to try some things on individual initiative and with a small competent team would provide the chance to finalize solutions faster" (c20, E3-G2).

In combination with the discussed elaboration of a digitization strategy, especially the time aspect is in focus and "delays" constitute the main aspect previewed by this (c22, E4-G1). To sum up, the first five challenges affect internal processes at the SMEs. Challenges number six and seven address the demand for new approaches in the development of value proposition and innovation within the service systems.

6   Discussion, Implications and Management-Oriented Research Areas

The study examines, using a multiple case study, the factors driving the integration of an industrial cloud and the challenges that exist in its integration. Thus, it explores the background of resource reconfiguration by resource integration in service systems and provides a part for analysis of digitization-enabled innovation in service systems. The service systems perspective allows an analysis of the interrelationships between the key elements of service systems: technology, actors and information, as well as value propositions (Spohrer et al., 2007). It places the human agents as decision maker in service systems at the center of the analysis and thus reveals their significance for the reconfiguration process in service systems and digitization-enabled innovation (Böhmann et al., 2014; Breidbach & Maglio, 2016).

The technology was defined by the restriction to industrial clouds in this study. As a consequence, this study outlines how the integration of an industrial cloud causes adaptations at entities, stakeholders, knowledge, skills and value propositions of the service system, to a dynamic interaction and (re)combination of different actors, resources and market offerings (Benkenstein et al., 2017; Lusch & Nambisan, 2015; Nambisan, 2013; Perks, Gruber, & Edvardsson, 2012). The restriction to SMEs provides an analysis field in which the actors tend to be limited in terms of resources and therefore gives greater emphasis to resource decisions (Vajjhala & Ramollari, 2016).

6.1   Discussion

As discussed in the literature, the main driver behind the integration of a new technology and behind improvements of the service systems is the enablement of innovation and the enhancement of service innovation (Kieliszewski et al., 2012; Maglio & Spohrer, 2008; Vargo & Lusch, 2017). This assumption gets encouraged by sorting the seven drivers for digital technology integration of this empirical study into the reconfiguration patterns in service systems according to Maglio et al. (2006). In their view, reconfiguration in service systems can be categorized in four changes in the service system. (1) First, reconfiguration can be fostered by the emergence of a completely new service system. (2) The second pattern is the connection of existing service systems to an emerging service system. (3) The third pattern targets new entities and stakeholders, which get connected to an existing service system. (4) The fourth pattern describes the distribution of current resources to other existing actors as well as the allocation of new resources to the involved actors of a service system (Maglio et al., 2006).

The identified drivers target the creation of new service businesses (6) to allow the emergence of new service systems. Additionally, the exchange between entities (1) and (2) the sharing of knowledge and data (3) to connect existing and new entities and service systems as well as improvements in data analysis (5), production (7) and processes (4) for a resource allocation of existing and new actors within the service systems have been named in the interviews. In this sense, the reconfiguration and the creation of innovation potentials is the overall driver for the integration of a new digital technology into service systems (Breidbach & Maglio, 2015; Siltaloppi & Vargo, 2014). The new digital technologies indeed serve as an enabler, promoter and improver of service systems (Fritzsche et al., 2018; Vargo & Lusch, 2017). The technological change remains important for innovation, particularly in service systems (Miles, 2007).

Following Barrett et al. (2015), digital technologies can act as operant and operand resources. The empirical research has shown that SMEs use industrial clouds, both, to provide new solutions such as predictive maintenance and remote monitoring, but also to use the technology as an independent innovation tool, for example to improve communication and data transport. The findings were thus able to reveal both roles of the industrial clouds and identify both as drivers for their introduction. Through the offerings on the industrial clouds, which include automated evaluation and tracking, the findings also contribute to smart service systems and demonstrate the role that industrial clouds can play in them (Beverungen, Müller, et al., 2017).

6.2 Implications for Practice

Integrating an industrial cloud affects entities and stakeholders within and outside the organizations. The presentation of the drivers and challenges creates a deep atmospheric picture of the integration of new digital technologies, in particular industrial clouds, in German manufacturing organizations and their connected service systems. The study focuses on the human agents within the service systems and thus reveals their decisive role for the integration of new resources. It is the task of human agents to weigh up the advantages and disadvantages of resource integration, in this case the decision whether the advantages which drive the decision exceed their challenges. Only with their decision for resource integration they start the reconfiguration of service systems and enable the innovation in them and pave the way for possible service innovations.

Moreover, the findings have not only shown that numerous SMEs are currently right before or in an integration process, but also that their drivers for integration are often similar. The main drivers here are to be seen in a transport function of the industrial cloud, to make knowledge and skills within the organization and beyond its borders available. The integration of different departments, but also of suppliers, partners and customers is a major aspect. SMEs can therefore count on the knowledge and experience of other organizations. Due to the similar conceptions in the drivers, it is highly probable that best practices of other organizations can also lead to a knowledge increase in their own company. Thus, the drivers are to be found primarily in the improvement of the service systems' core element information.

The same applies to the challenges that the integration of an industrial cloud brings with it. Here, too, very similar challenges were mentioned across the companies involved in the interview study. Most of these challenges relate to the management of the integration process in various aspects. For this purpose, the following areas are shown in which the management of SMEs needs additional support in the integration of new digital technologies and compares them with the current research landscape.

6.3 Areas Where Extra Management Support is Needed

In addition to the service systems perspective, this study thus consciously takes a further perspective on the discussion of the challenges in the integration of digital technologies and classifies the results into management-oriented research. This paradigm shift within the study has been calculated and will serve the further procedure of this research. In the following two studies (Part V and Part VI), the service systems perspective and a management orientation are integrated for the purpose of a design-oriented approach. This part of the discussion of the present study results is a first step into this direction. It serves to identify fields of action for management-oriented research by outlining areas where extra management support is needed in the resource integration, in particular when this deals with digital technologies as the integrated resource and intends digitization-enabled innovation in service systems.

As technology is one core element in every service system, the integration of a new digital technologies (being one new resource that is integrated into the service system) have to be understood and operated purposefully. The findings reveal, to ensure a targeted dealing with the occurring challenges, the initial situation and the problem needs to get structured. This is a step to be undertaken before the formal integration of the new resource. This enables the organizations to select the digital technology as new resource of the service systems in a targeted manner and determine the concrete requirements for it. Problem structuring methods can support to cope with challenges beforehand and help to identify the best fitting methods, frameworks and tools for later support for its overcoming (Cronin, Midgley, & Jackson, 2014). This approach is beneficial, as the identified challenges are diverse and the possible attempts to a solution vary in usability and direction.

One alternative in this field is a specific technology management (TM) for new digital technologies in a service systems setting. As TM affects applying technology within service systems and thereby the service systems as a whole, necessary changes on current TM practice – triggered by digitization and a service systems perspective – have to be identified and considered (Daim et al., 2010). To support unexperienced organizations, the activities of the TM can deliver guidance by process structures well known in organizations. The supporting activities of TM like knowledge management and innovation management (Cetindamar, Phaal, & Probert, 2009; Cetindamar et al., 2016; Phaal, Probert, & Farrukh, 2004) can encourage SMEs to overcome the current challenges named in findings of this study.

Nevertheless, initially the necessary adaptations to existing TM frameworks have to be derived to adjust the structured support on the requirements of digital technologies and service systems. For this purpose, the potentials of the new digital technologies for innovation have to be captured and converted through effective and dynamic TM (Cetindamar et al., 2009). As proposed by Daim et al. (2010), especially the application of TM theories, concepts and methodologies to the service systems can help firms to overcome current challenges. TM activities are required to realize the discussed technological capabilities for the resource integrating service systems. To this effect, also a service perspective in TM is required. On the one hand, a management perspective on the integration of new digital technologies into service systems leads to new viewpoints. On the other hand, taking a service systems perspective on the management of technologies reveals necessary adjustments to existing TM models and frameworks coming from the general alterations in service that led to service science, i.e. the general increased importance of service and a systems approach (Daim et al., 2010; Demirkan et al., 2016).

In the same vein, change management is required to cope with the challenges in the company philosophy adaption and the creation of a failure culture. This phenomenon is acquainted from past adaptations within organizations and remains present in service settings (Baines et al., 2016). To support organizations to overcome the challenges named in this study as the necessary adoption of the philosophy and the implementation of a failure culture, existing insights have to get transferred into a digital setting and a service systems perspective.

Finally, as the budget reclassification was named frequently through all group discussions and is closely related to the dealing with risk within the organizations, risk and budget management is obligatory for purposeful assimilations of digital technologies. In this context, not only the reallocation of budgets is gaining in importance, but also general financial planning (annual budget; planning of financial variables) and long-term planning (multi-year budget; deviation analysis) (Hungenberg, 2014, p. 49). These viewpoints have to be integrated within the considerations on resource integration. The following figure (Figure 16) summarizes the areas where extra management support in the organizations is needed.

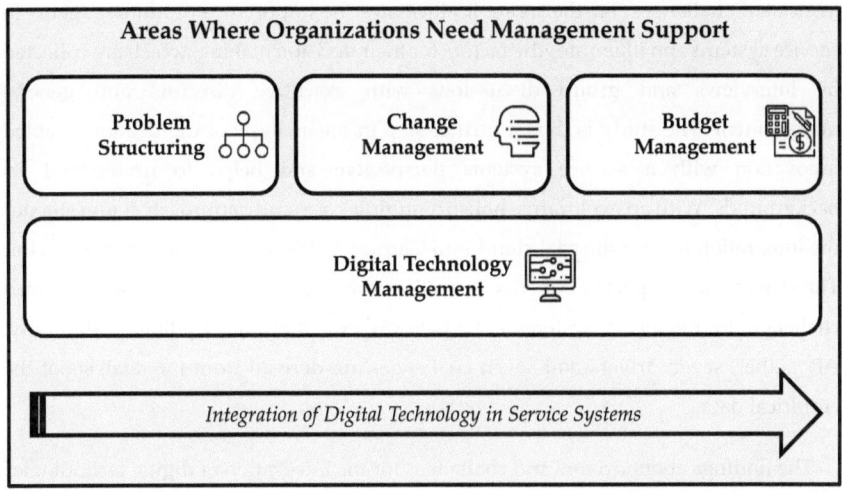

Figure 16: Areas where organizations need extra management support when integrating new digital technologies

7   Concluding Words About the Drivers and Challenges

The empirical study of Part IV explores the drives and challenges for the integration of a new digital technology into organizations with a service systems perspective. It thus reveals the reasons for integrating resources into service systems and identifies the associated challenges. Furthermore, it elucidates the importance of human agents in service systems and illustrates the factors for their decision making, which are collected by interviews and group discussions with executive directors and general management. The study is thus a further step in the analysis of digitization-enabled innovation with a service systems perspective and helps to understand its backgrounds. With an explorative holistic multiple case study approach, it investigates the integration of an industrial cloud into German SMEs in the manufacturing sector. The drivers and expected benefits as well as the occurring changes and perceived challenges for the service systems as a whole are presented in the findings of the study. Altogether, seven drivers and seven challenges are derived from the analysis of the empirical data.

The findings about drivers and challenges for the integration of digital technologies at German SMEs in the manufacturing sector show a thorough picture of the organizational level activities. Even if these findings are derived from a defined digital technology, for managers the drivers show the potentials for the individual entities and the service systems as a whole when integrating a new resource. The seven drivers aim to adjust, enhance, improve and extend the existing service systems (Kieliszewski et al., 2012; Vargo et al., 2008). The resulting innovation potentials for the service systems are the overall driver for the integration of a new digital technology in the investigated organizations (Breidbach & Maglio, 2015).

To the same extent, the challenges identified provide an overview of the fields in which companies find hurdles and barriers in the course of integrating new digital technologies into service systems. For the management, the findings thus create points on which they should pay particular attention. Since the drivers and challenges across the cases of the multiple case study were very similar, the empirical findings of the study also created a basis for best practice exchange and networking among several organizations to share benefits and overcome challenges.

By integrating management-oriented views in the discussion of the results, general areas with the need for structured support for the management of organizations during the integration of digital technologies have been identified. These fields constitute starting points for future academic work. The revealed challenges during the integration of new digital technologies show a need for management guidance, methods and tools. Necessary adaptions on current TM practice – triggered by digitization and a service systems perspective – have to be identified and considered (Daim et al., 2010). The next study of this research (Part V) takes up these points and integrates the findings into a design-oriented approach.

The data source and the method of sampling expose the multiple case study to a set of limitations. The findings about drivers and challenges for the integration of new digital technologies into service systems of German SMEs in the manufacturing sector have been identified during the integration of an industrial cloud and show a thorough picture of the organizational level with a service systems perspective. Nevertheless, the presented findings may be validated and extended by additional studies in different industries and research settings to draw generalizable conclusions (Yin, 2014).

The studies in Part III and Part IV provide a well-founded analysis of digitization-enabled innovation with a service systems perspective and build the "analyze" step of this research. Part III uses a broad data set to gain a general understanding of the current status-quo of digitization and uses the service systems perspective to understand the processes that lead to innovation in this context. With a view from outside, the study thus shows the interaction of the service systems' core elements and shows how the use of digital technology in this interaction leads to innovation and value propositions. Part IV analyzes the processes within service systems with a focus on the human agents relevant for decisions in the service systems. It is investigated which drivers are present to integrate a digital resource and which challenges are associated with it. The study contributes to knowledge about resource integration with a digitization view, focusing on the integration of a digital technology. Together, the first two studies form an understanding of digitization-enabled innovation with a service systems perspective. In this course, they reveal possible following research activities and show implications for management.

In a concluding management-oriented consideration of the results of this study (Part IV), areas are outlined in which design-oriented research would support management in the realization of digitization-enabled innovation. The following two studies (Part V and Part VI) follow a design-oriented approach and aim at designing the management of digitization-enabled innovation with a service systems perspective to support its realization. They use the findings of the first two studies as a basis and integrate them into method development and tool design. Moreover, the next study (Part V) will include the above intensively discussed management area of TM and promote the integration of TM and service innovation in the field of digitization-enabled innovation.

Part V

Managing Digitization-Enabled Innovation
in Service Systems:

Development of an Integrated Method for Digital Technology
Management and Service Innovation

© Springer Fachmedien Wiesbaden GmbH, part of Springer Nature 2020
S. M. Genennig, *Realizing Digitization-Enabled Innovation*, Markt- und
Unternehmensentwicklung Markets and Organisations,
https://doi.org/10.1007/978-3-658-28719-1_5

1   Needs and Objectives

"Technological innovation can alter the competitive status of firms and nations but its purposeful management is complex, involving the effective integration of people, organizational processes and plans" (Roberts, 1988, p.11).

Although Roberts gave this statement about three decades ago, the meaning behind it is nowadays as applicable as the day it was published. Technology continues to play an important role in companies' competitive advantage and technology management (TM) is still challenging, although these challenges have changed, particularly as a result of digitization (Demirkan et al., 2016). Thus, TM remains a factor in the realization of digitization-enabled innovation. The quote exemplarily illustrates the often predominant process view and still frequently existent lack of service focus in management-oriented research. In this research, Part V[7] is the first part of the design-oriented approach to support the realization of digitization-enabled innovation and aims at the integration of the service systems perspective with a management orientation, which also brings together two different research paradigms in order to derive the best possible benefit from both.

The previous parts of this research contribute to a better understanding of digitization-enabled innovation with the service systems perspective and to an understanding of the importance of the use of digital technology for innovation in service systems. They illustrate how the use of digital technology leads to innovation and opportunities for value increase through service innovation. In this way, the previous parts mainly add to service science and general service research. In this Part V, through the service systems perspective chosen in this research, new perspectives and aspects flow into management of digitization-enabled innovation. Conversely, the

---

[7] An earlier version of this research has been presented at the *11th Research Colloquium on "Innovation & Value Creation" (I+VC)* 2016 in Linz, Austria (Genennig, 2016) as well as in a further developed version at the annual conference of the *European Association for Research on Service (RESER)* 2018 in Gothenburg, Sweden (Genennig & Roth, 2018a). See Annex A for more information.

process thinking that is still present in management-oriented literature and corporate practice is introduced to service science. This also addresses the areas identified in Part IV in which management currently needs support for digitization-enabled innovation. In order to achieve this, service science and a management orientation are brought together in this study for the purpose of a design-oriented approach. The study aims at tackling the challenges occurring with digital technology integration as resource integration for innovation in service systems and takes up the aspects which are subject to change by digitization that got emphasized in the previous parts, in particular the management of digital technologies from its introduction to the achievement of value increase. With this focus, an integrated method is developed that provides companies with sound, fact-based and comprehensive support on the way to new digitization-enabled innovations and service innovations. The method helps with the reconfiguration of service systems and offers structured support for the orchestration of the three core elements of service systems (technology, actors and information) in the realization of digitization-enabled innovation and service innovation. To this end, this study is exploring the research question:

RQ 3: How does a structured method for supporting the management of digital technology for the purpose of service innovation in service systems look like?

The objectives of the study in Part V are therefore to identify the necessary adaptations in current TM methods brought to them by a digital technology focus and a service systems perspective. In this way, TM is adjusted to the introduction of digital technologies and the relevant activities to be carried out between the TM process steps are detected and assigned. These activities for the development of digitization-enabled innovations and resulting service innovations can then be reinforced by concrete tools that support the realization of digitization-enabled innovation in following research projects. In addition, the application of process thinking within service science represents another objective and aims at a better applicability of the method in management practice.

To explore the research question both a literature-based and an empirical approach is required. In this respect, the study follows the approach of systematic combining according to Dubois and Gadde (2002), i.e. an abductive approach to case research. In this course, an exploratory, multiple case study is set up for method development. The different cases deal with the integration of a new digital technology in an MDAX-listed company and its connected service systems. In this context, the processes from the first technology identification to the final specified value increase through new services is explored in real-world settings and the insights gained from this flow into method development. The individual cases of the multiple case study represent different technology integrations at a manufacturing oriented company. In the longitudinal multiple case study, the method was developed on the basis of the insights gained from the organization and then applied for iterative further development in the organization.

The study forms Part V of the research and represents the first study of the design-oriented part of this research. It consists of seven chapters. Following the introduction in chapter 1, chapter 2 and chapter 3 present the literature background and theoretical underpinning of the study. Chapters 4, 5 and 6 explain the empirical study, present the method as its results and discuss them. Chapter 7 concludes the study. Figure 17 places the study in the overall picture of this research.

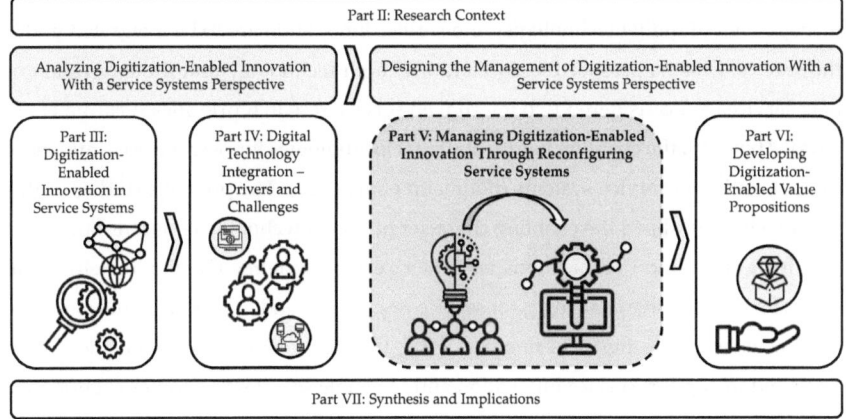

Figure 17: Part V within the overall research structure

2   Understanding the Context: Integrating Service Science and a Management Perspective

The increasing importance of service over the past decades has been highlighted in this research before. However, during that time not only the importance of service, but also the role of technology changed in major ways (Daim et al., 2010). Digital technologies became an essential part of companies´ value creation and service provision (Cetindamar et al., 2009; Yoo et al., 2010) and the characteristics of technology changed. Due to digitization, technologies have several roles and functions, on the one hand as knowledge transfer and knowledge source and on the other hand as outcome and medium of value co-creation and innovation (Coreynen et al., 2017; Legner et al., 2017; Vargo, Wieland, & Akaka, 2015). This evolution reinforces the importance of a digital technology consideration in service innovation (Akaka & Vargo, 2014) and expands the use of digital technologies in service development and execution (Barrett et al., 2015; Ostrom et al., 2010). Accordingly, the management of digital technologies is not only relevant for their introduction, but also for their later use for the purpose of service innovation (Davis, Spohrer, & Maglio, 2011).

Due to the importance of both for digitization-enabled innovation, in this study the management of digital technologies and service innovation are to be integrated under the service systems perspective. In literature, both technology and the innovation of new services are considered two interlinked service research priorities (Ostrom et al., 2015). Above all, the enabling nature of digital technologies for new services influences the innovation in service systems (Böhmann et al., 2018). The previous studies of this research have outlined the enabling character of digital technologies as a resource that gets integrated into organizations and their service systems. Grenha Teixeira et al. (2017) formulate three challenges for service researchers and in seeking to develop new services enabled by digital technology. First, the technology needs to be adequately deployed to support service innovation and to enable seamless customer experiences. Second, multidisciplinary contributions need to be further integrated in service research to support the orchestration of technology-enabled services. Finally, the integration of several perspectives will advance service research as an interdisciplinary field (Grenha Teixeira et al., 2017, p. 241). But in this context, numerous questions remain unanswered, such as the systematic method-based support of service innovation, particularly in digitization contexts and under consideration of digital technologies (Daim et al., 2010; Helm & Graf, 2018).

In addition, management orientation has scarcely been taken into account in service science so far. The apparent close connection between the management of digital technologies and service innovation remains largely unexplored in research. Daim et al. (2010) foster the integration of the two fields and specify the management-oriented aspects by a focus on TM. This study pursues this approach and follows the merging of TM and service innovation as up to now, no method exists which links TM and service innovation in a manner that both can be mapped and carried out in an interlinked approach (Daim et al., 2010; Kocaoglu et al., 2008). Within the diverse management fields, TM is considered the most relevant for digitization-enabled innovation, particularly through its focus on the development and the implementation of technological capabilities (Cetindamar et al., 2009), which can thus be incorporated into the service science's understanding of resource integration (Lusch & Nambisan, 2015). Furthermore, the TM field includes aspects of both innovation management and knowledge management (Cetindamar et al., 2009), which makes it a promising field to be considered in the context of digitization-enabled innovation. Thus, the decision in favor of TM is based on both, the empirical findings of the previous studies of this research and the characteristics of TM derived from literature. In the following, the theoretical foundations of the study are established and prepared by means of a literature review. The focus here is on the one hand on deriving a suitable general TM process and on the other hand on identifying relevant service innovation activities.

3   Theoretical Underpinning: Technology Management and Service Innovation

Within the realization of digitization-enabled innovation, the aim of this study is to develop a method that supports the management of the integration of new digital technologies with the purpose of service innovation. TM and service innovation are integrated with a design-oriented approach. This is done under the service systems perspective generally chosen in this research. The method aims at guidance and structure on the path from resource (digital technology) integration to value increase and thus concerns innovation in service systems and subsequent service innovation to achieve value increase (Breidbach & Maglio, 2014; Vargo & Lusch, 2017).

For this purpose, a literature review is created as theoretical foundation, which condenses a unified TM process from existing processes and defines an approach for service innovation and its activities. This is then used as a theoretical template for the empirical work of this study. The multiple case study later aims at parallelizing these two procedures in a new method and by adding the relevant adaptations applicable for digital technologies and a service systems perspective.

3.1   A Unified Technology Management Process

As a foundation for the following study, a general technology management process will be presented first by summarizing extant literature on the topic. The literature review of TM processes reveals that the TM process steps vary only marginally between authors and have remained unchanged over the years. So a general TM process is condensed out of existing TM processes. The underlying TM process consists of five sequential steps which originate from the greatest possible overlap of the existing processes. The following table (Table 4) shows the final TM process steps. Subsequently, the origin and meaning of the individual steps is outlined.

Table 4: The condensed steps of technology management and their origin

TM process step:	Derived from:
1. Identification & Tracking	NCR, 1987; Bhalla, 1987; Gregory, 1995; Tschirky, 1998; Spur, 1998; Cotec,1998; Phaal, Farrukh, & Probert, 2004; Rush, Bessant, & Hobday, 2007; Dodgson, Gann, & Salter, 2008; Cetindamar, Phaal, & Probert, 2009; Schuh, Klappert, & Moll, 2011; Cetindamar, Phaal, & Probert, 2016
2. Detection & Selection	NCR, 1987; Roberts, 1988; Brockhoff, 1998; Gregory, 1995; Tschirky, 1998; Spur, 1998; Cotec,1998; Bullinger, 2002; Phaal, Farrukh, & Probert, 2004; Rush, Bessant, & Hobday, 2007; Stebel, 2007; Dodgson, Gann, & Salter, 2008; Cetindamar, Phaal, & Probert, 2009; Schuh, Klappert, & Moll, 2011; Cetindamar, Phaal, & Probert, 2016
3. Acquisition & Development	Roberts, 1988; Gregory, 1995; Zahn, 1995; Tschirky, 1998; Spur, 1998; Cotec, 1998; Phaal, Farrukh, & Probert, 2004; Rush, Bessant, & Hobday, 2007; Strebel, 2007; Levin & Barnard, 2008; Dodgson, Gann, & Salter, 2008; Cetindamar, Phaal, & Probert, 2009; Schuh, Klappert, & Moll, 2011; Cetindamar, Phaal, & Probert, 2016
4. Exploitation & Diffusion	NCR, 1987; Bhalla, 1987; Roberts, 1988; Gregory, 1995; Zahn, 1995;Brockhoff, 1998; Spur, 1998; Cotec,1998; Bullinger, 2002; Phaal, Farrukh, & Probert, 2004; Rush, Bessant, & Hobday, 2007; Stebel, 2007; Dodgson, Gann, & Salter, 2008; Levin & Barnard, 2008; Cetindamar, Phaal, & Probert, 2009; Schuh, Klappert, & Moll, 2011; Cetindamar, Phaal, & Probert, 2016
5. Protection & Learning	Gregory, 1995; Zahn, 1995; Spur, 1998; Cotec,1998; Bullinger, 2002; Phaal, Farrukh, & Probert, 2004; Rush, Bessant, & Hobday, 2007; Stebel, 2007; Levin & Barnard, 2008; Cetindamar, Phaal, & Probert, 2009; Schuh, Klappert, & Moll, 2011; Cetindamar, Phaal, & Probert, 2016

1. Identification & Tracking

The first process step consists of the identification and tracking of technologies. In this context identification stands for both, finding new technologies being relevant for the organization (Cetindamar et al., 2009, 2016; Gregory, 1995; Phaal et al., 2004) and revealing innovation potentials and problem solutions that are inherent in technologies (Dodgson et al., 2008; Rush et al., 2007; Wellensiek, Schuh, Hacker, & Saxler, 2011). The first TM process step focuses on the search for triggers for innovation and change that may be signals from the market or within the organization resulting from new technological developments (Rush et al., 2007; Wellensiek et al., 2011). The other part of it, tracking, stands for the permanent implementation of this search, auditing, data collection and intelligence processes and exposes the importance for a recurring practice in intervals (Cetindamar et al., 2009).

2. Detection & Selection

Step two of the TM process consists of the decision-making process (Cetindamar et al., 2009). This process step summarizes numerous sub-steps in that note. The main task is the development of a strategic approach (Cetindamar et al., 2016; Dodgson et al., 2008; Phaal et al., 2004; Roberts, 1988; Rush et al., 2007). This contains the recognition of opportunities (Roberts, 1988), the generic strategic approach of the business (Phaal et al., 2004), the estimation and development of technological competences (Dodgson et al., 2008) and the formulation of a clear idea of where to change and why (Rush et al., 2007). Following the outcomes of TM process step one, the strategy development in this step focuses on business improvement and innovation or on the particular solution to a problem (Dodgson et al., 2008). If this has not already happened in advance, this process step involves formulating a value proposition for the intended solution made possible by the digital technology. The selection is then the alignment of the technology decision with the business strategy (Cetindamar et al., 2009). This is of critical importance as it may result in the allocation of resources and the restriction of the company's future options (Gregory, 1995). Dodgson (2008) includes the formation of collaborations by a shared commitment of resources and risk by a number of partners in this process step.

3. Acquisition & Development

The third process step describes the acquisition of the selected technologies and how to make them applicable in the integrating organization (Phaal et al., 2004). This entails the decision either to buy, collaborate, or do it oneself (Cetindamar et al., 2009). Gregory (1995) describes in this context two ways of technology acquisition. Technologies may be acquired internally, through organizational learning within the entities of the organization, or they may be acquired externally through the integration of new entities. Alternatively, acquisition by purchasing the technology remains an additional option (Gregory, 1995). The development of the new solution to be offered is the core element of this step (i.a. Cetindamar et al., 2009; Dodgson et al., 2008; Levin & Barnard, 2008; Phaal et al., 2004).

Development refers not to the evolution of a new technology itself, but relates to the individualization of the technology for the respective use (Wellensiek et al., 2011). This implies the transformation into artefacts (Levin & Barnard, 2008). The technology might need various stages of future development to final integration (Rush et al., 2007). Especially generic technologies have to be modelled into organization specific solutions.

4. Exploitation & Diffusion

Exploitation is the systematic conversion of the technological capabilities into marketable solutions (Gregory, 1995). The commercialization of the solution is the main goal of the exploitation and diffusion (Cetindamar et al., 2009; Dodgson et al., 2008). Here, the solution is matched with user requirements and the purpose which originates from the previous stages (Levin & Barnard, 2008). Schuh et al. (2011) distinguish between internal and external technology exploitation. Internal exploitation focuses on the use of unique technological capabilities within the value creation of a company. In this case, the company aims to generate a competitive advantage through the use of technology. Moreover, the integrated technology is used in a wider range of markets and for the provision of different services. In contrast, external technology exploitation stands for the supply of technologies to entities outside the company by e.g., cooperation, licensing or disposal (Wellensiek et al., 2011). Since the internal exploitation remains the main driver, innovation within the service systems is seen as the main driver for technology integration in this study.

5. Protection & Learning

The last step of the TM process includes the protection of the developed technology specific know-how (Cetindamar et al., 2009, 2016; Gregory, 1995; Phaal et al., 2004; Wellensiek et al., 2011) and the learning from the integration (Bullinger, 2002; Cetindamar et al., 2009, 2016; Phaal et al., 2004; Rush et al., 2007). The first part focuses on the protection of knowledge and expertise embedded in the developed technology-based solution (Cetindamar et al., 2009). This involves counteracting know-how-leakage to competitors to avoid imitation (Wellensiek et al., 2011).

Learning from the development & exploitation of technologies and from experiences of success and failure followed by resulting improvement constitutes the second part of this TM process step (Cetindamar et al., 2009; Cotec, 1998). A continuous development of competences and constant improvement of effectiveness, efficiency and strategy formulation are part of this (Rush et al., 2007). This is strongly linked to the field of knowledge management (Cetindamar et al., 2009). Although some publications divide protection and learning into two distinct steps (Cetindamar et al., 2009, 2016; Wellensiek et al., 2011), in the condensed general TM process they are summarized under one process step.

In conclusion, the five general TM process steps reflect the general process of technology integration. The process forces an all-embracing view of the complex connection of technological, economic and environmental aspects of technology (Wellensiek et al., 2011). The general TM process provides a basis for the subsequent method development.

3.2   Activities of Service Innovation

As discussed before, innovation within service systems does not automatically lead to service innovation and value increase. Therefore, the activities on the way to service innovation are identified in literature. These are outlined below and placed in the context of service systems. These will later serve as the basis for the design-oriented method development of this study.

3.2.1   Service Innovation Activities

The importance of service innovation activities is well recognized in service research (Edvardsson, Meiren, Schäfer, & Witell, 2013; Kelly & Storey, 2000; Kindström & Kowalkowski, 2014). In order to organize the activities of service innovation, this study is based on the four phases of service innovation: Discover, Define, Develop and Deliver. These are derived from the Double Diamond, which represents all creative processes as a number of possible ideas that get created ('divergent thinking') and later refined and narrowed down to the best of them ('convergent thinking'), what can be represented by a double diamond shape and contains these four phases (Design Council, 2013). Figure 18 gives an overview of the activities and the structure.

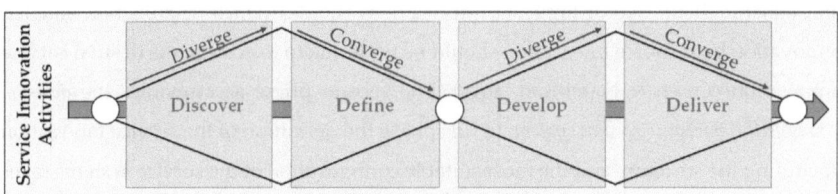

Figure 18: Service innovation activities after Design Council (2013)

In the context of service innovation, the possibilities for new solutions are explored in the first *Discover* phase. According to Den Hertog et al. (2010), there are five possible starting points: new service concepts, new customer interactions, new business partners, new revenue models and new delivery systems (Den Hertog et al., 2010). This phase represents the start of service innovation activities. In the second *Define* phase, the options of the previous Discover phase are concretized. For this purpose, in the service innovation activities the following questions will be investigated: which matters most?, which should be acted on first?, what is feasible?. The *Develop* activities follow in the third quarter in which the solutions are created, prototyped, tested and iterated. In the final *Delivery* phase, the service is finalized, produced and launched (Design Council, 2013).

3.2.2   Service Innovation Activities in Service Systems

The four phases of service innovation can be further specified for service systems. This helps to identify and allocate the activities even more precisely. To this end, Kleinschmidt et al. (2016) divide the service innovation process in service systems into four phases, particularly in a digitization-enabled context. They name the four phases: Understanding, Designing & Implementing, Operating & Changing and Value Capture. These phases are conceptually put together with the four phases of the Double Diamond, but are more specifically tailored to the needs of service systems and digitization.

According to Kleinschmidt et al. (2016), the first activities are undertaken to accompany the *idea to the decision*. In the first instance, the aim is to collect ideas for digitization-enabled service innovations and to decide which means should be used to implement them. Accordingly, a decision is made which digitization-enabled innovation by resource integration should be undertaken to achieve the desired service innovation (Lusch & Nambisan, 2015). The second phase accompanies the *decision towards the emerging service system*. In this phase the definition of the service innovation including the structure and the most suitable configuration of the service systems takes place. In this context it is determined which digitization elements will be implemented how and when to achieve the required reconfiguration of the service system and the desired digitization-enabled innovation. The third phase of the service innovation process then brings the *service system to usage*. This is about operating the new service system and applying the newly integrated digital resources. The fourth and final phase then describes the process from *usage to value increase*. This is about the systematic derivation of benefits from the service innovation that has been made possible by digitization-enabled innovation and also includes the measurement of the performance (Kleinschmidt, Peters, & Leimeister, 2016, p. 5).

Bringing this view together with the service innovation activities after Design Council (2013) as shown in the following figure (Figure 19), the activities start with the opening process of understanding, which takes up possible ideas and develops alternatives. This can be illustrated under the term *Discover* and describes the path from the idea to decision preparation. These diverging activities are followed by the converging step *Define*. Here the decision is made and transferred into a service system. The selected alternative is designed and implemented. The results of the activities of the definition are a conceptual service and a first service system configuration. This is followed by the second divergent step with the activities described under *Develop*. Here the conceived service system is operated and adapted accordingly. The divergent nature is particularly evident when prototyping, trying out and adapting digitization-enabled innovations for service innovation. The fourth group of activities creates the convergence of the service innovation process in the concrete increased value capture based on the innovated service. These activities are referred to as *Deliver* and are primarily concerning the specific value of the solution. Ultimately, these activities are aimed at value increase and value capture. In the following, the general TM process and the framework of service innovation activities are used as a basis for an integrating method. The design-oriented part of this study encompasses both fields relevant for digitization-enabled innovation: TM and service innovation.

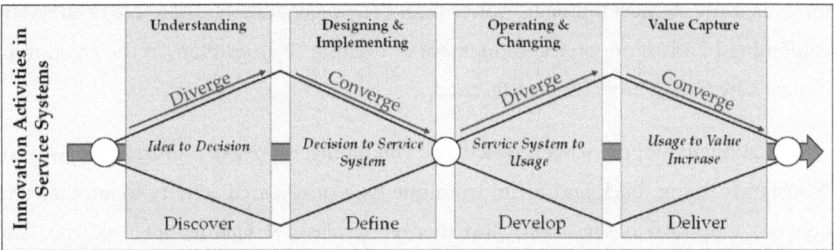

Figure 19: Service innovation activities in service systems, inspired by Design Council (2013) and Kleinschmidt et al. (2016)

4   Research Design

This study is part of the design-oriented step of this research and aims to develop a method for supporting and structuring digitization-enabled innovation for service innovation with a service systems perspective for management. This should take into account the role of TM in service innovation and support both, the steps of TM and the activities of service innovation on the way to new solutions. For this purpose, a method is designed and evaluated using an explorative qualitative research approach, as it aims to close a gap in present practice (Eisenhardt, 1989; Miles et al., 2013). In particular, systematic combining with a multiple case study with four individual cases serves as a basis for the development, iteration and later application of the method (Dubois & Gadde, 2002; Eisenhardt & Graebner, 2007).

Systematic combining allows a stronger theory dependence than induction and is at the same time more open to empirical research than deduction. The approach suggested by Dubois and Gadde (2002) is closer to an inductive than a deductive approach and forces a continuous interplay between theory and empirical observation that is stressed more heavily than in the grounded theory approach. It is therefore a form of abduction that is different from only a mixture of deductive and inductive approaches. The proposed abductive approach is fruitful if the research objective aims to discover new things, for example new relationships. Similar to grounded theory, the main concern is related to the generation of new concepts and the development of theoretical models, rather than confirmation of existing theory and it approaches more towards a theory development, rather than theory generation. Therefore, systematic combining builds more on the refinement of existing theories than on the creation of radical new ones (Dubois & Gadde, 2002).

The abductive approach of systematic combining represents an iterative way of "constantly going 'back and forth' from one type of research activity to another and between empirical observations and theory" (Dubois & Gadde, 2002, p. 555). The ingredients of systematic combining that get matched during research are therefore the theory and its frameworks as well as the empirical world through the cases. In this case, the TM process and the service innovation activities acquired from the theory are thus combined and supplemented by the relevant adaptations through empirical findings from the multiple cases. Theory and empirical findings are combined to form the objective of an integrated method. Here the theoretical foundations and knowledge constantly provide assistance. In the course of traceability and in view of compliance with the quality criteria of qualitative research, the present study follows a structured research process (Chapter 4.1) that continues to take into account the iterative nature of systematic combining, but also provides the necessary structuring.

4.1   Research Process

The research process was inspired by the approach used by Frow et al. (2015) and consists of workshops and interviews structured in three phases, as shown in Figure 20. In the sense of the systematic combining approach, an iterative approach was adopted within the phases and both theory and empirical findings were consulted (Dubois & Gadde, 2002). In phase 1, three cases were analyzed in order to identify requirements for the method to be developed and to identify necessary adaptations to the process steps and activities derived from the theory. Another case was analyzed in phase two to develop and refine the method and to accompany the parallelization of the two approaches of technology management and service innovation through empirical findings by method application. The study concluded with the third phase. Following the argumentation of Frow et al. (2015), interviews and a facilitated workshop process should be chosen when the study aims to facilitate immediate feedback and assist the efficient flow of information (see also: Linstone & Turoff, 2002), which is also in line with the generally applied systematic combining approach. In this sense, each of the three phases was outlined interactively and iteratively and applied a qualitative abductive approach. The first two phases were concerned with the iterative development of the method itself, while the third phase was targeting the evaluation and finalization of the method and its application within an organization.

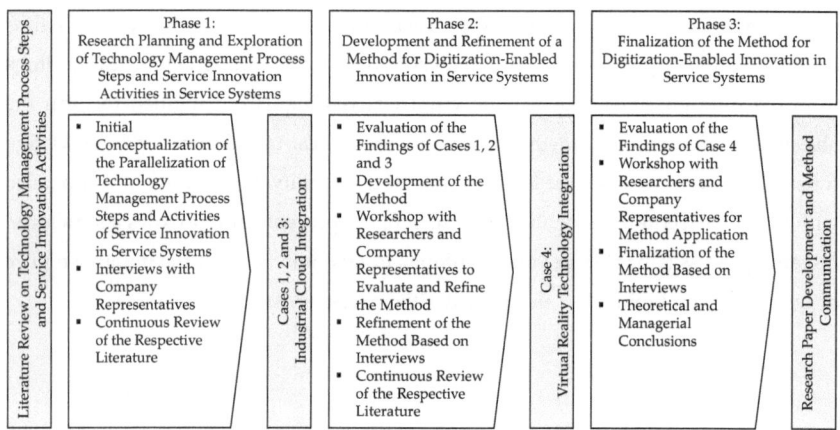

Figure 20: Outline of the empirical study

Phase 1: Research Planning and Exploration of Technology Management Process Steps and Service Innovation Activities in Service Systems

The focus of this phase was the identification and refinement of the relevant TM steps and the service innovation activities in service systems. For this purpose, an extensive literature review was conducted beforehand, which resulted in a condensation of the relevant TM process steps as well as a four-tier innovation procedure in service systems (as presented in chapter 2). Building on this, three different cases were analyzed, integrating three digital technologies into different service systems. The design of the four cases of this multiple case study is explained in detail in the following chapter (4.2 Data Collection).

The qualitative data was collected and analyzed to enrich the output of the literature review. The qualitative findings were iteratively reflected with the literature. The main focus was put on the identification of special features of the TM of digital technologies as well as on the identification of linking approaches of TM steps and service innovation activities. The synthesis of these findings formed the decisive input for the next phase.

Phase 2: Development and Refinement of a Method for Digitization-enabled Innovation in Service Systems

Based on the analysis of literature and cases 1, 2 and 3, a first version of a method for digitization-enabled innovation in service systems was developed and refined further. In a workshop with participants from research and practice, the first version of the method was presented and intensively discussed for refinement. A concluding group discussion summarized the remarks and the feedback. Subsequent interviews also served to pick up the points of the feedback and further specified them for implementation. A continuous review of the respective literature based the method adaptations on both qualitative findings as well as on literature.

Phase 3: Finalization of the Method for Digitization-Enabled Innovation in Service Systems

In the third and final phase, the method was further adapted on the basis of the feedback gained. During a final workshop, the method application was evaluated. The workshop included the contents of case four and gained findings about the application of the developed method. Concluding interviews specified feedback and discussed managerial implications of the method application. Subsequently, the method was prepared for scientific publication and communicated on practice-oriented events.

4.2   Data Collection

Within the multiple case study, four individual case studies were conducted. Eisenhardt (1989) recommends the investigation of four to ten cases. In this way, multiple case studies provide a stronger foundation for theory development and are more generalizable and robust in comparison with single case research (Eisenhardt & Graebner, 2007; Yin, 2014). All four cases deal with the integration of a new technology into a service system, but in four different applications and four different contexts (Yin, 2009). The case studies were all conducted at a family-run component manufacturer, examining four different service systems into which different digital technologies were integrated. The company is part of the German MDAX and thus functions as an exemplary company for Germany's most important form of medium-sized companies. The four cases were each accompanied over longer periods of time. Data on the various cases was collected over a period of three years. In the first three cases, the introduction of numerous cloud solutions was accompanied. These affected different parts of the company – in one case the entire company and in two other cases individual departments – and thus also different service systems. The introduction of the digital technologies was not parallel but offset, so that knowledge could be drawn from the previous cases. The fourth case intentionally dealt with an additional technology that had different characteristics. In this case, the integration of a virtual reality application was accompanied.

Data was collected by semi-structured interviews (Parker, 2012) and workshops with group discussions and feedback circles. The suitable respondent candidates were identified by an evaluation with a company representative identifying the experts of the technology integration processes. Eisenhardt and Graebner (2007) recommend interviewing people who view the phenomenon from diverse perspectives to limit the bias. Therefore, is was taken care to select the interview participants across departments and competencies. The interviews always started with a short introduction to the themes and to the objectives of the interview and dealt with the process steps of the TM, the specific service innovation activities, the processual changes triggered by digitization and parallelization of the TM process steps and service innovation activities. Later, the interviews helped to evaluate the method on different development stages. New data was collected until saturation occurred and additional interviews and group discussions were not providing new insights. Following the guidelines of Eisenhardt (1989) and Miles et al. (2013) who see adjustments during the data collection process as essential, the interview guideline was continuously improved and adapted according to insights from the interviews before.

At first, the interviews were conducted face to face in order to allow the observation of the non-verbal communication. However, due to geographical distances and the wish of some interviewees, some interviews were conducted by phone. In phase 1, altogether, eleven 60 - 90 minute interviews were conducted with relevant actors involved in the integration of different industrial clouds. Some of the interview partners were involved in several of the three cases at the same time and could therefore also be used as cross-case respondents. In phase 2, the workshop took place with six researchers and company representatives who contributed to the group discussion. Two additional 60-90 minute interviews evaluated the method application and the method itself. In phase 3, five researchers and company representatives reviewed and reached agreement on a final version of the method in a workshop and a concluding group discussion. The participants were all involved in the integration of the new technology. The workshop and two additional interviews allowed an iterative refinement of the method and the innovation activities in particular. The table in Annex E illustrates the participants of the group discussions and interviews of the multiple case study.

4.3   Data Analysis and Interpretation

To track the interviews and group discussions in the workshops, an audio recording device was used to capture the answers. Afterwards, the interviews and discussions were transcribed and analyzed following the general principles of data analysis and reduction brought forward by Miles et al. (2013). The transcripts of the interviews and group discussions were put together and notes and pictures were scanned. The transcripts were double checked to ensure their accuracy and freedom of typographical errors. The extended text was condensed and rearranged into a more comprehensible and manageable form in line with the research objectives.

The data were then structured according to the abductive coding process prescribed by the systematic combining approach. To support the organization of the data, it was decided to use MAXQDA as a computer aided qualitative data analysis software (CAQDAS) to ensure a systematic approach and increase both transparency and methodological rigor. According to the guidelines of Miles et al. (2013), data condensation took place in form of manual first- and second-cycle coding. The first cycle of coding clustered the statements in thematic groups while the second coding cycle revealed patterns in the data.

In phase 1, the five TM process steps and the four service innovation activities served as first order categories. The relevant passages were collected among these. The unit of analysis were sentences and short paragraphs. In phases 2 and 3, the general statements on the method were collected and subdivided into the general first-order coding categories "parallelization", "applicability" and "improvement".

5   Method for Digitization-Enabled Innovation in Service Systems

Based on the findings of the multiple case study, the research goal of developing a structured method for supporting the management of digital technology for the purpose of service innovation in service systems was addressed with a method integrating TM processes and service innovation activities in a parallelized approach. This maps the synchronization of both integrating a new digital technology as a resource to the service systems for innovation and innovating services through the reconfiguration of the service systems. In this way, the innovation potentials created by the integration of a new digital technology into service systems are to be turned into service innovation potentials. At the same time, the process of integrating digital technologies as new resources to the service systems is methodically guided. Thus, the method supports the realization of digitization-enabled innovation. In the following, the adjustments to the TM process steps, which are based on the empirical data, are first explained. With the help of interviews and group discussions, guiding questions were formulated for each TM process step, which meant a sharpening of the content towards digital technologies and the integration of the TM process steps into the service systems perspective. The method is afterwards presented in detail and its empirical anchoring made explicit. In this course the interplay of TM and service innovation is outlined. It is shown in detail how the TM process steps and service innovation activities interlock.

5.1   Digitization Forced Changes in Technology Management

As a result of the multiple case study, guiding questions were formulated for each TM process strep which reflect the adaptations to digital technologies as well as the service systems perspective. Digitization brings changes in terms of implementing and performing these steps when integrating a new digital technology:

"There are many reasons why we are slow. One reason is, it is very, very complex for typical industrial companies. This means that an industrial company must first build up the competence to understand this. So, many don't understand what it means to connect machines at all. They don't know what it means to have a platform, build the infrastructure and build the data models" (i11).

It is the perspective and the flexibility in the application of the TM process steps that changes though digitization. Jumps and setbacks within the steps are simpler and are therefore carried out continuously.

"However, steps 1 and 2 were used strongly iteratively. We went always back and forth. Do we prefer to take AR from the provider or do we prefer VR from the other provider or do we even take VR or over all AR? That merged into each other, so 1 and 2 have been really iterating" (i12).

This reached so far that one interviewee generally summarized the two steps under the term introduction and described their integration as very closely connected:

"Identification/observation of possible technologies we have already done in part before. [...] Well, if you look at this as planning and selection, then from my point of view it is rather a kind of general introduction. In my eyes, we couldn't really separate that" (i11).

This shows the close link between the first two TM process steps in the context of digital technologies. Nevertheless, the other interviewees emphasized the separation of the first two steps. With regard to the TM process steps, this also means changes in practices and to a certain extent a rather unstructured approach. For example, there is a lack of *"a kind of guideline such as we have for basic machine purchases where we have a specification book with technology needs and actions"* (i09).

As a result of the interviews and group discussions, the guiding questions were formulated with respect to the intensified iterative character of the TM process steps. Moreover, the service systems perspective was included in the questions in the form that the questions should be answered for a specific service system. This creates a specification which helps in the discussion of the background and in the decision processes, so the consensus of the first group discussion. The iterative nature of the TM process steps in the context of digital technologies was also illustrated in the sequence of the TM steps. Decisions at individual process stages which later turn out to be inappropriate can usually be corrected more easily and quickly. Back steps in the process are possible at any time. For example, the entire process can be restarted from the beginning even before it has been completed. Although Protection & Learning is the last step, it does not mean learning from the process, but rather improving the use of digital technology and the service developed. The learning and adaptation of digital technology and perhaps also the selection of an alternative digital technological solution takes place in all identified process steps. Figure 21 gives an overview of the adapted guiding questions and the adapted process operation. The guiding questions of the respective TM process steps are as follows:

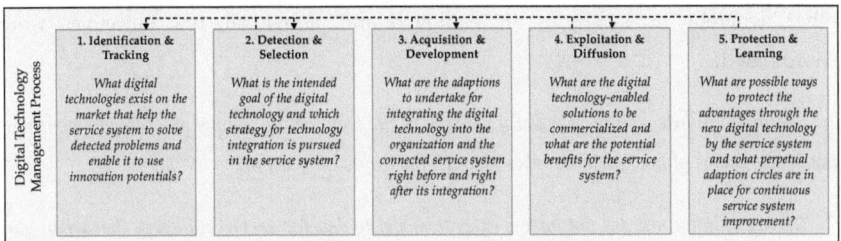

Figure 21: Digital technology management process in service systems

1. Identification & Tracking: *What digital technologies exist on the market that help the service system to solve detected problems and enable it to use innovation potentials?*

2. Detection & Selection: *What is the intended goal of the digital technology and which strategy for technology integration is pursued in the service system?*

3. Acquisition & Development: *What are the adaptions to undertake for integrating the digital technology into the organization and the connected service system right before and right after its integration?*

4. Exploitation & Diffusion: *What are the digital technology-enabled solutions to be commercialized and what are the potential benefits for the service system?*

5. Protection & Learning: *What are possible ways to protect the advantages through the new digital technology by the service system and what perpetual adaption circles are in place for continuous service system improvement?*

5.2   Method for Digitization-Enabled Innovation in Service Systems

The developed method (method for **DIGIT**ization-En**Ab**Led Innovation in Service Systems = **DIGITALISS**) maps the process of digitization-enabled innovation and service innovation comprehensively. As a result of systematic combining of theory and empirical findings, the five TM process steps and four service innovation activities are carried out in parallel, alternating respectively between one process step and one activity. This way, the integration of new digital technologies as a new resource in service systems is parallelized with the activities of service innovation.

First and foremost, the coordinated activities and process steps were identified in the cases of the multiple case study in order to parallelize the two approaches in the method. This started from the fact that the two processes were independent of each other, whereby no synergies are exploited and, above all, few objectives were coordinated:

"Technology integration is usually the task of the technology management department and the development of new services takes place in the innovation department" (i13).

"In my opinion, we did not have a process model to develop services. Except that when you don't know what to do, you form a task force" (i15).

The TM process steps form the upper part of the method (Figure 22). The lower half of the method consists of the service innovation activities already adapted to service systems in the literature as presented in chapter 2.

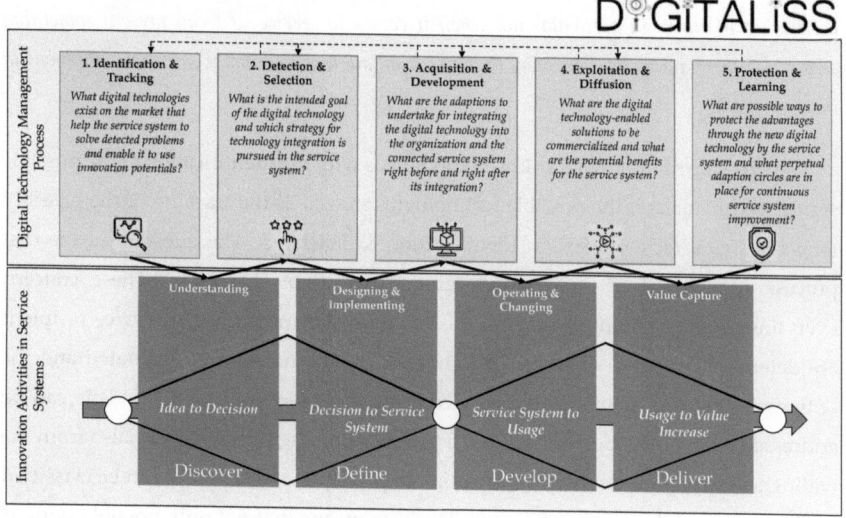

Figure 22: Method for digitization-enabled innovation in service systems – DIGITALISS

Located between the TM process steps, the service innovation activities describe the activities which are conducted in the service systems on the way to newly innovated services. As defined and outlined in chapter 2, in this research the activities are based on the Double Diamond of the Design Council (2015) and are embedded in the TM process through the DIGITALISS method. They form an interplay between diverging and converging activities and thus accompany the process steps both in the creative development of new digitization-enabled solutions as well as in the selection of the best possible alternative. This understanding was mainly derived from literature and brought to the cases of the multiple case study as a theoretical basis.

In this context, the interviews have shown that converging activities in the organization are gaining in importance. These help to present service concepts that have been formulated in terms of content and thus go beyond traditional cost accounting:

"Content based decision-making, i.e. converging methods, are, in my opinion, also becoming increasingly important for our company. At the moment it is the case that decisions are taken

at higher management exclusively via cost and economic calculation. It is not possible to express everything in euros, in particular not when it comes to service. If I can present something structured there, it will help me more than the calculation of how many euros will jump out in the end" (i15).

The first step of the DIGITALISS method deals with the identification of the possible service recipients and the possible technologies as well as the tracking of the possibly relevant digital technologies (1. Identification & Tracking). The question of the first process step thus leads to the diverging activities of "Discover". These concern everything related to understanding the situation. The needs of the service recipient are determined, the possible digital technological alternatives are evaluated and the options for starting points of the service to be designed are identified. This can be addressed from both sides, either from a problem-solving perspective or also from the willingness to exploit innovation potential. In principle, the activities can be classified on the way from the *"idea to decision"*. This also means that not only possible options are raised, but also the integration of a decision preparation. For this purpose, initial feasibility assessments are made. In the VR case, specific definition questions such as *"What is VR?", "What is augmented reality?", "What is mixed reality?", and "What else is on the market that goes in this direction?"* were answered (i12).

The "Discover" activities initiate the technology management process step 2. Detection & Selection. In the specific case of digital technology, this means selecting the best possible solution. In this context, however, the question of the availability of the chosen digital technology also arises:

"In this respect, we always had to look at a technology range and determine whether it is available at all. A year ago, availability meant finding an industry cloud that could be deployed. That wasn't even noticeable from the outset with the industry clouds, because at the time they weren't even in the development status that we could have rolled them out directly" (i15).

Triggered by the specific selection of the digital technology, the subsequent activities of service innovation are launched. These are summarized under the "Define" term and primarily aim at the design and implementation of the solution to be developed. This concerns both the concrete extension of a service system on the one hand and the specification of the service on the other. The activities of the "Define" block thus accompany the path of service innovation from *"decision to service system"*. The "Define" activities thus converge the alternative solutions into a concrete service system and deliver as essence a digitization-enabled service concept and a respective service system. In the VR case, the service system was developed in the first workshop. Based on this, the relevant entities and stakeholders were identified. First of all, the desired value proposition had to be emphasized *"in order to know who to talk to" (do3)*. The service architecture of the later service was here created. The questions raised were summarized as follows by an interview partner who was actively involved in the design of the service concept:

"We aimed to develop a transparent basis for decision making. Where will this service be located later? How does it look like later? Where will this service be implemented and offered? [...] how is the service running so far, what is the difference to the new service, what simplifies it? What skills do I need in which position? Where in a company structure does it make sense to locate the service?" (i14).

After the solution has been conceptualized and the service system specified, the third step of the TM process is attained. Under the heading Acquisition & Development, the adaptation requirements of the digital technology and the service system are collected and processed. This third step of the TM leads to the "Develop" activities of service development. They pave the service systems´ way from the previous configuration of the *"Service System to Usage"*. In the empirical study, possible usage scenarios were evaluated in this phase. *"We have identified a total of 10 different use cases that we could theoretically roll out in our service system" (i12).* From these, the modalities for their implementation were then determined.

The activities are concerned with getting the conceptualized service now into the conversion. For example, the implementation possibilities are tested and evaluated by means of prototyping or various tests. The activities are therefore concerned with the points Operating & Changing. Through the withdrawal of various alternatives and the opening of the solution space, the activities of "Develop" are again of a divergent nature and open up the scope of the concrete solution.

The fourth step of TM, Exploitation & Diffusion, follows the "Develop" activities of service innovation. This questions the concrete solution arising from the digital technology and focuses on the commercial use of digital technology in connection with the developed solution. After dealing with the exploitation aspects of digital technology, the activities of the service innovation also take a look at value capture. In the context of the final "Deliver" activities, the service systems' path from *"Usage to Value Increase"* is taken. The final converging activities explore, for example, the service delivery options and possible revenue models. The result is not only the concrete digitization-enabled innovation for service innovation but also the value increase that can be achieved for the actors of the service system through its implementation. In the VR case, the cost evaluation was undertaken:

"We have already selected a concrete data set which we have already worked with and implemented as a prototype. But the real world also dictates that we must first draw up a cost-benefit calculation" (i11).

The final fifth step of the TM is Protection & Learning. As already mentioned before, digitization enables permanent learning and short-lived adaptation of the technology. Learning is therefore included at all levels of the TM. Adaptation cycles can also accelerate permanent learning and adjustment. The focus of the last TM step is therefore rather the protection of the own (further) developments in relation to the digital technology. This emphasizes that the TM process does not reach a final conclusion but is continued after the introduction of the service. Permanent adjustments and fine-tuning are intended and will be enforced. The empirical data has also shown that this was iteratively integrated into resource integration and service innovation as a continuous process. The last TM step is thus an ongoing one that remains present above all in the continuation of the project and in the opening of the technology for further use cases and in the expansion of the service portfolio.

The advantage of the parallelization of TM and service innovation and thus also the bundling of activities in one department was summarized in the interview on the VR use case of DIGITALISS by one interviewee form service development:

"When it comes to technology management, we have the advantage that we handle this part ourselves in the VR case. When we introduced the cloud, we always had to rely a lot on other departments, and now we can tackle this comprehensively" (i15).

This also reflects how the individual cases of the multiple case study learned from each other and how the VR case learned from the insights of cloud integration. The parallelization of TM and service innovation and the integration of these into one department was thus highlighted as operationally feasible and valuable.

6   Discussion and Implications

The developed method merges the two fields of TM and service innovation in a digital context and with a service systems perspective. It aims at two objectives: on the one hand, the stimulation and expansion of service research with a concrete technological impact and, on the other hand, the support of digitization-enabled innovation-oriented activities in practice.

6.1   Discussion

The DIGITALISS method thus takes a concrete step towards the integration of TM into the service sector and service science as requested by research (Daim et al., 2010). With the specification on service systems and the support of service innovations in these, the DIGITALISS method feeds the in service science likewise required tool and method support with concrete artifacts (Böhmann et al., 2014; Helm & Graf, 2018; Kleinschmidt et al., 2016). The method supports resource integration in service systems and the subsequent transfer of the resulting innovation through reconfiguration of the service systems into new solutions, service innovation and value increase for the service systems (Lusch & Nambisan, 2015; Vargo & Lusch, 2017). DIGITALISS structures and manages the reconfiguration process in service systems and considers all three core elements (Breidbach & Maglio, 2015; Vargo et al., 2008). The main focus of the method is on the integration of digital technology as a new resource of the service system, which is why the method in all steps reflects the activities with the service systems core element *technology*. The knowledge and skills associated with reconfiguration, i.e. the *information*, are mainly dealt with in the service innovation activities of the DIGITALISS method. These imply the adaptations within the service systems core element innovation. The core element *actors* is in the middle of the method at the center of consideration when it comes to transferring the decision for a new digitization-enabled solution into a specific service system in the "Define" activities. In addition, the service systems perspective generally ensures a broader consideration of all actors involved and of the overall system. To support this further, the service systems orientation of the activities within the method provides approaches for future substantiation through specific service systems tools for the respective service innovation activities. Part VI of this research addresses this with the design of a tool. Conversely, the DIGITALISS method also transfers the service focus to the TM discipline, which still tends to be more product-oriented (Cetindamar et al., 2016; Lee, 2015). The forced change of perspective can lead to a stronger service orientation in TM and to subsequent academic discourse, which will further stimulate the field of research.

In the context of smart service systems, the DIGITALISS method also offers an approach to guided service innovation and takes up the specifics which result from the technologies used in them (Beverungen, Müller, et al., 2017). It thus provides an answer to one of the major challenges in smart service systems, namely supporting the development and design of such systems (Demirkan et al., 2015, p. 734). In this context, the DIGITALISS method also makes a contribution to general service innovation research and addresses a currently still fragmented field by process-related support of innovation activities and conception (Carlborg, Kindström, & Kowalkowski, 2014). Moreover, the DIGITALISS method supports the human agents as decision-makers in service systems with a structured and guided approach (Peters et al., 2016). It takes up the findings of the previous study (Part IV) and follows the view of human impact within service science (Breidbach, Antons, & Salge, 2016).

6.2   Implications for Practice

The permanent interplay between TM steps and service innovation activities represents a close intermeshing of the two fields. The method picks up on the process thinking expressed in management-oriented literature and operational organizational practice. However, the TM process is used more as a structure for the service innovation activities located below and the iterative nature of the process steps is emphasized. Thus, the DIGITALISS method sees itself less as a process model than as a guided procedure that points out the relevant aspects and thus ensures that the respective questions are considered along the way.

The multiple case study has shown that the two processes in companies are often located separately in different departments. This makes it more difficult to exploit potential synergies and focus on common goals. With the developed DIGITALSS method, digital technology is closely linked to the service developed. This ensures a purposeful use of digital technology and accelerates the emergence of digitization-enabled innovation for service innovation. This became particularly clear in the application of the method, in which the organizations emphasized the permanent critical reflection of the use of digital technology. The VR case has shown that an early determination of the later value proposition has an influence on the technology integration. In this context, the guiding questions encourage the continuous control of the sense and suitability of digital technology for service innovation. The outstanding importance of the value proposition development which was recognized in the multiple case study will be taken up in the next study with a design-oriented approach.

Moreover, the multiple case study has demonstrated the advantage of conscious opening and closing activities in service innovation through divergent and convergent activities. The transfer of the principles of the double diamond into service innovation (Design Council, 2013) accordingly raises awareness of opening and closing activities in the process of resource integration in service systems and concluding service innovation. In particular, the reopening of the alternatives after the agreement on a concept represents the many possible solutions that still exist at this point in time. This is also relevant due to the digital aspects of the technologies and solutions which still leave sufficient room for changes at this time. In the identification of digital technologies and the associated competence-based selection of new partners for the organization, the service systems perspective included in the DIGITALISS method led to an early consideration of the role of the new partners in the service systems. The service systems perspective thus leads management to consider all actors involved in the realization of digitization-enabled innovation and strengthens the importance of their positioning in the service systems.

7 Concluding Words About the Developed Method

Part V takes up the previous findings of the research and represents its first design-oriented part. A method is developed by systematic combining (Dubois & Gadde, 2002) of theory and an empirical multiple case study. As a result, the DIGITALISS method parallelizes the two procedures of TM and service innovation. Process steps of TM are parallelized with activities of service innovation and put into an integrated approach within the service systems perspective. It helps to reconfigure service systems by the introduction of digital technologies as a new resource and traces the path from innovation to value increase. The reconfiguration of service systems is thus initiated, realized and continued in a targeted manner and the adaptations of the three service systems core elements technology, information and actors are converted into service innovation. The method consequently covers the spectrum of new digitization-enabled innovation and resulting service innovation in service systems and supports the realization of digitization-enabled innovation.

The study contributes to the research landscape due to the mutually conflated perspectives of a management orientation and a service systems perspective and by consciously bringing together the two paradigms. It expands the service science by the aspects of TM and provides an application-oriented method which is complemented by real-world knowledge in its development. On the other hand, it also highlights the importance of service systems for management-oriented literature and provides an additional perspective for future research activities.

For management, the study highlights the importance of parallelizing TM and service innovation. This offers advantages for the mostly separate processes for closer coordination and the use of synergy potentials that arise. The scientific accompaniment of the integration of new digital technologies for service innovation in the multiple case study has highlighted the importance of a not only coordinated but also integrated approach of technology management and innovation departments. In addition to their parallelization, these must be bundled if possible in order to act in a targeted and coordinated manner. The DIGITALISS method therefore strives for a change of perspective in management, which is decisive for the realization of digitization-enabled innovation and the resulting service innovation.

Nevertheless, the study is subject to some limitations due to its orientation and approach. The multiple case study was conducted in a single company, yet dealt with four different cases in diverse service systems with different size and characteristics. In order to demonstrate the broad applicability and to make further possible adjustments to the method, a broad application is foreseen. This will both stimulate scientific discourse and further demonstrate its practical applicability.

The DIGITALISS method does not represent the completion of the innovation activities. It moderates, structures and supports the management of digital technologies for the purpose of service innovation. However, digital transformation also serves to develop completely new business models (Zolnowski, Christiansen, & Gudat, 2016). The subsequent transformation of digitization-enabled innovation into comprehensive business models is a possible path for future research.

The contents and elements of the DIGITALISS method were collected from both literature and empirical findings, as the main purpose of this study was to develop and prototype the present method. Now it is up to future research projects to continue applying and evaluating the method. In this way, the generalizability and cross-industry applicability of the method must be emphasized and further evaluations and possible refinements of the method must be carried out. Qualitative follow-up projects can thus further refine the elements and promote possible sharpening.

Furthermore, the transfer of innovation potentials into value increase is an essential element of the DIGITALISS method. The multiple case study has shown that early development and concretization of value propositions is advantageous. Appropriate approaches and tools in the context of digitization-enabled innovation in service systems remain objects of future research activities. To this end, the following study (Part VI) designs a tool for developing digitization-enabled value propositions from scratch. The purpose of this is then to cover the first two activities of service innovation and to provide support through both converging and diverging characteristics. The study in Part VI thus refers to the findings from this study.

Part VI

Developing Digitization-Enabled Value Propositions in Service Systems:

Design of a Supporting Tool

1 Needs and Objectives

"To succeed in the digital economy, companies must offer a unique value proposition that is difficult for both established competitors and start-ups to replicate" (Ross, Sebastian, & Beath, 2017, p. 9).

The development of such a value proposition is the attention of every company. Digitization also has a great impact on value propositions through the availability of data and the sharing of information, forcing companies to make adjustments to stay successful (Amit & Han, 2017; Coreynen et al., 2017). The study in Part III has shown that either completely new value propositions are created as a result, or existing value propositions are extended and adapted. A decisive finding from the previous study in Part V is the great importance of value proposition development in the course of reconfiguration of service systems and for subsequent service innovation. The previous study has also shown that there is a need for supporting tools that take into account the various relevant aspects of value proposition, as well as at the same time the changes resulting from digitization. Part IV has also uncovered the need for structured support in this context and outlined the importance of human agents in the decision-making.

As second step of the design-oriented part of this research, the focus of this study in Part VI[8] is on the design of a specific tool for the development of value propositions which are made possible by digitization, i.e. which include digital technology as an essential component. The development of these value propositions is a decisive step along the path of realizing digitization-enabled service innovations, as described and located in the DIGITALISS method above. As the previous study in Part IV, this study also puts SMEs in the center of the investigation. Especially for these organizations with

---

[8] An earlier version of this research has been presented at the *12th Research Colloquium on "Innovation & Value Creation"* (I+VC) 2017 in Hamburg, Germany (Genennig, 2017) and is published as further developed version in the *Journal of Service Management Research* (Genennig, Roth, Jonas & Möslein, 2018). See Annex A for more information.

resource restrictions and niche competence (Vajjhala & Ramollari, 2016), an often used alternative to the development of new digitization-enabled value propositions by their own is the simple copy of an existing successful value proposition, for example of a competitor (Priem, Wenzel, & Koch, 2018). More promising, however, is the development of a new digitization-enabled value proposition by the organization that takes into account both the strengths of the organization and its connected service systems and the specific needs of the recipients. Either way, both the copy of an existing value proposition for the own organization and the development of an own new value proposition require a structured approach for an all-embracing consideration of all relevant aspects. SMEs – but also other forms of companies – would then benefit from this approach. In order to meet this and the challenges identified in the previous studies of this research, the following study of Part VI aims to explore the fourth sub-research question:

RQ4: How can digitization-enabled value propositions in service systems be systematically developed?

Under the overall chosen service systems perspective, the previous parts of the research have dealt with the integration of digital technologies as a resource in service systems and the resulting digitization-enabled innovations. These innovations can lead to service innovation and value. In order to support this path, the objectives of the study are to identify the relevant elements of digitization-enabled value propositions and to transfer them into an encompassing tool which is subordinated to the previously developed DIGITALISS method and which can be used both physically and digitally. In this way, the findings concern both management and research. On the one hand the study aims to design a tool that supports management along the systematic development of digitization-enabled value propositions and enables widespread use of the tool through physical and digital distribution. On the other hand, though the use of service science as the theoretical foundation, service research gets promoted by evidence-based knowledge on real-world service systems and on digitization-enabled value proposition development for service systems through a concrete artifact. This is also intended to stimulate and foster academic discussion on this topic.

To explore the research question, a design science research (DSR) approach is chosen (Peffers et al., 2007; Walls, 2013). In the DSR approach, by means of a six-stage iterative research process, an artifact becomes designed – in this case a tool for the development of digitization-enabled value propositions. The DSR research process is supported by qualitative research elements. Thus, interviews and group discussions in workshops provide empirical insights on the further development and evaluation of the tool. A final application of the tool at three different companies shows its applicability and delivers best-practices.

The study forms Part VI of the research and consists of eight chapters. Following the needs and objectives in chapter 1, chapter 2 and chapter 3 present the research context and theoretical underpinning of the study. Chapter 4 then explains the research design in detail. Chapters 5 and 6 explain the designed tool and show it in practical application. Chapter 7 discusses the insights gained and reveals practical implications. The final chapter 8 concludes the study. The following figure (Figure 23) illustrates the study in the general structure of this research.

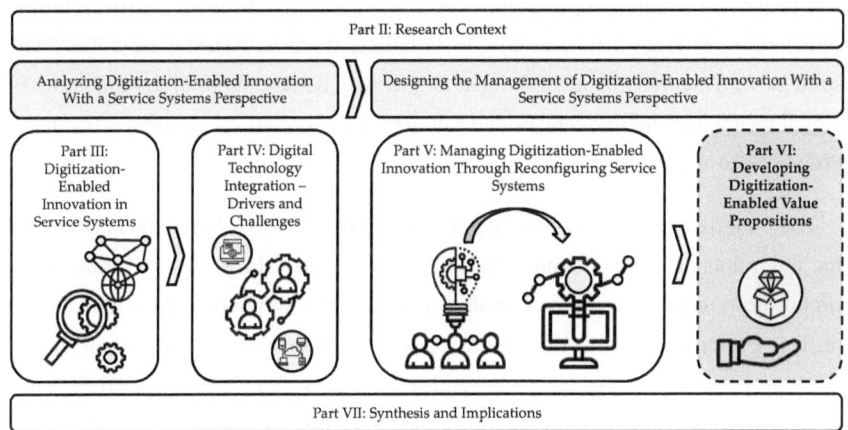

Figure 23: Part VI within the overall research structure

2 Understanding the Context: Technology and Value Propositions in Service Systems

A survey conducted by IBM already in 2006 found that in terms of operating margins companies successfully focused on the innovation of value propositions rather than direct innovation of products or services (Amit & Zott, 2012). In line with this argumentation, a comparison of innovation frameworks conducted by Hartmann et al. (2014) identified value propositions to be present in all of their analyzed works, while other components, such as key resources, key activities, or cost structure, were excluded in certain models (Hartmann, Zaki, Feldmann, & Neely, 2014). Value propositions play the key role in companies´ offerings (Reymen, Berends, Oudehand, & Stultiëns, 2017) and consequently, the concept of value propositions is widely used in academia as well as in management (Anderson, Narus, & van Rossum, 2006). Literature suggests to start service and business model innovation with the development of the value proposition and confirms the influence of technological innovations on value propositions (Cortimiglia, Ghezzi, & Frank, 2016; Johnson, Christensen, & Kagermann, 2008). Nevertheless, there is a strong need for "new strategic frameworks that are aiming at deliberately harnessing unique capabilities of digital technology that are embedded into [services] to gain competitive advantage" (Yoo et al. 2010, p. 730).

The underlying service systems perspective of this research forms the background for the value proposition understanding in this study. In service systems, value propositions request engagement of all connected actors and require them to make use of their competences (Chandler & Lusch, 2015). The service systems are aligned to value propositions which their entities and stakeholders offer (Peters et al., 2016). Value propositions connect the different actors and resources on a content-related basis (Vargo et al., 2008) and are invitations from actors to each other to mutually engage in service and involve human agents as active actors in their formation (Ballantyne, 2003; Beverungen et al., 2018). The development of new value propositions serves as a crucial step in service innovation and value creation and is an essential element for downstream processes and activities (Pawar, Beltagui, & Riedel, 2009). According to Schüritz et al. (2017), new services are being built around value propositions that reflect the changes brought about by digitization.

New digital technologies enable innovation and value creation within service systems and thus affect the alteration of their value propositions (Demirkan et al., 2011). As shown in Part III, digital technology forces the advancement of existing or the development of new value propositions, for example through an altered composition of the actors of the service systems (Breidbach & Maglio, 2016). In this sense, new digitization-enabled value propositions can evolve from already existing value propositions inside or outside the service systems (Priem et al., 2018) or emerge as new value propositions. Consequently, changes in the value propositions of service systems have significant impact on the service architecture and can change the configuration of actors, resources, and activities of value (co-)creation (Böhmann et al., 2014). Although the influence of digital technologies on service systems and especially on the development of new value propositions is frequently discussed in literature, existing tools for the development of value propositions lack on both, a service systems perspective and the consideration of changes through digital technologies (Chandler & Lusch, 2015). Both, however, represent a need in practice and are therefore considered in the tool design in this study.

3   Theoretical Underpinning: Development of Digitization-Enabled Value Propositions

The development of digitization-enabled value propositions constitutes the starting point in the line of action to purposeful service innovation (Ballantyne, 2003; Chandler & Lusch, 2015). The inherent innovation potentials of digital technologies likewise lead to altered and new value propositions (Kindström et al., 2013; Payne, Frow, & Eggert, 2017; Peters et al., 2016; Skålén et al., 2015). In this context, especially the structured development of digitization-enabled value propositions for service innovation in service systems still requires more scientific attention (Akaka & Vargo, 2014; Breidbach & Maglio, 2016). Although there are general contemplations of value propositions in service systems (Chandler & Lusch, 2015), current literature lacks a deeper understanding of value creation and innovation in service systems (Ostrom et al., 2015). A predominant question for service systems in this context is how technology influences the ways in which value can be created (Vargo et al., 2008).

The development of value propositions is a structuring element within the reconfiguration of service systems and allows an early modelling of the entire service system (Kieliszewski et al., 2012). Value propositions thus provide the decisive human agents with references for a targeted resource integration and service systems reconfiguration and provide guidance in the path from innovations to following service innovation in service systems (Maglio et al., 2015; Siltaloppi & Vargo, 2014; Spohrer & Maglio, 2008). In this sense, active development of new digitization-enabled value propositions represents a decisive step in the realization of digitization-enabled innovation and service innovation.

In order to get an overview of the existing tools for the development of value propositions, a review was conducted within this study (see *Table 5*). Value proposition tools were identified from scientific and practitioner oriented publications and evaluated for their suitability for the development of digitization-enabled value propositions in service systems. Initially, the tools were evaluated according to their service orientation. Then their suitability for service systems and a digitization context was examined. On the one hand it was pointed out whether they are dyadic oriented tools or whether they represent a network or even a system perspective. On the other hand, the consideration of technology and data in the tools was identified in order to demonstrate their inclusion of digitization conditions. Finally, the focus on value proposition development was examined and assessed whether the tools are supporting their development or if they are pursuing a different orientation, such as simple mapping.

The review shows that there are several existing tools, but mostly with a dyadic character and a simplified perspective that neither fully considers the system character nor a service focus. None of the tools includes technology or data as an important element of the value proposition. Furthermore, all tools remain in the perspective of the organization and do not take into account the service systems behind the value propositions. Despite the large amount of research dedicated to identifying and creating value proposition frameworks, there is still a lack of research which focuses on the use of digital technologies to alter value propositions into digitization-enabled value propositions and a transformation of this into applicable tools. In addition, the adaptation of value proposition tools to digitization-related alterations lags behind. Even if there are individual elements in some existing frameworks that are still relevant for the development of digitization-enabled value propositions, a comprehensive solution is not available. The findings of the tool review are used as a basis for the design of a new tool for the development of digitization-enabled value propositions in this study.

Table 5: Overview on the derived results from the parts of this research

Frameworks	Service orientation	Customer / Recipient focus	Network reflection	Service Systems reflection	Technology reflection	Data reflection	Supports VP development
Buyer Utility Map (Kim & Mauborgne, 2005)	+	++					+
Customer Fulfillment Lifecycle (Hamilton, 2013)	+	++					+
Deconstructing the Value Proposition (Payne & Frow, 2014)	+	++	+	+	+		+
Design Space for Value Facilitation (Alter, 2013)	+	++					+
Needmining (Kuehl, 2016)	++	++				+	+
Value Blueprint (Alter, 2013)	++	++	++	++			++
Valueprop Checklist (Horton, n.d.)	+	++					+
Value-Focused Enterprise Model (Barnes, Blake & Pinder, 2009)	+	++	+				++
Value Map (Osterwalder et al., 2014)	+	++	+	+			+
Value Proposition Builder (Barnes, Blake & Pinder, 2009)	+	++					++
Value Proposition Canvas (Osterwalder et al., 2014)	+	++					++
Value Proposition Framework (Kambil, Ginsberg & Bloch, 1996)	+	++	++				+
Value Stream Discovery (Cooper, Vlaskovits & Ries, 2013)	+	++					+
Value Stream Loop (Rother & Shook, 1999)	++	++					+
Value Stream Mapping (Rother & Shook, 1999)	+	++	++	+	+		+

Explanation of the table:

++ fully represented; + partially represented; "*empty*" no consideration.

4 Research Design

To design a tool for the development of digitization-enabled value proposition, this study is following a design science research (DSR) approach (Peffers et al., 2007; Walls, 2013). Originated in information systems, DSR is considered a valuable method to advance service research and innovate service innovation (Beloglazov, Banerjee, Hartmann, & Buyya, 2015; Ostrom et al., 2015). DSR is reflected as suitable method due to its technology background and its focus on designing methods and tools for the development of new solutions for complex problems (Gregor & Hevner, 2013). This study emphasizes the complexity of the development of digitization-enabled value propositions by combining management perspectives and service design elements.

Following Gregor and Hevner (2013), DSR can contribute even to highly mature application domains through the evolvement of new artefacts. While service design practitioners may create new services that solve specific problems at the recipient side, DSR generates novel models and tools that advance the process of service design and service research fields through its iterative process of conceptualization and validation (Grenha Teixeira et al., 2017).

4.1 Design Science Research Process

Following Hevner et al. (2004), the DSR approach encompasses two main activities that are performed iteratively: building and evaluating. The new artefact is constructed in the building phase (always considering its specific purpose) and is assessed in the evaluation phase (with attention to its successful performance) (Hevner, March, Park, & Ram, 2004). Both process activities require an iterative approach which involves design science and social science (Peffers et al., 2007). Therefore, qualitative research can be one part of the DSR method to consolidate the context and to evaluate the artefact (Hevner et al., 2004). This study uses qualitative research based on Corbin and Strauss (1990) to evaluate the usefulness of the developed tool (Corbin & Strauss, 1990).

For the general tool design, the six steps of the DSR Methodology Process Model by Peffers et al. (2007) have been applied:

1. Identify the problem & motivate: A literature review on digitization-enabled value propositions in service systems, as well as a structured review of existing tools to develop value propositions supported the problem formulation and motivation. Hereby, the fundamental importance of digitization-enablement as a key factor for developing new value propositions and the promising approach of combining technology and service for innovation within a service systems perspective was brought to life.

2. Define objectives for a solution: The overall goal of the tool is to support practitioners along the systematic development of digitization-enabled value propositions. Thus, a management perspective is chosen. Additionally, service research gets promoted by taking the service systems perspective of this research, considering service as the fundamental basis of exchange and emphasizing the altered role of technology in the value proposition development for service systems.

3. Design and development: During the development of the tool for digitization-enabled value proposition development ($V^{di}P$-developer), the theoretical foundations supported the unification of management contributions and service science. Regarding research methodology, DSR was followed throughout this research with the support of qualitative research to develop the applications and to evaluate the tool. The elements of the tool were mainly derived out of intensive interaction processes between several researches and practitioners and were partly inspired by existing value proposition tools as well as some approaches for value proposition development in literature. As can be seen in detail in the following section of this chapter (4.2 Qualitative Data Collection, Analysis and Interpretation), first two workshops were held to iterate the respective form of the tool. In this way, both the relevance of the newly developed tool for the research field and its later practical applicability were already taken into account in the design phase. Subsequently, three workshops with different companies and three feedback cycles with practitioners were carried out. In these development and feedback cycles, the tool was developed and applied iteratively

and to a company-specific situation in the respective status and checked for its applicability. The feedback was then included in the iterative revision of the tool.

In this way, an iterative interplay of literature and practice was made possible. Based on the findings of the literature review, the needs identified in practice were addressed either by elements of existing value proposition tools or by newly developed elements. These were then tested again and were integrated into the tool to be designed. The design of the tool followed the design research criteria by Forlizzi et al. (2008): process, invention, relevance, and extensibility. First, this research project details the design process so that it can be replicated and improved. Additionally, the quality criteria of qualitative research have been applied with increased focus on procedural reliability (Wrona & Gunnesch, 2015). The invention and relevance have been identified by a sound literature review, showing that there is a lack in research about the purposeful use of technology for service innovation in service systems. This highlights the relevance and novelty of the artifact, being a tool for the development of digitization-enabled value propositions in service systems and supporting the overall service innovation activities in organizations. Extensibility refers to the leverage of the artefact to different application situations and challenges. The use of the tool in different organizations with different strategic objectives tested its extensibility to other contexts. Figure 24 outlines the research process and summarizes the activities carried out in the third step.

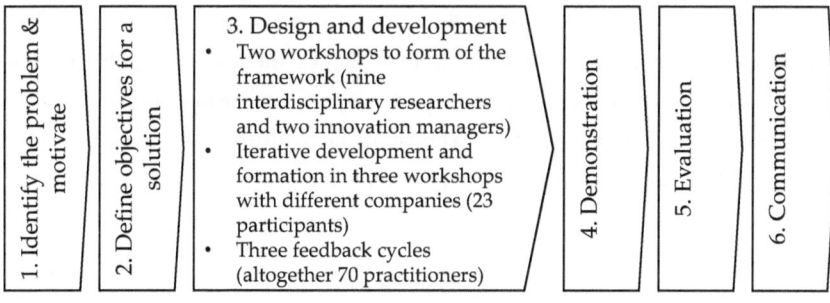

Figure 24: Outline of the research process

4. Demonstration: The tool was demonstrated by its application to solve the identified problem. The tool was applied in different organizations and settings, showing how the tool supports the development of digitization-enabled value propositions. After its application, qualitative interviews and focus groups were used to study the experiences at the use of the tool.

5. Evaluation: The tool was evaluated using the criteria of DSR (Hevner et al., 2004) and qualitative elements. Including feedback cycles in the workshops and interviewing participants subsequent to the workshops, the experiences with the implementation of the tool have been collected and assessed. Following Gregor and Hevner (2013), the evaluation is discussed after presenting the applications in the application section.

Figure 25: Impressions from the workshops on tool design and evaluation

6. Communication: Scholarly and professional presentations and publications have been selected to spread the tool among the targeted audience. So far, the tool was repeatedly discussed with both practitioners and academic audiences. In addition, the tool was transferred into a digital form and is available as an application for desktop and mobile use (V^diP Konfigurator)[9]. By adding the necessary explanations and by using guided process steps, the application allows the user to apply the tool independently and allows its use in interested companies at any time. In order to make the application of the tool accessible to a broad public, to further support its application and processing, and to identify existing potential for improvement, it was placed in an open innovation lab for three months and made available for visitors to use. This open

---

[9] The digital implementation of the V^diP-developer can be found under the following link: vdip.innovationresearch.eu

innovation lab is located in the city center of Nuremberg (JOSEPHS)[10] and thus ensured a broad and multi-layered user base for the application. The application was installed on a tablet and integrated into an environment that drew visitors' attention to digitization-enabled innovation. The following pictures show the setting of the application deployment in the open innovation lab (Figure 26). Screenshots of the application can be found in the annex (Annex H).

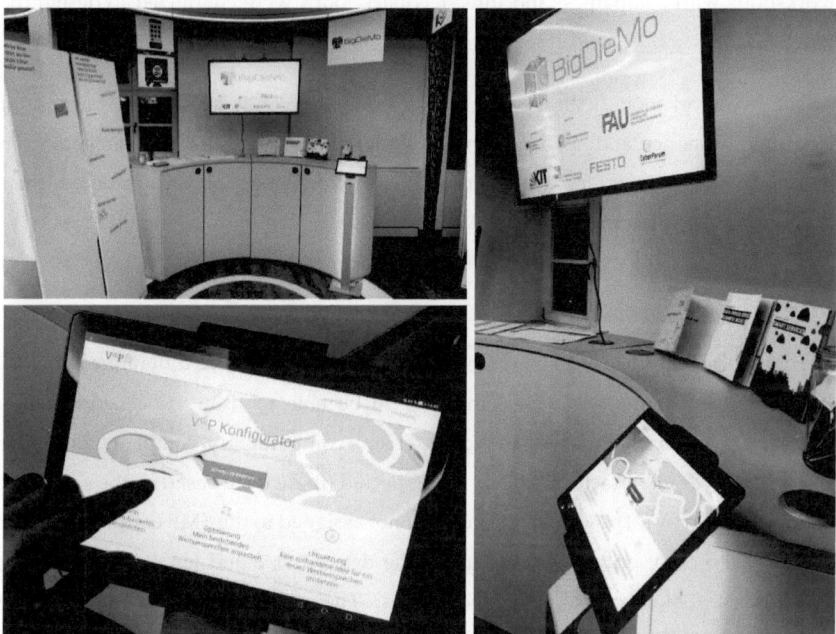

Figure 26: The V^{di}P application in the open innovation lab JOSEPHS in Nuremberg

---

[10] For further details, see: www.josephs-innovation.de

4.2   Qualitative Data Collection, Analysis and Interpretation

Qualitative data was used to support the DSR approach in its two main activities: building and evaluating. Due to their characteristics, SMEs in particular require special support in the development of new digitization-enabled value propositions. For this reason this study focuses on SMEs and targets the applicability of the designed tool in organizations of this characteristic. Five workshops (two research workshops and three workshops with companies) and three feedback loops were conducted to design the tool.

The two workshops with a focus on research were conducted for the purpose of identifying theories and setting general foundations. In total, nine researchers from different backgrounds took part in the two workshops and contributed their experiences on value propositions. Additionally, two company representatives were also present at these workshops to integrate practical findings into the tool design at an early stage.

Subsequently, three workshops were held at companies. Three different companies were selected for the workshops in order to be able to draw conclusions across company boundaries. However, in order to ensure comparability, companies of similar size with a clear manufacturing focus were selected (these were based on the size of the company in Part V). These were deliberately not assigned to the SME category in order to be able to carry out the workshops in the desired size and length. A total of 23 participants took part in these workshops. The detailed characteristics of the participants can be found in Annex G. In order to ensure the applicability of the tool for SME, three feedback cycles were conducted with companies of this size. In these, the tool was presented and used independently by the SMEs. The SMEs came from all sectors and were not subject to any thematic preselection. A total of 70 practitioners participated in the feedback cycles.

After each workshop and feedback cycle the results were evaluated. In order to achieve this, recording devices were used in the workshops to secure the feedback and additional notes were taken. This also applied to the qualitative interviews and focus groups which took place after the tool application. In the feedback cycles, the participants were first asked for oral feedback and were also given the possibility of anonymous written feedback. The respective findings led to a permanent further development of the tool in the iteration steps already described before. Chapter 5 introduces the structure of the tool, followed by the three application samples. Later, the tool is evaluated and research contributions are detailed.

5   The Digitization-Enabled Value Proposition (V^{di}P-) Developer

Figure 27 shows the final digitization-enabled value proposition (V^{di}P-) developer that was deducted from the DSR research process. The tool serves the systematic development of digitization-enabled value propositions in service systems and contains the core elements of value propositions as well as a focus on digital technologies. The V^{di}P-developer is presented as a tool with eight boxes for a step by step development of digitization-enabled value propositions. A consecutive completion of the boxes, starting with box one and ending with box eight, is recommended but not necessary. Each of the boxes contains specific interrogations according to the intended problem-solving approach. The left part of the V^{di}P-developer focuses on the recipient side of the digitization-enabled value proposition while the right part of the figure applies to the whole service systems. The segmentation in two parts should be understood as emphasis rather than a separation.

The Digitization-Enabled Value Proposition (V^{di}P) Developer						V^{di}P
Recipient	**Pains**	**Gains**	**Solution**	**Technology & Data**	**Partner**	
Who will be targeted by the new digitization-enabled solution?	What are the pains of the potential recipients of a digitization-enabled solution?	What are the gains of potential recipients of a digitization-enabled solution?	What is the offered digitization-enabled solution?	What digital technology and what data is used for the solution?	Who else is involved in the solution creation and delivery?	
Existing or new recipient?	*Is there a specific problem situation?*	*Which improvements would make the recipients happy?*	*Is there an answer to the pains or a solution to increase gains?*	*What digital technology will be deployed for the solution?*	*Existing or new partners?*	
B2B or B2C?	*What barriers keep the recipients from adopting a solution?*	*What would increase the likelihood of the adoption of a solution?*	*Is there solution potential from the key resources or key activities of the service system?*	*What data is necessary and is this data accessible?*	*What new partners emerge through the change in technology?*	
How can the recipients be concretized?						
Recipient benefit			**Unique characteristics**			
What are the specific benefits for the recipients of the digitization-enabled solution?			What are the unique characteristics of the digitization-enabled solution?			
How does the digitization-enabled solution relieve pains or exceed gains of the recipients?			*How can the service system differ themselves from other solutions?*			
How can the recipients perceive the specific benefits?			*What are alternative solutions and how does the solution differentiate from existing solutions?*			
			How can the advantages of the digitization-enabled solution over other solutions be proved?			

Figure 27: The digitization-enabled Value Proposition (V^{di}P-) developer

As a development tool, the applying organization can use the proposed $V^{di}P$-developer to identify viable digitization-enabled value proposition alternatives by answering the respective questions with the applying situation-related perspective. The title of some boxes of the $V^{di}P$-developer rests on elements of existing tools. Even though the contents of these boxes have been completely reworked and aligned to the service systems and digitization context, the familiarity of some key words is still an anchor in later use. In the following, the eight boxes are explained in detail, building on the relevant components of the workshops and feedback cycles and on the underlying and supporting literature.

5.1 The Boxes of the $V^{di}P$-Developer

(1) Recipient: This box serves to discuss the addressee of a possible digitization-enabled solution. It defines the starting point for the development of the digitization-enabled value proposition and serves as foundation for the following steps. In the workshops as well as in the feedback rounds, a recipient-focused approach was clearly preferred, which sees the identification of possible recipient groups as a starting point. Nevertheless, it is well aware that these can still adapt and change in the further course of the tool.

This is also in line with single elements of some existing value proposition tools. In the value proposition builder of Barnes et al. (2009, p. 60), the definition of the "market" implies the first of their six step model where the target group of customers gets defined (Barnes, Blake, & Pinder, 2009). This approach goes along with the value proposition canvas (Osterwalder, Pigneur, Bernarda, & Smith, 2014, p. 8) in which the definition of the targeted customer segment is the task to start with. Moreover, Alter (2013) gives the service recipient a dominant position in his value blueprint. In his tool the customer value and the customer activities are defined in detail (Alter, 2013). The presented tools also propose the definition of the service recipient as starting point.

The wording is adapted to "recipient" to sharpen the service focus and the system view of this tool, taking the encompassing view of service within service systems

(Chandler & Lusch, 2015). In this work, the recipients will be rather considered as the customer or user. The application of the tool has shown that all receiver types can be found here, from individual receivers to receiver groups to general receiver segments. The concretization depends on the respective use case and then defines the view for the following boxes. The recipient identification is the key question of this box: *Who will be targeted by the new digitization-enabled solution?* Further possible sub questions that lead to a better understanding address the separation between existing and new recipients, a distinction between B2B or B2C interactions and a possible categorization of recipient groups.

(2) Pains: The idea behind the following boxes "pains" and "gains" is already known from an existing tool – the value proposition canvas (Osterwalder et al., 2014) which discusses in one of its elements the general pains and gains of potential recipients. The V^{di}P-developer slightly dissolves from this tool as the recipient activities are not in the focus of this box and the pains have already a clear solution orientation, differing from the customer segmentation view of the value proposition canvas. Additionally, the results of the workshops indicated to separate the two elements "pains" and "gains" and to work out a sharpening of the content.

Despite a generic collection of pains, the clear recipient definition of box one keeps a focus on digitization-enabled pains. Consequently, it is recommended to define the recipient in advance and to elaborate box one beforehand. Together with the next box, this action helps to define the digitization-enabled solution in the following steps and supports the definition of the recipient benefits in box six in the ongoing process. Box two explores the question *"What are the pains of the potential recipients of a digitization-enabled solution?"* Supporting questions to be answered are what specific problem situation exists and what barriers (can) refrain the recipients from adopting possible solutions.

(3) Gains: Box three can be regarded as counterpart of the antecedent box. Like box two it is inspired by the value proposition canvas (Osterwalder et al., 2014) and takes up the idea of the value proposition builder (Barnes et al., 2009), but again differs in its general alignment. Step three builds the value experience by collecting perceived

customer benefits and deducts the costs of their creation. It aims to answer the question: *What are the gains of potential recipients of a digitization-enabled solution?* This might raise the chance of the adoption of a possible solution.

(4) Solution: This box (pre)defines the digitization-enabled solution. It has been positioned at this point to allow the essence of the previous boxes to flow into the solution finding process and to guide and inspire the following boxes. The workshops have shown that the location of this box at this point of the $V^{di}P$-developer is most suitable and that a definition of the solution can already be successfully carried out here. Being one of the core elements of every value proposition development process, this step is also partially present in existing tools. In the value proposition canvas it is addressed in the "product and services" box (Osterwalder et al., 2014). In the value proposition builder it is named "offerings" and it is explained as the product and service mix the company is selling (Barnes et al., 2009). Nonetheless, these tools take a product-service mix view while still sticking to a product centric orientation. The $V^{di}P$-developer takes the service-dominant view and names this box "solution" keeping in mind that products may be used as service enabler (Barile & Polese, 2010; Ostrom et al., 2015; Vargo & Lusch, 2017). Moreover, through its formulation, the $V^{di}P$-developer is able to approach both, technology driven (address customer job and gains) and market pulled (react on customer problems and pains) solutions (Osterwalder et al., 2014). In fact, the tool makes no distinction between the two streams. Therefore this box poses the following question: *What is the offered digitization-enabled solution?* Possible solutions might be a result of the pains and gains. The key resources and key activities are part of one additional sub-question, keeping in mind that solutions might also originate from specifics of the organization. If organizations have a clear pre-set solution beforehand, the "solution" box can constitute a starting point in the $V^{di}P$-developers' application. In this case, the recipient box and the other boxes would be filled according to the solution. The remaining boxes of the $V^{di}P$-developer are then used for specification and structuring of the solution.

(5) Technology & Data: In this box, the implicated technologies are chosen and necessary data to be used for the development of value proposition is defined and collected. These steps are missing so far in other value proposition development tools.

They have been added here as a result out of argued practical needs and research perspectives during the workshops. It was important for the companies using the V^(di)P-developer to identify and record the technologies and data required for value proposition at an early stage. The level of granularity depends on the application situation. The joint treatment of technology and data issues was seen as essential, as technology and service are closely related (Daim et al., 2010) and the use of technology for innovation has to be conducted purposefully (Breidbach & Maglio, 2016). The selected technology entails specific tasks and influences the decisions within the following boxes, e. g. the consultation of additional actors to the service systems (Essén, 2009). Additionally, the digital transformation leads to potentials for data usage in service provision (Schüritz et al., 2017). In data-driven services, technology constitutes the source of data. The box collects the deployed technology and the used data by exploring the question: *What digital technology and what data is used for the solution?* It collects all technologies and evaluates the accessibility of the conceived data.

(6) Partner: Box six collects the involved actors in the provision of the digitization-enabled solution. In this point the V^(di)P-developer is following the logic of the service business model canvas, which integrates an encompassing "partner" perspective into value proposition development (Zolnowski, Weiß, & Böhmann, 2014). After the recipients have been selected in step one, the "partner" box serves to identify all connected actors of the service systems participating in the service provision (Maglio & Spohrer, 2008). The approach was also endorsed by the practitioners in the workshops, who appreciated the overview of the entire group of internal and external actors in this box. Although this view is not present in most value proposition tools, it is partly included by Golnam et al. (2014) who integrate the network of all parties involved in their value map tool. The value map incorporates a distinction between the actors of service provision, including all organizations and connected suppliers, developers and others, as well as the service recipients (Golnam, Viswanathan, Moser, Ritala, & Wegmann, 2014). Although this box deals mainly with the overall service system, the wording was left with the term *"Partner"*, since this term is more intuitive and widely used in practice. To collect all entities and stakeholders of the service systems involved in value proposition, the V^(di)P-developer explores the following question in this box: *Who else is involved in the solution creation and delivery?* In this

context "else" refers to all other actors except the actual editing party as well as to already defined recipients. This may imply other actors (entities and stakeholders) inside as well as outside the organization. In this box, all existing and new partners are collected. New partners might come along with new technologies and might require extended data analysis.

(7) Recipient benefit: The formulation of the clear recipient value as benefits is the essence of this box. The $V^{di}P$-developer uses box seven to substantiate the clear benefits of the digitization-enabled solution. The workshop participants saw this box as the starting point for following discussions, for subsequent marketing activities and as a conclusion of the recipient perspective of the $V^{di}P$-developer. This box was also inspired by existing tools like the value proposition builder (Barnes et al., 2009) which targets benefits and the recipient's value of the solution as one element. This view is also part of the first swim lane of the value blueprint (Alter, 2013) and gets expressed in the value map (Golnam et al., 2014). In the $V^{di}P$-developer the box focuses on the following question: *What are the specific benefits for the recipients of the digitization-enabled solution?* This can be an answer to the recipients' pains or exceed the recipients' gains. In addition to that, the formulation of approaches to enable these benefits for the recipients can also be part of this box.

(8) Unique characteristics: The last box of the $V^{di}P$-developer focuses on the unique characteristics of the digitization-enabled solution. This box was designed to reflect the developed solution. It is also a summary of step five and six of the value proposition builder (Barnes et al., 2009) in which it targets "alternatives & differentiation", as well as "proof". The "alternatives & differentiation"- step represents the differentiation from other solutions and the characteristics that make the solution better than other offerings. "Proof" underpins the arguments by collecting the substantiated credibility and believability of these points (Barnes et al., 2009). With this box, the $V^{di}P$-developer purposefully amalgamates existing elements in a new sense giving way and goes much further than other tools for value proposition development which stop after the general solution development. By claiming a proof for the developed solution components, the $V^{di}P$-developer ends with a sparring element for critical reflection. Consequently, the "unique characteristics"-box constitutes a recap of the solution features and explores

the following question: *What are the unique characteristics of the digitization-enabled solution?*

5.2   Creating Value Propositions With the V^{di}P-Developer

To apply the V^{di}P-developer a systematic approach is recommended. According to Hartmann et al. (2014), general analysis can be either descriptive, prescriptive, or predictive. This view of analysis – originated in data analytics – can be carried to the act of value proposition development. Descriptive analytics describe the current state of what is happening or has happened so far. Prescriptive analytics aim to provide guidance on how to best proceed or fix a problem. Predictive analytics combine past knowledge with models and learning to predict what will happen in the future. Taking this approach as the perspective of analysis, the V^{di}P-developer is completed three times with one of these perspectives at a time on the way to value proposition development. It starts with a status-quo analysis and the capturing of the current situation, guided by the question: *How is the situation right now (descriptive)?* In a second cycle, the possibilities of improvement will be gathered, contributing to the question: *How can the situation be better (prescriptive)?* Finally, the last cycle combines the status-quo with all possibilities and identifies the preferred solutions: *How will the situation be (predictive)?* This last cycle is the essence of the V^{di}P-developer and derives new value propositions. This approach is particularly suitable in situations where the organization has no pre-existing solution in mind and aims to make use of the digital transformation. In this case, the V^{di}P-developer is first enhancing creativity and opens up options ('divergent thinking') before it then translates the options with the predictive question into concrete decisions and takes on a closing character ('convergent thinking') on the way to the final value proposition (Design Council, 2013).

If individual boxes – like "recipient, "technology & data" or even "solution" – are predefined in advance, the three-step process described above can be shortened. In this case, the empty boxes are filled with orientation on the predefined elements. The process described above has proven itself in the application of the tool in practice. The developed results were more substantiated and the way to get there was well-founded.

These findings were also taken into account in the mobile application of the $V^{di}P$-developer. This offers the user three different starting points, depending on the initial situation. The starting point "inspiration" is aimed at situations in which the user needs creative support. In several alterations, possibilities are first collected and then their feasibility and practicability questioned. The starting point "optimization" is applied for the transformation of an existing analogue value proposition into a digitalization-enabled value proposition. In a first iteration, the existing value proposition and its core aspects are recorded before subsequently possible digitization-enabled optimizations are worked out. The third starting point "implementation" helps to elaborate a value proposition which has already been conceived in its basic features and to consider all its core aspects. The outcome of the $V^{di}P$-application is always a completely filled out $V^{di}P$-developer which can be downloaded as PDF. An overview of the possible paths through the $V^{di}P$-application can be found in the annex (Annex I).

In addition to its actual application, upstream and downstream activities can support the $V^{di}P$-developer. Building a suitable recipient definition for the first box of the $V^{di}P$-developer, the application of a creativity support tool for recipient analysis, e. g. the personas service design tool (Pruitt & Adlin, 2006), can facilitate the entry to the $V^{di}P$-developer. In the same vein, the collection of accessible key resources can establish a basis for the following value proposition development (Osterwalder et al., 2014; Zolnowski et al., 2014). Moreover the clear formulation of the problem situation according to the problem definition template of Kimbell (2015) or fishbone diagrams, can support the start of the $V^{di}P$-developer.

The formulation of a positioning statement, e. g. the common framing by Moore (2006), constitutes a suitable method to recap the results of the seven boxes of the $V^{di}P$-developer. With the expressed statement the developed value propositions become more replicable and tangible. The workshops showed that it is easy for companies to formulate Moore's statement after applying $V^{di}P$-developer, as the individual elements represent the essence of some of its boxes.

To be successful, the digitization-enabled value proposition must "fit". This means that is has to respond to a specific job-to-be-done of a targeted recipient (Johnson et al., 2008). In this context, tools to identify and match the jobs-to-be-done, e. g. the universal job map (Bettencourt, 2010), can provide guidance and ensure the consideration of all relevant points. Fitting to the specific job-to-be-done, the value proposition has to act as one part of a strong business model (Osterwalder et al., 2014). Figure 28 provides an overview of possible upstream and downstream activities.

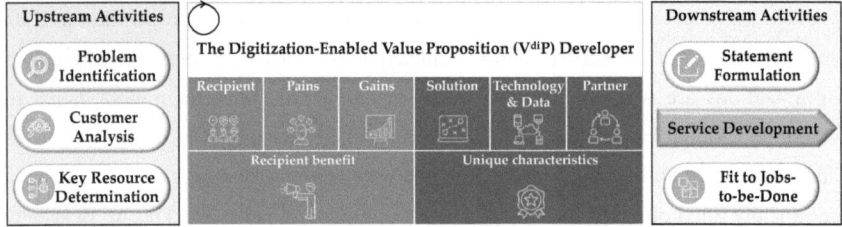

Figure 28: Upstream and downstream activities of the V^{di}P-developer

Thus the V^{di}P-developer presents a tool for the conception phase of digitization-enabled solutions and supports the encompassing development of new value propositions. It supports the organizations in the first two activities of service innovation, *Discover* and *Define*, and brings an idea to a decision and transforms it into a service system. In the following, the developed value propositions have to undergo the subsequent activities of service innovation, *Development* and *Delivery*, and have to be transferred into usage and concrete value increase (Design Council, 2013; Kleinschmidt et al., 2016).

6 Application and Evaluation of the V^{di}P-Developer

Often, conceptual tools lack a practical proof and do not show how executives might benefit from them (Payne & Frow, 2013). Responding to this concern, this chapter illustrates how three companies used the V^{di}P-developer to derive new value propositions to their business to evaluate and refine the tool. It thus provides best practices and illustrative material for other companies and also shows the tool in actual application.

6.1 Application of the V^{di}P-Developer

The three companies intended to develop a digitization-enabled service, solving a complex issue by the purposeful integration of digital technology into their connected service systems. All of them are manufacturing companies, one component manufacturer (company 1), one system manufacturer (company 2) and one plant manufacturer (company 3). The V^{di}P-developer was applied with two iterations at every company. In all three companies, the V^{di}P-developer was used as a boundary object to bridge between different groups in the workshops. The points presented in the following constitute the most essential points of the V^{di}P developer's application. The results of the application can be found in the figure below (Figure 29).

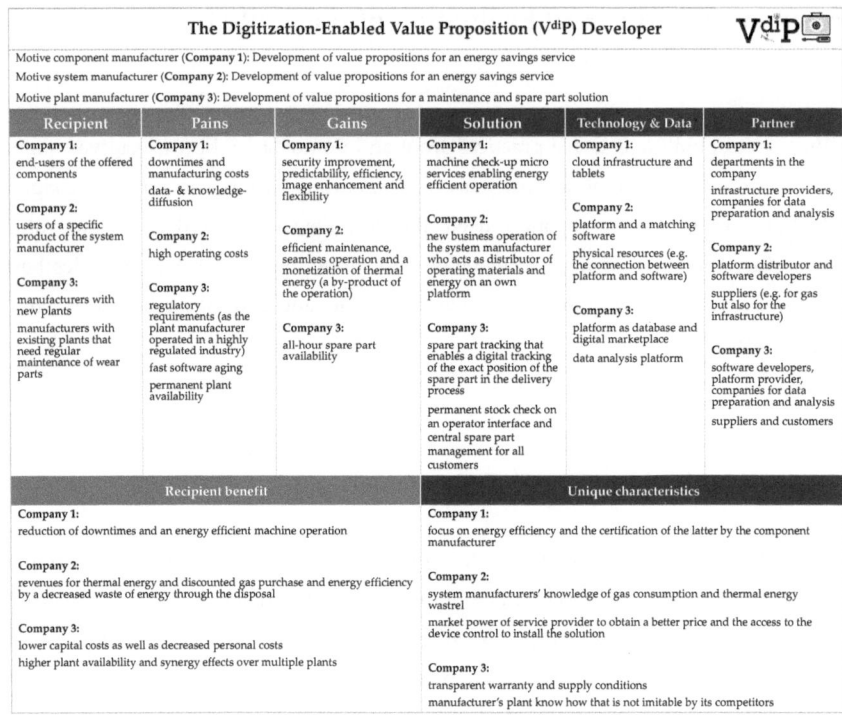

Figure 29: Application of the V^{di}P-developer in three organizations

6.1.1 Application at a Component Manufacturer (Company 1)

The main motive for the component manufacturer was the development of digitization-enabled value propositions for an energy savings service. The developed digitization-enabled solution is a machine check-up containing micro services that enable energy efficient operation at machine commissioning and operation. During the value proposition development, especially the partner box was intensively discussed within and between the groups. Finally, the required partners were identified as departments in the company and new partners at the infrastructure provision level (knowledge provider, infrastructure data, supply chain data), in the data analysis process (consultancy in the data selection, data transformation, data mining) and during the service setup (cloud platform, programmer). Despite the structuring function of the V^{di}P-developer, in this case the tool paved the way from brainstorming to consensus.

6.1.2 Application at a System Manufacturer (Company 2)

Also for the system manufacturer the development of digitization-enabled value propositions for an energy savings service was the leading motive for the application of the V^{di}P-developer. The solution is a new business operation of the system manufacturer which acts as distributor of operating materials and energy on an own platform. The manufacturer sells gas to his users and in return buys their thermal energy for reselling. The required technologies consist of a platform and a matching software. The platform should act as intermediary and the software is needed to identify the price optimum for buying and selling the resources through matching commodity exchange prices.

As the system manufacturer developed a new business model in the solution box, the V^{di}P-developer assisted in the ascertainment of the value proposition of the new business model. In this way the tool fostered both, creativity and the following structuring.

6.1.3 Application at a Plant Manufacturer (Company 3)

The development of digitization-enabled value propositions for a maintenance and spare part solution was the main motivation of the plant manufacturer. The developed digitization-enabled solution is a spar part tracking that enables a digital tracking of the exact position of the spare part in the delivery process and a permanent stock check on an operator's interface. The plant manufacturer enables the solution through a central spare part management for all customers. Cost savings are realized by cumulating spare part orders over numerous plants.

During the application of the $V^{di}P$-developer, the company was very detailed in the description of its digitization-enabled solution. This also led to a quick but detailed formulation of the recipient benefits and the unique characteristics. All three companies used the $V^{di}P$-developer in a successive manner, starting with the recipient box and concluding with the recipient benefits and the unique characteristics.

6.2 Evaluation

Following a DSR approach, the $V^{di}P$-developer was evaluated on its usefulness for supporting the development of a digitization-enabled value proposition. Following the recommendations of Hevner et al. (2004), the tool was validated through six applications in three different organizations. These applications provided a test of the tool in a real-world context and ensured its' comprehensibility, applicability and expedience.

Compared to the other companies, the first company had the most undefined objectives beforehand. This resulted in large differences in the specificity of the results of the $V^{di}P$-developer. Nevertheless, the first round of applications led to two very concrete solutions. In a subsequent discussion, the pros and cons of the respective results were discussed and finally a final value proposition was developed from the essence. The *"clear service mindset"* (c1, wsp4) and the *"targeted use of technology and especially of already available data for new value propositions"* (c1, wsp2; wsp5) were mentioned as strengths of the tool. One critical point mentioned by the first company was the perceived need to generate a quick solution. One employee expressed the desire for *"several loops that make it possible to adapt the later solution again and make it more concrete"* (c1, wsp3). From the following feedback, refinements of the structure and the wording of the tool were made. At the beginning, the tool suggested a gradual application. The discussion in company one showed that it is important to be able to move freely in the tool and so the former numbers of the individual steps were removed for more flexibility. In addition, the three-step approach described above was included as a critical reflection step in the development of the solution.

In companies two and three, the specifications of intended solutions were more concrete and thus the acquired results of the groups were much more similar. The highlighted positive aspects of the tool were the recipient orientation and the match of the solution with technology and data. One workshop participant stated: *"By taking the customer's perspective and identifying concrete needs, we were subsequently able to develop many possible solutions. The match with our existing data enabled an early feasibility assessment"* (c2, wsp1). The feedback-based changes in the tool were therefore fewer and related to modifications of the wordings and explanations of the boxes. At first the desired contents of the boxes were explained by detailed descriptions as there was a wish for a more concrete designation of the intended field contents (c2, wsp3). This has been changed into questions after the first two iterations. The adjustments became less after every application of the $V^{di}P$-developer. The subsequent extensive feedback rounds led to minor changes in the wording of the explanations and questions. The feedback suggested (based on feedback of company 1 and 2) translating the tool into the respective native language of the users (based on feedback from the subsequent feedback cycles with practitioner groups). Above all, the feedback rounds showed the usability of the $V^{di}P$-developer in real-world settings and proved its structuring characteristics in this context.

The design research criteria after Forlizzi et al. (2008) were evaluated through the feedback received by the organizations. This evaluation focused on the outcome of the $V^{di}P$-developer (relevance and extensibility) and on the tool characteristics (process). A continuous assessment of the application was evaluated in a stepwise manner throughout the whole process and its result.

Supporting activities amplified the application of the $V^{di}P$-developer by setting the stage for its implementation with familiar elements beforehand und afterwards. The organizations used either a problem identification tool or a tool for the identification of key resources in advance. For Companies that first collected their data treasure it was easier to assess the feasibility of the possible value proposition. Company 3 appreciated this as *"a good entry into the tool"* (c3, wsp2). Neither advantages nor disadvantages were identified for one or the other approach, as the best fit depends on situational circumstances. However, this is not a constraint, for example, Company 1 *"lost sight of the existing data and developed new value propositions independently of this"* (c1, wsp1). All three organizations formulated a positioning statement in consequence of the application of the $V^{di}P$-developer. As the statement consists of several elements of the $V^{di}P$-developer, the formulation was performed fast and efficiently and the organizations benefit from the succinct summary.

Finally, all organizations appreciated the supporting characteristics of the $V^{di}P$-developer and its contemporary perspectives of technology influence as well as the service systems perspective. The consideration of only dyadic offerings in other tools have been identified as an essential lack of existing models, which is in vein with the adaptions of Zolnowski et al. (2014). The separation into a recipient and a service systems side supported the organizations in the consideration of all connected entities.

7   Discussion and Implications

The aim of this study is to design a tool for the development of digitization-enabled value propositions in service systems. A DSR field-based research process was used to design the artefact and to identify the best fitting process steps. In this regard, engaging researchers and practitioners in the design and evaluation of the DSR project has operationalized this research. The designed tool is the first tool to consider two essential elements in the value proposition development, a service systems perspective and the influence of (digital) technology and data (see Annex J). The objective of the $V^{di}P$-developer is to foster the discussion in academia and to support management.

7.1   Discussion

According to Gregor and Hevner (2013), the $V^{di}P$-developer can be regarded as improved solution in a known context. The development of new value propositions has always been the core of entrepreneurial activities (Anderson et al., 2006; Frow & Payne, 2011). However, as the influencing factors altered with the growing digitization in organizations, solutions and all parts of the value chain (Coreynen et al., 2017), adaption to practice has been driven by external factors and new emerging problems. Although the changes brought about by digitization have led to numerous new research activities (Ostrom et al., 2015), they have hardly produced concrete methods and tools to guide and support the service innovation activities. The $V^{di}P$-developer contributes to the research priorities of service science by Ostrom et al. (2015) through the stimulation of activities in service innovation (p. 131) and by a specific support in the development of service systems (p. 135).

Since Maglio et al. (2008) have highlighted the particular importance of value in service systems, numerous publications have been published in this regard. However, there is still a need to consider technology for the further development of service systems and, in particular, tools that capture and map current developments. With the integration of a management perspective, a service science perspective, and particularly the consideration of the strong need of the targeted use of technology for innovation in service systems (Daim et al., 2010), the tool connects various research streams. It reflects the significance of new digital technologies for innovation processes and the value creation in service systems (Demirkan et al., 2011). Decisions taken by a human agent within a service system affect the service system as a whole (Breidbach & Maglio, 2014), which is why the service systems to be created are already designed during the development of new value propositions. Value propositions connect the relevant actors and resources to a service system which is aligned to the common value proposition (Maglio & Spohrer, 2008). The consideration of this system perspective, not present in other value proposition tools, represents an extension of the value proposition development in the $V^{di}P$-developer.

A second problem the $V^{di}P$-developer is approaching is the targeted use of the opportunities of digitization, especially digital technologies and data (Benkenstein et al., 2017; Beverungen, Matzner, et al., 2017; Schüritz et al., 2017). The integration of new digital technologies constitutes an enabler for the new value propositions and thus an enabler for innovation and resulting service innovation in the service systems. In this context, the conclusions drawn from the application of the $V^{di}P$-developer help to find answers to the question posed by Vargo et al. (2008), how information technology influences the ways in which value can be created. The $V^{di}P$-developer closely connects technology use with value propositions. With its data consideration, the tool also supports the value proposition development in smart service systems and contributes to this field of service science (Maglio & Lim, 2016).

In addition, the tool has opened up new perspectives in the management of digital technologies with its service innovation focus (Lusch & Nambisan, 2015). Since the technologies are taken into account with a clear sense of purpose, the $V^{di}P$-developer, for example, opens up the question of in-house development or external procurement of the required technologies and data from the very beginning. This strengthens the system perspective within the context of technology management.

7.2 Implications for Practice

The application of the $V^{di}P$-developer underlined its intelligible design and adaptability in corporate context. All three companies reallocated the actors within and connected to their organizations to provide the digitization-enabled solution and used digital technologies to connect the entities and stakeholders of the service systems (Breidbach & Maglio, 2016; Vargo et al., 2008). Moreover, innovation was driven by a new orchestration of the mix of information (knowledge and skills), actors and technology, and was enabled by the integration of new digital technology to the service systems (Grenha Teixeira et al., 2017). The resulting value propositions varied from adaptions of existing ones to the creation of incremental new value propositions, resulting in new solutions and new service opportunities.

Moreover, human interaction remained present in all solutions. In this effect, the definition of digitization-enablement could be adopted and the remarks of Breidbach et al. (2013) were supported. Especially in the knowledge-intensive solutions, the presence of physical interaction next to digital parts of the solution supported the explanations of Breidbach and Maglio (2016). Additionally, digital technology enabled the provision of new solutions in all companies. The use of digital technologies has become an essential part for service provision and supply (Demirkan et al., 2011). All three organizations strived to use a digital platform to offer the new value proposition. On the one hand, this has underlined the importance of digital platforms for innovation and, on the other hand offers best practices for management.

In addition, the use of data was an essential part of many new value propositions created with the $V^{di}P$-developer in the feedback cycles with SMEs. Due to its distinct perspective, the $V^{di}P$-developer supports the development of value proposition for future data-driven services (Schüritz et al. 2017). The interweaving of digital technology and data makes the consideration of both elements in a $V^{di}P$-developer box advisable.

The development of new digitization-enabled value propositions represented the starting signal for subsequent service innovation in the organizations. This underlines the location of the $V^{di}P$-developer in the first two service innovation activities of the DIGITALISS method from Part V and shows at the same time how the tool can be used for the "Discover" as well as for the "Define" phase. The VdiP-developer creates on the one hand the way from the idea to the decision, on the other hand it also supports the development of a concrete service system on the basis of the decision for the digitization-enabled solution to be implemented (Kleinschmidt et al., 2016).

Concluding, the $V^{di}P$-developer supports the course from divergence to convergence. This was particularly noticeable in applications with workshop participants from different backgrounds. In these cases, the tool was first used for creative idea generation and afterwards for consensus building. In a first step, different solution variants were developed, followed by a discussion in order to find the most promising solution for the further procedure. The individual elements of the value proposition helped with the feasibility analysis. Ideas often failed in the subsequent discussion due to unrealizable assumptions in the boxes about technology or partners. In general, the tool represents a structured way to lead to convergence.

8   Concluding Words About the Value Proposition Tool

Part VI is the second design-oriented study in this research. As "the real power of value proposition thinking is in the process" (Barnes et al., 2009, p. 53), the study in Part VI designs a tool for the systematic development of digitization-enabled value propositions in service systems. To achieve this structured development, the relevant components of digitization-enabled value propositions in service systems have been identified based on literature and practice. As a literature review revealed, current tools for value proposition development lack an encompassing view and neither unite digitization-enabled solutions with specific recipient needs, nor consider the system behind service provision. Nevertheless, existing value proposition tools also have elements that are still relevant for the development of value propositions, but need to be adapted to the changed circumstances that result from the digitization and from a service systems perspective for management. These changes were empirically collected in the context of this study. The designed tool, the V^{di}P-developer, considers the alterations through digitization as well as the service systems perspective in value proposition development. The encompassing consideration of all relevant elements of digitization-enabled value propositions is the particular characteristic of the V^{di}P-developer tool. The design and iteration of the tool followed a DSR process with the inclusion of qualitative research (Corbin & Strauss, 1990; Peffers et al., 2007).

For research, the study in Part VI of this research is particularly relevant, since it designs a specific tool for the further development of service systems and thus addresses a specific research gap within service science (Beverungen et al., 2018; Böhmann et al., 2014; Ostrom et al., 2015). The study provides real-world findings for the fertilization of scientific discourses in the areas of service systems reconfiguration and service innovation. In addition, it provides an overview of the strengths and weaknesses of existing tools for value proposition development and transfers existent elements into the selected research context through adaptation. In this way, the study also highlights the fundamental need for adaptations to existing tools in order to meet the challenges of digitization. These empirical findings can consequently also provide inspiration for the adaptation of other management-oriented tools.

For management, this study is relevant as it provides support in and facilitates the development of new digitization-enabled value propositions. On the one hand, the V^{di}P-developer is a tool that guides and accompanies the process of value proposition development and, on the other hand, provides real-world best practices that offer inspiration and orientation. In addition, the designed tool serves the need for support in the first two activities of the service innovation, "Discover" and "Define", as highlighted in the previous study (Part V). Thus, the results of the tool's application offer a possible direction in the reconfiguration of service systems or can accompany it. The positioning of the V^{di}P-developer in the DIGITALISS method also places it in a big picture of the realization of digitization-enabled innovation and the resulting service innovations.

Despite this, the study is subject to certain limitations due to its theoretical underpinning and research approach. First, this research project focused on the design of the V^{di}P-developer. The tool was then applied in three manufacturing organizations for further evaluation and demonstration. Its generic formulation and open structure suggest the fit to numerous settings and situations when it comes to the development of digitization-enabled value propositions in service systems. Nevertheless, the tool has to be evaluated by additional workshops and discussions in the future. In the course of this, also different sectors and settings need to proof its broad applicability and its advantages over existing tools. Additionally, the alterations to general service development, triggered by the digital transformation, have to be identified in further research projects. This would support the merger of the V^{di}P-developer with its following processes.

The present study takes a service systems perspective on a meso level. As changes are expected on a micro level perspective, the additional entities and stakeholders involved, for example in-house departments, have to be considered in a next step. To get a comprehensive view of service systems and their actors, the changes in the processes of all entities and stakeholders constitute one research implication (Akaka &

Vargo, 2014). Therefore, the applicability of the designed tool in all these settings and the findings of this study prepare the way for further applications and analyses.

This study also explored numerous upstream and downstream activities of the $V^{di}P$-developer. The design of these supporting activities was not the focus of this research project. The close link to these activities will support the targeted use of the $V^{di}P$-developer in organizational practice. Future research projects should adapt these supporting activities to the changes brought about by digitization and to the service systems perspective. This would provide even better support for the use of the $V^{di}P$-developer and would also enable the supporting activities to be located under the DIGITALISS method.

The study in Part VI forms the final point of the empirical activities in this research and also completes its design-oriented part. The study uses the findings from the analysis of digitization-enabled innovation with a service systems perspective in the first two studies in Part III and Part IV and answers therein identified challenges. The tool designed in this study is a possible element within the DIGITALISS method and addresses the digitization-enabled value propositions development as decisive activity in service systems reconfiguration and service innovation as highlighted in Part V. This study and the $V^{di}P$-developer tool designed in it represent a further step in the realization of digitization-enabled innovation and service innovation. In the following Part VII of this research, the insights gained are summarized and considered in a cross-study discussion.

Part VII

Synthesis and Implications:

Realizing Digitization-Enabled Innovation in Service Systems

1   Summary of Findings

Technological advancement caused by digitization and the increasing importance of service have changed the perspective of service research, especially in the last decade. The promoted shift to a service-dominant view, digitization facilitated alterations and a systematic approach forced a science for service (Akaka & Vargo, 2014; Barrett et al., 2015; Breidbach & Maglio, 2014; Vargo & Akaka, 2009). This discipline puts emphasis on the interdisciplinary nature of service (Böhmann et al., 2014) and a systematic approach of service innovation (Spohrer et al., 2007). In this context, service systems are seen as the basic abstraction of service science and provide a perspective for analysis in this field, e.g. to derive a scientific understanding or to develop evidence-based methods and tools (Maglio et al., 2009).

This research takes a service systems perspective for the analysis of digitization-enabled innovation and for design-oriented approaches for the development of a management method and the design of a management tool in this context. Thus, it operationalizes the service systems perspective for the purpose of realizing digitization-enabled innovation by a management orientation. Furthermore, it puts the management-oriented view into the perspective and aims towards exploring the question of how organizations can manage the use of new digital technologies for digitization-enabled innovation in service systems. This research pursues this objective with four empirical qualitative studies. The first two studies aimed at the analysis of digitization-enabled innovation in service systems and the second two at the design of management artifacts.

In the first study (Part III), a manual document analysis by qualitative content analysis is used in a desk research approach to take an external perspective at organizations and their connected service systems. This reveals the digitization facilitated alterations in service systems and examines how these enable innovations. The data are drawn from the annual reports published by companies listed in the German MDAX index and also reflect how these companies perceive themselves in dealing with digitization. Thus, the digitization approach of different industries and the specific digital technologies being used were examined. Furthermore, the changes of the actors and the improvements of knowledge and skills through the use of digital technologies were explored. In addition, the study outlines how the use of digital technology leads to improvements in value propositions which in turn enable the innovation of service offerings. The analysis shows that the integration of digital technologies leads to innovation in service systems and changes all their core elements, i.e. besides technology also actors (internal and external) and information (knowledge and skills).

The second study (Part IV) takes a look at the organizations and their associated service systems from inside with the focus on human agents as their decision-makers. In a multiple case study among SMEs exploring their technology integration, the practices in organizations dealing with digital technologies are examined. In particular, the integration of an industrial cloud is explored and the drivers behind the integration as well as the challenges surveyed. The determined drivers point out different fields of the desired objectives and thus show the multifaceted innovation potentials. These innovation potentials apply to all core elements of service systems and the development of new value propositions, which therefore contain potentials for new service offerings and overall value increase. In addition, the challenges affect all core elements of the service systems and can also be found in the development of new value propositions. The findings illustrate the motives for human agents as decision-makers in digital technology integration. Moreover, by combining the findings in a second step with a management-oriented perspective, the challenges involve concrete research demands, as they include areas where extra management support is needed for the organizations to overcome current challenges. This consideration is also the first step in bringing together the two paradigms of service science and management orientation. Therefore, the following two studies are taking up these challenges and develop ways to meet them with design-oriented approaches.

Study three (Part V) reinforces the interdisciplinary nature of service science and combines technology management (TM) and service innovation, the two essential fields for the integration of new digital technologies for the purpose of innovation in service systems. It aims to transform the innovations through the reconfiguration of service systems into service innovations and value increase. Through systematic combining of existing elements in theory and a multiple case study, the DIGITALISS method is developed iteratively. The method parallelizes TM process steps and service innovation activities in an integrated approach. This provides the management with guidance, support and structure along an innovation-promoting and target-oriented approach that maps and accompanies a process from digital technology identification to value increase. The developed DIGITALISS method illustrates the path to digitization-enabled innovation and subsequent service innovation and value increase.

In the fourth study (Part VI), a design science research (DSR) approach is applied to design a tool for developing digitization-enabled value propositions. As a service systems encompassing arc, value propositions define the boundaries of the service systems and constitute an early stage in service innovation activities. The designed physical and digital tool, the $V^{di}P$-developer, provides a supporting structure which covers the core elements of value propositions. These elements are developed in the study on the basis of theory and empirical findings. In addition, the application of the $V^{di}P$-developer shows best practices and illustrates the development of digitization-enabled value propositions in three different companies. The tool is an element of the DIGITALISS method and addresses the digitization-enabled value propositions development as decisive activity in targeted service systems reconfiguration and service innovation. The $V^{di}P$-developer thus supports the realization of digitization-enabled innovation with a management-oriented tool which lays the foundation for following service innovation and simultaneously considers the service systems perspective.

In a nutshell, the cumulated findings of this research are summarized in the following figure (Figure 30). For this purpose, six summarizing sentences are formed from the findings of the four qualitative empirical studies to nurture and inspire research and management.

Part III	The integration of digital technologies leads to reconfiguration and thus innovation in service systems and changes all core elements of service systems , i.e. besides technology also actors (stakeholders and entities) and information (knowledge and skills).
Analyzing the digitization facilitated alteration in service systems and their enabling character for innovation	Innovations through the reconfiguration of service systems lead to new or improved value propositions which in turn enable the innovation of services.
Part IV *Analyzing the integration of digital technologies in service systems by drivers and challenges of human agents as decision-makers*	The integration of new digital technologies aims at reconfiguration and thus innovation in service systems and opens potentials for service innovation and general value increase. The innovations have to be transformed into new service offerings for value increase.
Part V *Developing a method for parallelized TM and service innovation in a digitization context*	The challenges in the integration of new digital technologies can be met with methods and tools for guidance, support and structuring. These methods and tools guide the reconfiguration of service systems and support the transformation of innovation into new service offerings.
	The parallelization of TM and service innovation leads to an innovation-promoting, target-oriented and integrated approach that maps and accompanies a path from technology identification to value increase.
Part VI *Designing a tool for the development of digitization-enabled value propositions*	The development of new digitization-enabled value propositions is a potential starting point of service innovation activities, forms the service systems and sets the direction for the subsequent steps of the TM.

Figure 30: The key findings of this research in a nutshell

Table 6 below presents the findings of this research on a more detailed level, and points out the parts of the thesis they originate from. It thus represents a more precise list of the results and localizes them in the overall context of the research. The findings are associated with the respective study of their origin. This also shows that some findings were tracked throughout the whole research and thus viewed from different angles. The dark-colored boxes next to the statements indicate the location of the results in the respective study. This also shows how results raised early in this research inspired and guided later studies.

Table 6: Overview of the derived results from the parts of this research

Summarized Findings	Part III – Digitization-Enabled Innovation in Service Systems	Part IV – Digital Technology Integration	Part V – Managing Digitization-Enabled Innovation	Part VI – Digitization-Enabled Value Propositions
The integration of a new digital technology in organizations leads to reconfigurations in their connected service systems and thus to innovation.	■			
Digitization-enabled reconfigurations affect all core elements of service systems and enable new and improved value propositions.	■			■
Digital platforms, such as industrial clouds, can act as an operand and operant resource in the reconfiguration of service systems.	■			
The reconfigurations in service systems and the resulting innovation lead to potentials for value increase, but to achieve this, innovation must be transferred into new service offerings.	■			■
The integration of new digital technologies aims at innovation in service systems and opens up potentials for value increase.	■			■
The challenges in the integration of digital technologies can be met with methods and tools that guide, support and structure before, during and after technology integration.		■		■
Applying TM and its processes to the services sector can help companies overcome the challenges in integrating digital technologies for new service offerings.		■	■	
The parallelization of TM and service innovation leads to a targeted, management-oriented and supporting approach to the innovation of new service offerings.		■	■	
Tools that support a specific methodological approach to the development of digitization-enabled innovation in certain steps help facilitate its application.		■	■	
The development of digitization-enabled value propositions is a potential starting point in service innovation and needs a structured approach to consider all relevant elements.			■	■
The application of methods and tools with a service, service systems and digitization focus leads to an organized development of innovation potentials.			■	■

2   Theoretical Contributions

After summarizing the four empirical studies of this research in the previous chapter, their theoretical contributions are integrated in this chapter. To this end, the four studies are first considered separately before a cross-study examination of their contributions follows.

2.1   Summarized Theoretical Contributions

This section highlights the study-specific contributions for each of the four empirical studies. These are presented under the particular part in which they are arranged in this research and get referred to respective literature.

2.1.1   Theoretical Contributions of Part III

Study 1, which forms Part III of the research, analyzes the reconfiguration processes in service systems, in particular through the use of digital technologies. The results provide real-world insights on the service systems definitions of Vargo et al. (2008). The innovations resulting from the reconfiguration of service systems, as stated by Breidbach and Maglio (2015), were collected empirically and allocated to the core elements of service systems. The findings of the study reveal the specific innovations from the reconfiguration of service systems. Thus, they also show how digitization leads to reconfiguration in service systems and new value propositions and hereby represent empirical findings for research on technology-enablement, in particular digitization-enablement (Beloglazov et al., 2015; Breidbach, Kolb, et al., 2013; Breidbach & Maglio, 2016; Grenha Teixeira et al., 2017). The findings contribute to the disagreement in current publications whether digital technology use in service systems initiates and/or enables service innovations by improving the integration of resources and value increase (Kleinschmidt et al., 2016) by highlighting the enabling character of digital technologies. This follows literature which perceives digitization as innovation enabled (Demirkan et al., 2016; Matt et al., 2015).

Through the service systems perspective, the study makes a contribution to the Service Research Priorities according to Ostrom et al. (2015), which highlight "technology, particularly digital technology, as one of the key opportunities and challenges related to service innovation" (Ostrom et al., 2015, p. 131). The findings provide insights into this direction, as they emphasize new digitization-enabled value propositions which in turn can form the basis for new service offerings and thus lay the foundation for service innovations.

2.1.2 Theoretical Contributions of Part IV

Study 2 (Part IV) contributes to research about innovation in service systems. It outlines the importance of technological change for innovation, particularly in service systems and follows the argumentation of Miles (2007), transferring his views in current operations in organizations with a digital technology as example. It elucidates the importance of human agents in service systems (Peters et al., 2016) and illustrates the factors for their decision making by outlining drivers for and challenges in the integration of new resources in service systems. The assumptions of Siltaloppi and Vargo (2014), according to which the integration of resources is initiated by actors in order to achieve a general improvement of the state of others, and reciprocally, the state of oneself, were empirically supported (Siltaloppi & Vargo, 2014, p. 1279). This encourages the role of human agents as decision-making actors in the reconfiguration of service systems.

The selected digital technology in this study is an industrial cloud, which is therefore contributing to research about digital platforms and follows the suggestions of Barrett et al. (2015) for research about the digital platforms' abilities to support the design of services, particularly in service systems. In addition, the study contributes to the research activities on value creation through platforms and shows how industrial clouds are located as a resource in service systems (Cusumano, 2012; Henfridsson &

Bygstad, 2013). Here, their operand and operant properties are highlighted in the identified drivers (Lusch & Nambisan, 2015; Nambisan, 2013), which contributes to the argumentation of Akaka and Vargo (2014) defining technology as an operant resource in service systems and in this regard provides empirical results "to better understand the nuances of technology as a dynamic and influential resource [...] and its role in service systems" (Akaka & Vargo, 2014, p. 382).

In addition to that, the identified challenges that occur during the introduction of digital technologies are also viewed with a management orientation and thus determine general areas in which management relies on additional research support. In this regard, the study followed the research agenda of Lusch et al. (2016) to foster the interdisciplinary perspective of service-dominant logic by using its inherent strategic management perspective. Thus, the results of the study structure the identified need for supporting methods and tools for the management in the development of new services, particularly in digital contexts (Böhmann et al., 2014; Grenha Teixeira et al., 2017; Kleinschmidt et al., 2016; Matt et al., 2015; Skålén et al., 2015) by outlining specific fields.

2.1.3   Theoretical Contributions of Part V

Study 3 (Part V) brings together TM and service science, as forced by Daim et al. (2010). They suggest positive effects and state that "the application of TM theories, concepts and methodologies to the service sector can help firms to overcome some of the major challenges they are facing today" (Daim et al., 2010, p. 5). The service systems perspective is operationalized by a management-oriented view and a design-oriented approach. In this regard, it also supports the notion of Kocaoglu et al. (2008) that TM is a discipline well suited for the service economy due to its broad conceptualization and its focus on efficient and effective management of technology (Kocaoglu et al., 2008). On the other hand, it highlights the importance of services for TM. Since TM still has a rather product-oriented focus (Cetindamar et al., 2016; Lee, 2015), the results of the study thus provide new perspectives for TM.

The findings of the two previous studies were brought together with this approach and transformed into an integrated method that parallelizes TM process steps and service innovation activities. This responds to the need in literature for a systematic method-based support of services innovation, particularly in digitization contexts (Daim et al., 2010; Helm & Graf, 2018; Kleinschmidt et al., 2016). This contributes to service research and enriches it with a concrete methodical approach as demanded by Böhmann et al. (2014).

Furthermore, through the digital technology focus of the DIGITALISS method, it supports the development of smart service systems as particularly digital technologies have accelerated the development of these service systems and it contributes to research on their formation (Beverungen, Müller, et al., 2017; Medina-Borja, 2015). In this sense, the method represents a step towards transferring the in research existing interdisciplinary convergence about the service systems of the future into practice, as demanded by Medina-Borja (2015).

2.1.4   Theoretical Contributions of Part VI

As the previous study, study 4 (Part VI) aims at extending service science by a supportive artifact. By designing a tool for the development of digitization-enabled value propositions ($V^{di}P$-developer), the study also contributes to the service sciences´ need for targeted support for innovation activities (Böhmann et al., 2014; Daim et al., 2010; Kleinschmidt et al., 2016). The tool, which focuses on the development of digitization-enabled value propositions, provides support for the service innovation activities at an early stage. The study therefore contributes to the research priorities of service science by Ostrom et al. (2015) through the stimulation of activities in service innovation (p. 131) and by supporting the development of service systems (p. 135).

The designed tool strengthens the service systems view in the development of digitization-enabled value propositions. Distinct from a firm-based perspective, the system-based view of the $V^{di}P$-developer is characterized by considering the value propositions for all value-creation participants and follows the views of Amit and Han

(2017). At the same time, the tool reflects the significance of new digital technologies for innovation and value creation in service systems (Demirkan et al., 2011).

Thus, the study supports the research agenda of Chandler and Lusch (2015) in the intensive investigation of value propositions in service systems and in particular the engagement of actors. The authors see value propositions as invitations from actors to other actors to engage in service systems and aim to guide the study of service systems through concrete questions in their research (Chandler & Lusch, 2015). Two of these questions are touched by the findings of the study: "How do actors in their roles as consumers, employees, parents, spouses, or partners offer value propositions? How do actors accept, evaluate, or act on value propositions?" (Chandler & Lusch, 2015, p. 16). In this context, the study followed the viewpoint of Vargo and Lusch (2011) and Barrett et al. (2015) who see the resource-integration and service provision with an actor-to-actor (A2A) perspective. This means that all actors are involved in the same, generic activities. In the study, the integration of partners and recipients into the development of value propositions in service systems followed this A2A way of thinking and, through the application of the $V^{di}P$-developer, it provides empirical insights on the engagement of different actors in service systems as well (Chandler & Lusch, 2015; Vargo & Lusch, 2011).

Finally, the study provides findings about the development and the characteristics of digitization-enabled value propositions through the application of the designed tool in the real-world. In this regard, it supports the exploration of the question formulated by Vargo et al. (2008), how new technology influences the ways in which value can be created.

2.2   Cross Study Contributions

This research creates an understanding of the reconfiguration of service systems and the processes behind their emergence and creates interdisciplinary methods and tools for the innovation and service innovation for value increase in service systems. It thus follows the research of Patrício et al. (2011) with empirical and design-oriented studies on service systems and takes an additional management perspective on them. In order to integrate this perspective into service research, the areas with need for management support were first identified in study 2 and then the field of TM was emphasized as particularly suitable due to the extraordinary importance of technology in service systems (Daim et al., 2010; Kocaoglu et al., 2008) and the changes brought about by digitization (Barrett et al., 2012, 2015). The subsequent studies then applied this perspective in method development and tool design.

The structure and the analyses performed in this research are based on the core elements of service systems, technology, actors and information (Maglio et al., 2006) and thus provide sound insights into their content and their interaction in the reconfiguration processes. This research thus provides empirical results on research directions formulated by Frost and Lyons (2017), which suggests that more intensive research should be carried out on the components of service systems. Following the remarks of Siltaloppi and Vargo (2014), the changes within the knowledge and skills, i.e. the service systems core element information, were additionally explored. This research presents empirical studies and provides real-world insights, which in turn serve the research opportunity 1 of Frost and Lyons (2017), calling for additional empirical studies in this context.

In addition, this research provides insights into how organizations can be seen as service systems and to what extent such a perspective is useful in their exploration (Lyons & Tracy, 2013). The empirical studies used a meso perspective of analysis and examined organizations and their service systems. In this context, the focus was also put on human agents, which supports the research of their role in service systems through empirical studies on their decision-making during service systems' reconfiguration and with methods and tools for their support, following the research agenda of Maglio et al. (2015).

In studies 1 and 2, the use of digital technologies in the reconfiguration process of service systems was analyzed to identify the specific digitization-enabled innovations in service systems (Akaka & Vargo, 2014; Breidbach & Maglio, 2015). This contributes to the comments by Frost and Lyons (2017), who emphasize resource integration and the resulting innovations as a crucial field of research on service systems.

The digital technology that was present in all studies were digital platforms, more precisely industrial clouds for their enablement. Their importance was already recognized in study 1. Study 2 focused on them by outlining the drivers behind their integration as well as the challenges during their integration. The use of the tool in study 4 once again underscored their importance and showed in three applications how the use of digital platforms can lead to new value propositions. This research thus adds to the remarks of Demirkan et al. (2015) on cloud computing and adds empirical knowledge. As a consequence, this research provides an exploration of the questions formulated in the research agenda on digital platforms by de Reuver et al. (2018) of how digital platforms transform industries by exemplified new value propositions and intended services (de Reuver, Sørensen, & Basole, 2018).

On the way to the actual realization of innovation potentials and to transforming them into service innovations (Kleinschmidt et al., 2016), study 3 has developed a method for a structured approach from technology identification to value increase. Study 4 has designed a tool that supports the value proposition development as decisive activity of service innovation. The tool contains all relevant elements of value propositions and suggests a procedure for their development. It is part of the method developed in study 3 and supports two activity steps of the DIGITALISS method, the service innovation activities *Discover* and *Define* (Design Council, 2013). Consequently, this research makes a contribution to research direction 3 derived from the current trends in the literature by Frost and Lyons (2017), which recommends developing a better general understanding of innovation in service systems.

The summarized contributions of this research provide a general understanding of the use of digital technologies for innovation and the operationalization of a service systems perspective through an added management orientation. With specific artefacts, it supports the realization of digitally-enabled innovation and paves the way for service innovation and value increase. The following table (Table 7) briefly summarizes the main research directions covered in this research.

Table 7: Summary of the main research directions addressed in this research

Author(s)	Research direction
Akaka & Vargo, 2014, p. 382.	Call for research *"to better understand the nuances of technology as a dynamic and influential resource [...] and its role in service systems".*
Barrett et al., 2015, p. 149.	Research to *"consider how service innovation theory informs and may be applied in the design of services, of service systems and of service ecosystems".*
Böhmann et al., 2014, p. 78.	Call for research *"leading to actionable design theories, methods and approaches for systematically designing, developing and piloting service systems, based upon understanding the underlying principles of service systems".*
Breidbach et al., 2013, p. 439.	Call for research on *"how to plan, build, and manage service systems".*
Breidbach & Maglio, 2015, p. 7.	Call for research on the *"exploration of service system reconfigurations through resource shifting or resource access as a key mechanism for service innovation. [...] How do service systems reconfigure resources, and how can this reconfiguration process be implemented and governed"?*
Daim et al., 2010, p. 5.	Call for research to proceed *"the application of TM theories, concepts and methodologies to the service sector".*
Frost & Lyons, 2017, p. 224.	*"The lack of research focused on applying service system theories and methods to specific domains indicates a gap to be filled in future studies".*
Frost & Lyons, 2017, p. 225.	Call *"for researchers to create holistic service system frameworks".*
Maglio et al., 2015, p. 4.	Call for research on *"new methods and new approaches for understanding complex human-centered service systems".*
Ostrom et al., 2015, p. 131.	Understand the role of *"technology, particularly digital technology, as one of the key opportunities and challenges related to service innovation".*

3   Implications for Practice

The objective of this research is to support management in the realization of digitization-enabled innovation by introducing a service systems perspective to it. In this respect, this research aims to help organizations, and particularly SMEs, with the integration of digital technologies to force innovation in their connected service systems and to guide the path to following service innovation and value increase. This research meets this objective through empirical investigations of digitization-enabled innovation in real-world service systems as well as through the design of artifacts for their management. As a result, three main fields for practical implications can be derived from this research, i.e. an understanding of the role of digitization, the path from digitization-enabled innovation to service innovation and value increase and the operationalization of the service systems perspective for the management of digitization-enabled innovation.

3.1   Understand the Role of Digitization in Service Systems

First, this research can support SMEs which are currently involved in digitization processes or which are striving to do so. It shows the changes in service systems brought about by the use of digital technologies and focuses its analysis on the three core elements of service systems: technology, actors and information (Maglio et al., 2006). It equips the management with the possible characteristics and thus offers illustrative material and orientation. Therefore, the digital technologies in use in the companies are examined and the alterations of the internal and external stakeholders and entities as well as the alterations in the knowledge and skills of the service systems through digitization are highlighted in study 1.

With the drivers and challenges highlighted in study 2, the process of digitization in service systems is examined from a decision-makers view. The reasons for the integration of a digital technology are pointed out to the management and the obstacles resulting from it are emphasized. Consequently, SMEs can compare their own drivers with the drivers worked out in study 2 and can assign a purpose to the introduction of a digital technology.

The application of the method in study 3 and the tool in study 4 top off the understanding of the role of digitization in service systems in this research. Here, cases of the introduction of a digital technology are pointed out. These can also serve as illustrative examples and provide insights into best practices.

3.2   Transform Innovation into Value and Service Innovation

Current literature, research reports and also the results of the first study of this research show how digitization brings innovation into organizations and their connected service systems. The integration of a digital technology enables reconfiguration within the service systems and improvements in it. For the management, however, it is then crucial to transform these innovations into value increase and possibly into service innovation in order to strengthen the competitiveness of the organization (Breidbach & Maglio, 2014; Kleinschmidt et al., 2016; Spohrer & Maglio, 2008).

The research shows a comprehensive approach to the realization of digitization-enabled innovations on the one hand and the subsequent steps to value increase and service innovation on the other. The importance of their connection is explicitly pointed out. The results demonstrate management the path from the identification of digital technologies to the realization of value increase. In study 3 and 4, this research illustrates how the early linking of technology integration and service innovation plays a decisive role. This reveals different starting points for innovative activities. These can be either focused on the later recipient of digitization-enabled solutions, or technology-driven. For the management it is therefore crucial to have a goal in mind that should be achieved with the integration of digital technology. The application of the DIGITALISS method and the use of various tools to support the individual service innovation activities – such as the $V^{di}P$-developer for value proposition development –

support management on the path from digitization-enabled innovation to service innovation and value increase.

3.3   Manage the Digitization-Enabled Innovation

In addition, this research aims at the support of management in the context of digitization-enabled innovation through an operationalization of the service systems perspective by a design-oriented approach for concrete artifacts. For this purpose, a management orientation is brought to the service systems perspective. Study 2 identified the areas in service systems where extra management support is required and allocated them to management fields. This also shows the management general aspects that should be considered when integrating digital technologies into service systems and can therefore provide orientation in this context.

Based on this, study 3 and 4 design artifacts for operating these areas and to support organizations in the management of digitization-enabled innovation. In this regard, TM was selected from the identified management fields, on the one hand because technology is of explicit importance in service systems and digitization leads to changes at the technology element of service systems and on the other hand through the focus on the development and implementation of technological capabilities in TM (Cetindamar et al., 2009), which can thus be incorporated into the service science understanding of resource integration (Lusch & Nambisan, 2015). To integrate a management orientation into the service systems perspective, the developed DIGITALISS method combines TM and service innovation to an integrated method which parallelizes both processes. The reciprocal method alternates TM process steps with service innovation activities of service systems and unifies two paradigms of importance in the management of digitization-enabled innovation in service systems.

For management, the combination of TM and service innovation can also mean the breaking with existing structures in companies, as shown in study 3. The method then requires a cross-departmental approach and can lead to more intensive exchange and synergy potential within organizations.

Furthermore, the start of digitization-enabled innovation is often difficult for management and – as discussed previously – is often postponed. For management, the development of new digitization-enabled value propositions can be a starting point in this context. Study 4 identified the relevant components of digitization-enabled value propositions in service systems. By tailoring these components to a structured approach with consecutive steps, the designed physical and digital tool ($V^{di}P$-developer) supports the structured development of these value propositions. A broad application of the $V^{di}P$-developer has distinguished its fit in the early stages of digitization-enabled innovation activities. The tool is thus located under the DIGITALISS method and supports the first two activities of service innovation "Discover" and "Define". An application of the $V^{di}P$-developer therefore supports organizations in the conception of the service and at the same time in the conception of the necessary service system. By allocating the $V^{di}P$-developer under the DIGITALISS method, the required digital technology is identified and selected for integration. The identification of suitable upstream and downstream activities supports the integration of the tool to organizational practice and also shows further tools for positioning under the DIGITALISS method. The open design of DIGITALISS aims at locating all tools for digitization-enabled innovation currently in use in organizations and is thus intended to organize and support the innovation activities carried out in SMEs.

For organizations undergoing digital change, the targeted use of digital technologies is a key factor in the development of new services and in the development of new unique selling points for their compettitive advantage. With the described multifaceted view on innovation in service systems as well as through the developed method and the designed tool, this research offers management a comprehensive approach to the realization of digitization-enabled innovation with a service systems perspective.

4   Limitations and Future Research

The limitations of the four studies are necessary addendums to the contributions and implications of this research. Besides the limitations already discussed in the last chapter of every study, in the following the limitations of the four studies and of the overall research are once again briefly outlined and used to identify avenues for future research. In all its four empirical studies, this research opens up possibilities for linking up with the respective results and can thus initiate research activities based on these results. As a result of the findings of study 1, the companies in studies 2, 3 and 4 are mainly located in the manufacturing industry. Future research can take up the findings from the studies presented here and transfer them to other contexts and industries, thus testing their relevance and applicability across industries.

This also applies the digital technology focus. Consequently, another avenue for future research is the exploration of further digital technologies and comparative studies with the results of this research. The digital technologies examined here were largely oriented towards the field of digital platforms and industrial clouds for their realization. Further research projects could follow up here and accompany additional digital technologies, for example technologies identified in study 1, in their integration. The reconfigurations of the service systems could then be compared with the insights gained in this research, which on the one hand would examine their generalizability and emphasize their unique characteristics. As discussed, there is currently no consensus in the literature on the role of digital technologies as operant and/or operant resources (Akaka & Vargo, 2014; Lusch & Nambisan, 2015), which makes comparative research with other resource integration for the purpose of service innovation appear promising.

This research combines the paradigms of TM and service science and thus serves the needs of management research and research on service systems and service innovation. The decision for TM as the applied management discipline was derived from theory, the characteristics of TM and the empirical results of this research in the previous studies. Nevertheless, there are other management disciplines that promise the overcoming of current challenges by their application. In this context, future research should focus on the connection of other management fields with service innovation in complex service systems, as already outlined by Barile and Polese (2010). Study 2 provides a first approach by empirically identifying areas in which managers need extra support and by underpinning these with concrete management fields. Future research can follow up here.

The initiated connection of service science and management (Daim et al., 2010) is promoted with the contribution of a method and a tool in this reasoning and advanced by adding the neglected subject of digitization to the field. The focus of this research was the development and prototypical application of artifacts. Cross-company applications and a broad implementation of the method and the tool were not part of the objectives. The use of the designed artifacts in further fields of application as well as design-oriented studies for the extension of the tool pool are possible avenues for future research. The developed DIGITALISS method represents a further element of service science and in particular of research on service systems. For the placement of the method into service systems research, this research reinforces the research opportunity 1 of Frost and Lyons (2017), who see a major gap to be filled by further empirical studies in collecting the value of different service systems methods (p. 224). Accordingly, the application of DIGITALISS and also the application of the $V^{di}P$-developer in combination with other methods and tools in future empirical studies represents a promising research avenue. In addition, future research projects should design further tools for positioning under the DIGITALISS method. In particular, the financial component was not considered in this research, but represents an important perspective for future research activities and tool development due to its importance for management.

Finally, the meso perspective chosen for this research represents a limitation. The service systems perspective was applied to organizations and their service systems. Thus, the consideration of macroeconomic impacts of digitization from a macro perspective as well as the examination of the effects on individuals from a micro perspective remains the task of future research projects.

5   Final Consideration

The entire work of this research was motivated by the question of how companies can benefit from the changes brought about by digitization. In particular, digital technologies sprout up from the ground as almost infinite offerings and provide companies with ever new opportunities. Many companies feel more and more overwhelmed and are increasingly uncertain about future decisions. The main motives of this research were to better understand this situation on the one hand and to provide targeted support based on this understanding on the other hand. Companies need supportive guidance to identify, select and introduce digital technologies in a targeted manner and to be clear in advance about the planned value. The desired innovation and planned service innovation should be linked to technology integration at an early stage. In this spirit, this research explores the research question: *How can organizations manage the use of new digital technologies for digitization-enabled innovation in service systems?*

To this end, this research consists of two major steps. First, digitization-enabled innovation was analyzed and their respective roots revealed. Subsequently, the management of digitization-enabled innovation was supported by a method and a tool as results of design oriented approaches. The service systems perspective, which underlies the entire research, has been strengthened by considering the digitization-enabled innovation from the three service systems core elements – technology, actor and information – and by focusing in the tool design on value propositions which form service systems and constitute a starting point in service innovation. On the one hand, the analysis was led by the elements of service systems and structured accordingly. On the other hand, the integration of the service systems perspective into the designed artefacts has promoted the operationalization of service systems and thus service science.

Moreover, in order to achieve the objective of realizing digitization-enabled innovation, the management-oriented view and service science were brought together. Thus a parallelization of TM and service innovation was accelerated and brought together in one method. By combining the two paradigms, new perspectives were brought into research, but also into organizational practice. The development of digitization-enabled value proposition was supported by a tool which can be applied both digitally and physically. These two artifacts support the actors who are crucial in the context of digitization-enabled innovation, namely human agents.

Particularly in SMEs, the pressure in the course of digitization is high and due to scarce resources and risk aversion, decisions in this field are often postponed. The results of this research support the development of own digitization-enabled innovations and thus avoid the simple copying of solutions of others – for example competitors. The innovations developed in-house are assumed to be better tailored to the respective companies and the intended service innovation and value increase. The results of this research, and above all the DIGITALISS method and the $V^{di}P$-developer, are thus accelerating the development of own digitization-enabled innovation and are aimed at strengthening what has made SMEs the decisive business form in Germany, the development of company-specific unique solutions which represent the unique selling propositions and competitive advantages of SMEs.

References

Agarwal, R., & Selen, W. (2011). An Integrated View of Service Innovation in Service Networks (pp. 253–273). In *Service systems implementation*. Boston, USA: Springer.

Akaka, M. A., & Vargo, S. L. (2014). Technology as an operant resource in service (eco)systems. *Information Systems and E-Business Management, 12*(3), 367–384.

Alam, I., & Perry, C. (2002). A customer-oriented new service development process. *Journal of services Marketing, 16*(6), 515–534.

Alshamaila, Y., Papagiannidis, S., & Li, F. (2013). Cloud computing adoption by SMEs in the north east of England: A multi-perspective framework. *Journal of Enterprise Information Management, 26*(3), 250–275.

Alter, S. (2013). Value Blueprint and Service Design Space for Facilitating Value Creation Value Blueprint and Service Design Space for Facilitating Value Creation. In *Americas Conference on Information System (AMCIS) 2013 Proceedings*, 1–10.

Amit, R., & Han, X. (2017). Value Creation through Novel Resource Configurations in a Digitally Enabled World. *Strategic Entrepreneurship Journal, 11*(3), 228–242.

Amit, R., & Zott, C. (2012). Creating Value Through Business Model Innovation. *MIT Sloan Management Review, 53*(3), 41–49.

Anderson, J. C., Narus, J. A., & Van Rossum, W. (2006). Customer value propositions in business markets. *Harvard business review, 84*, 1–4.

Arthur, W. B. (2009). The Nature of Technology. What It Is it and How It Evolves. New York, USA: Simon and Schuster.

Baden-Fuller, C., & Haefliger, S. (2013). Business Models and Technological Innovation. *Long Range Planning, 46*(6), 419–426.

Baines, T., Ziaee Bigdeli, A., Bustinza, O. F., Shi, V. G., Baldwin, J., & Ridgway, K. (2016). Servitization: revisiting the state-of-the-art and research priorities. *International Journal of Operations and Production Management, 37*(2), 256–278.

Ballantyne, D. (2003). A relationship-mediated theory of internal marketing. *European Journal of Marketing, 37*(9), 1242–1260.

Barile, S., & Polese, F. (2010). Smart Service Systems and Viable Service Systems: Applying Systems Theory to Service Science. *Service Science, 2*(1–2), 21–40.

Barnes, C., Blake, H., & Pinder, D. (2009). *Creating and Delivering Your Value Proposition: Managing Customer Experience for Profit.* London and Philadelphia, England and USA: Kogan Page Publishers.

Barras, R. (1986). Towards a theory of innovation in services. *Research Policy, 15*(4), 161–173.

Barrett, M., Davidson, E., Fayard, A.-L., Vargo, S. L., & Yoo, Y. (2012). Being Innovative about Service Innovation: Service, Design, Digitalization. In *International Conference on Information Systems (ICIS) 2012 Proceedings*, 1–22.

Barrett, M., Davidson, E., Prabhu, J., & Vargo, S. L. (2015). Service innovation in the digital age: Key contributions and future directions. *MIS Quarterly, 39*(1), 135–154.

Beloglazov, A., Banerjee, D., Hartmann, A., & Buyya, R. (2015). Improving Productivity in Design and Development of Information Technology (IT) Service Delivery Simulation Models. *Journal of Service Research, 18*(1), 75–89.

Benkenstein, M., Bruhn, M., Büttgen, M., Hipp, C., Matzner, M., & Nerdinger, F. W. (2017). Topics for Service Management Research-A European Perspective. *SMR-Journal of Service Management Research, 1*(1), 4–21.

Bettencourt, L. (2010). *Service innovation: How to go from customer needs to breakthrough services.* New York, USA: McGraw Hill Professional.

Beverungen, D., Lüttenberg, H., & Wolf, V. (2018). Recombinant Service Systems Engineering. *Business & Information Systems Engineering*, 1–15.

Beverungen, D., Matzner, M., & Janiesch, C. (2017). Information systems for smart services. *Information Systems and E-Business Management, 15*(4), 781–787.

Beverungen, D., Müller, O., Matzner, M., Mendling, J., & vom Brocke, J. (2017). Conceptualizing smart service systems. *Electronic Markets*, 1–12.

Bhalla, S. K. (1987). The Effective Management of Technology – A Challenge for Corporations. Columbus, USA: Battelle Press.

Bitner, M. J., Zeithaml, V. A., & Gremler, D. D. (2010). Technology's Impact on the Gaps Model of Service Quality. In P. P. Maglio, J. Spohrer, & C. A. Kieliszewski (Eds.), *Handbook of Service Science* (pp. 197–218). Boston, USA: Springer.

Bleicher, J., & Stanley, H. (2016). Digitization as a catalyst for business model innovation a three-step approach to facilitating economic success. *Journal of Business Management*, (12), 62–71.

BMWi. (2018). Wirtschaftsmotor Mittelstand Zahlen und Fakten zu den deutschen KMU. Received from: https://www.bmwi.de/Redaktion/DE/Publikationen/Mittelstand/wirtschaftsmotor-mittelstand-zahlen-und-fakten-zu-den-deutschen-kmu.html.

Böhm, M., Müller, S., Krcmar, H., & Welpe, I. (2018). Auswirkungen der digitalen Transformation auf den Wettbewerb. In *Digitale Transformation* (pp. 35–47). Wiesbaden, Germany, Springer Gabler.

Böhmann, T., Leimeister, J. M., & Möslein, K. (2018). The New Fontiers of Service Systems Engineering. *Business & Information Systems Engineering, 1–3*.

Böhmann, T., Leimeister, J. M., & Möslein, K. M. (2014). Service Systems Engineering. *Business & Information Systems Engineering, 6(2)*, 73–79.

Bowen, G. A. (2009). Document analysis as a qualitative research method. *Qualitative research journal, 9(2)*, 27–40.

Breidbach, C. F., Antons, D., & Salge, T. O. (2016). Seamless Service? On the Role and Impact of Service Orchestrators in Human-Centered Service Systems. *Journal of Service Research, 19(4)*, 458–476.

Breidbach, C. F., Kolb, D. G., & Srinivasan, A. (2013). Connectivity in Service Systems. *Journal of Service Research, 16(3)*, 428–441.

Breidbach, C. F., & Maglio, P. P. (2015). A Service Science perspective on the role of ICT in Service Innovation. In *European Conference on Information Systems (ECIS) 2015 Proceedings, 1–9*.

Breidbach, C. F., & Maglio, P. P. (2016). Technology-enabled value co-creation: An empirical analysis of actors, resources, and practices. *Industrial Marketing Management, 56*, 73–85.

Breidbach, C. F., Smith, P., & Callagher, L. J. (2013). Advancing innovation in professional service firms: Insights from the service-dominant logic. *Service Science, 5(3)*, 263–275.

Brosius, H.-B., Haas, A., & Koschel, F. (2016). Inhaltsanalyse I: Grundlagen. In *Methoden der empirischen Kommunikationsforschung* (pp. 137–152). Wiesbaden, Germany: Verlag für Sozialwissenschaften.

Bryman, A. (2012). *Social research methods*. Oxford, Englad: Oxford University Press.

Bullinger, H.-J. (2002). *Technologiemanagement*. Berlin and Heidelberg, Germany: Springer.

Bullinger, H.-J., Fähnrich, K.-P., & Meiren, T. (2003). Service engineering—methodical development of new service products. *International Journal of Production Economics, 85(3)*, 275–287.

Calza, F., Gaeta, M., Loia, V., Orciuoli, F., Piciocchi, P., Rarità, L., Spohrer, J., &

Tommasetti, A. (2015). Fuzzy Consensus Model for Governance in Smart Service Systems. *Procedia Manufacturing, 3*, 3567–3574.

Carlborg, P., Kindström, D., & Kowalkowski, C. (2014). The evolution of service innovation research: A critical review and synthesis. *Service Industries Journal, 34*(5), 373–398.

Cetindamar, D., Phaal, R., & Probert, D. (2009). Understanding technology management as a dynamic capability: A framework for technology management activities. *Technovation, 29*(4), 237–246.

Cetindamar, D., Phaal, R., & Probert, D. (2016). *Technology management: activities and tools*. London, England: Palgrave.

Chandler, J. D., & Lusch, R. F. (2015). Service Systems: A Broadened Framework and Research Agenda on Value Propositions, Engagement, and Service Experience. *Journal of Service Research, 18*(1), 6–22.

Chandler, J. D., & Vargo, S. L. (2011). Contextualization and value-in-context: How context frames exchange. *Marketing Theory, 11*(1), 35–49.

Chang, C. M. (2010). *Service systems management and engineering: creating strategic differentiation and operational excellence*. New Jersey, USA: John Wiley & Sons.

Chesbrough, H., & Spohrer, J. (2006). A research manifesto for services science. *Communications of the ACM, 49*(7), 35–40.

Corbin, J., & Strauss, A. (1990). Grounded Theory Research: Processes, Canons, and Evaluative Criteria. *Qualitative Sociology, 19*(6), 418–427.

Coreynen, W., Matthyssens, P., & Van Bockhaven, W. (2017). Boosting servitization through digitization: Pathways and dynamic resource configurations for manufacturers. *Industrial Marketing Management, 60*, 42–53.

Cortimiglia, M. N., Ghezzi, A., & Frank, A. G. (2016). Business model innovation and strategy making nexus: evidence from a cross-industry mixed-methods study. *R&D Management, 46*(3), 414–432.

Cronin, K., Midgley, G., & Jackson, L. S. (2014). Issues Mapping: A problem structuring method for addressing science and technology conflicts. *European Journal of Operational Research, 233*(1), 145–158.

Cusumano, M. A. (2012). Can services and platform thinking help the U.S. Postal Service? *Communications of the ACM, 55*(4), 21–23.

Daim, T. U., Jetter, A., Demirkan, H., & Maglio, P. P. (2010). Perspective: Technology

Management in the Service Sector. *International Journal of Services, Technology and Management, 13*(1–2), 3–19.

Davis, M. M., Spohrer, J. C., & Maglio, P. P. (2011). Guest editorial: How technology is changing the design and delivery of services. *Operations Management Research, 4*(1–2), 1–5.

de Reuver, M., Sørensen, C., & Basole, R. C. (2018). The digital platform: a research agenda. *Journal of Information Technology, 33*(2), 124–135.

Demirkan, H., Hp, C. B., Spohrer, J., Rayes, A., Don, C., & Cisco, A. (2015). Innovations with Smart Service Systems: Analytics, Big Data, Cognitive Assistance, and the Internet of Everything. *Communications of the Association for Information Systems, 37*(1), 733–752.

Demirkan, H., Spohrer, J. C., & Welser, J. J. (2016). Digital Innovation and Strategic Transformation. *IT Professional, 18*(6), 14–18.

Demirkan, H., Spohrer, J., & Krishna, V. (2011). *Service systems implementation*. New York, USA: Springer Science+Business Media.

Den Hertog, P., Van Der Aa, W., & De Jong, M. W. (2010). Capabilities for managing service innovation: towards a conceptual framework. *Journal of Service Management, 21*(6), 490–514.

Design Council. (2013). Design methods for developing services. In U. Davies & K. Wilson (Eds.), *An introduction to service design and a selection of service design tools*, 1–23.

Dodgson, M., Gann, D., & Salter, A. J. (2008). *The management of technological innovation : strategy and practice*. Oxford, England: Oxford University Press.

Dubois, A., & Gadde, L.-E. E. (2002). Systematic combining: An abductive approach to case research. *Journal of Business Research, 55*(7), 553–560.

Edvardsson, B., Meiren, T., Schäfer, A., & Witell, L. (2013). Having a strategy for new service development – does it really matter? *Journal of Service Management, 24*(1), 25–44.

Eisenhardt, K. M. (1989). Building Theories from Case Study Research. *Academy of Management Review, 14*(4), 532–550.

Eisenhardt, K. M., & Graebner, M. E. (2007). Theory Building from Cases: Oppurtinities and Challanges. *The Academy of Management Journal, 50*(1), 25–32.

Essén, A. (2009). The emergence of technology-based service systems: A case study of a telehealth project in Sweden. *Journal of Service Management, 20*(1), 98–121.

Falkner, E. M., & Hiebl, M. R. W. (2015). Risk management in SMEs: a systematic review of available evidence. *The Journal of Risk Finance, 16*(2), 122–144.

Flick, U. (2004). Zur Qualität qualitativer Forschung − Diskurse und Ansätze. In *Qualitative Datenanalyse: computergestützt* (pp. 43–63). Wiesbaden, Germany: Verlag für Sozialwissenschaften.

Forlizzi, J., Zimmerman, J., & Evenson, S. (2008). Crafting a Place for Interaction Design Research in HCI. *Design Issues, 24*(3), 19–29.

Frost, R., & Lyons, K. (2017). Service Systems Analysis Methods and Components: A Systematic Literature Review. *Service Science, 9*(3), 219–234.

Frow, P., McColl-Kennedy, J. R., Hilton, T., Davidson, A., Payne, A., & Brozovic, D. (2014). Value propositions: A service ecosystems perspective. *Marketing Theory, 14*(3), 327–351.

Frow, P., Nenonen, S., Payne, A., & Storbacka, K. (2015). Managing Co-creation Design: A Strategic Approach to Innovation. *British Journal of Management, 26*(3), 463–483.

Frow, P., & Payne, A. (2011). A stakeholder perspective of the value proposition concept. *European Journal of Marketing, 45*(1/2), 223–240.

Fundación Cotec para la Innovación Tecnológica. (1998). *Temaguide: a guide to technology management and innovation for companies.* Madrid, Spain: Cotec.

Glückler, J., & Hammer, I. (2011). A pragmatic service typology: capturing the distinctive dynamics of services in time and space. *The Service Industries Journal, 31*(6), 941–957.

Golnam, A., Viswanathan, V., Moser, C. I., Ritala, P., & Wegmann, A. (2013). Designing value-oriented service systems by value map. In *International Symposium on Business Modeling and Software Design* (pp. 150–173). Cham, Switzerland: Springer.

Gregor, S., & Hevner, A. R. (2013). Positioning and presenting design science research for maximum impact. *MIS Quarterly, 37*(2), 337–355.

Gregory, M. J. (1995). Technology Management: A Process Approach. *Proceedings of the Institution of Mechanical Engineers, Part B: Journal of Engineering Manufacture, 209*(5), 347–356.

Grenha Teixeira, J., Patricio, L., Huang, K.-H., Fisk, R. P., Nobrega, L., & Constantine, L. (2017). The MINDS Method: Integrating Management and Interaction Design Perspectives for Service Design. *Journal of Service Research, 20*(3), 240–258.

Grove, S.J. and Fisk, R.P. (1992). Observational Data Collection Methods for Services Marketing: An Overview, *Journal of the Academy of Marketing Science*, 20 (3), 217–224.

Hammer, M. (2019). Digitization Perspective: Impact of Digital Technologies in Manufacturing. In *Management Approach for Resource-Productive Operations* (pp. 27–68). Wiesbaden, Germany: Springer Gabler.

Hartmann, P. M., Zaki, M., Feldmann, N., & Neely, A. (2014). Big Data for Big Business? A Taxonomy of Data-driven Business Models used by Start-up Firms. *Cambridge Service Alliance Whitepaper*, 1–29.

Hauschildt, J. (2004). *Innovationsmanagement* [Management of innovation], 3., völlig überarbeitete und erweiterte Aufl. München, Germany: Vahlen.

Helm, R., & Graf, Y. (2018). A capabilities-based service development process for industrial manufacturers. *International Journal of Knowledge Management Studies*, 9(1), 85–102.

Henfridsson, O., & Bygstad, B. (2013). The Generative Mechanisms of Digital Infrastructure Evolution. *MIS Quarterly*, 37(3), 907–931.

Hevner, A. R., March, S. T., Park, J., & Ram, S. (2004). Design Science in Information Systems Research. *Design Science in IS Research MIS Quarterly*, 28(1), 75–105.

Höckmayr, B., & Roth, A. (2017). Design of a Method for Service Systems Engineering in the Digital Age. In *International Conference on Information Systems (ICIS) 2017 Proceedings*, 1–23.

Hungenberg, H. (2014). *Strategisches Management in Unternehmen*. Wiesbaden, Germany: Springer Gabler.

Johnson, M. W., Christensen, C. M., & Kagermann, H. (2008). Reinventing your business model. *Harvard Business Review*, 86(12), 59–68.

Johnson, S. P., Menor, L. J., Roth, A. V., & Chase, R. B. (2000). A Critical Evaluation of the New Service Development Process: Integrating Service Innovation and Service Design. In *New Service Development: Creating Memorable Experiences* (pp. 1–32). Thousand Oaks, California, USA: Sage Publications Ltd.

Kagermann, H. (2015). Change Through Digitization—Value Creation in the Age of Industry 4.0. In *Management of Permanent Change* (pp. 23–45). Wiesbaden, Germany: Springer Fachmedien.

Kelly, D., & Storey, C. (2000). New service development: initiation strategies. *International Journal of Service Industry Management*, 11(1), 45–63.

Kieliszewski, C. A., Maglio, P. P., & Cefkin, M. (2012). On modeling value constellations to understand complex service system interactions. *European Management Journal, 30*(5), 438–450.

Kimbell, L. (2015). *The Service Innovation Handbook: Action-Oriented Creative Thinking Toolkit for Service Organizations*. Amsterdam, Netherlands: BIS Publishers.

Kindström, D., & Kowalkowski, C. (2014). Service innovation in product-centric firms: a multidimensional business model perspective. *Journal of Business & Industrial Marketing, 29*(2), 96–111.

Kindström, D., Kowalkowski, C., & Sandberg, E. (2013). Enabling service innovation: A dynamic capabilities approach. *Journal of Business Research, 66*(8), 1063–1073.

King, N., & Horrocks, C. (2010). *Interviews in qualitative research*. London, England: Sage Publications Ltd.

Kleinschmidt, S., Peters, C., & Leimeister, J. M. (2016). ICT-enabled service innovation in human-centered service systems: A systematic literature review. In *International Conference on Information Systems (ICIS) 2016 Proceesings*, 1–18.

Kocaoglu, D. F., Daim, T. U., & Jetter, A. J. (2008). Defining the Research Agenda: Technology Management as a Contributor to Service Sciences, Management and Engineering. In *Service Science, Management and Engineering Education for the 21st Century* (pp. 55–60). Boston, USA: Springer.

Kowalkowski, C., Witell, L., & Gustafsson, A. (2013). Any way goes: Identifying value constellations for service infusion in SMEs. *Industrial Marketing Management, 42*(1), 18–30.

Kwan, S. K., & Hottum, P. (2014). Maintaining Consistent Customer Experience in Service System Networks. *Service Science, 6*(2), 136–147.

Le, S., Dong, H., Hussain, F. K., Hussain, O. K., & Chang, E. (2014). Cloud service selection: State-of-the-art and future research directions. *Journal of Network and Computer Applications, 45*, 1–17.

Lee, H. (2015). Uncovering the multidisciplinary nature of technology management: Journal citation network analysis. *Scientometrics, 102*(1), 51–75.

Legner, C., Eymann, T., Hess, T., Matt, C., Böhmann, T., Drews, P., Mädche, A., Urbach, N., & Ahlemann, F. (2017). Digitalization: Opportunity and Challenge for the Business and Information Systems Engineering Community. *Business & Information Systems Engineering, 59*(4), 301–308.

Levin, D. Z., & Barnard, H. (2008). Technology management routines that matter to technology managers. *International Journal of Technology Management, 41*(1-2), 22–37.

Leyh, C., & Bley, K. (2016). Digitalisierung: Chance oder Risiko für den deutschen Mittelstand? – Eine Studie ausgewählter Unternehmen. *HMD Praxis Der Wirtschaftsinformatik, 53*(1), 29–41.

Lusch, R. F., & Nambisan, S. (2015). Service Innovation: A Service-Dominant Logic Perspective. *MIS Quarterly, 39*(1), 155–175.

Lusch, R. F., Vargo, S. L., & Gustafsson, A. (2016). Fostering a trans-disciplinary perspectives of service ecosystems. *Journal of Business Research, 69*(8), 2957–2963.

Lusch, R. F., Vargo, S. L., & O'Brien, M. (2007). Competing through service: Insights from service-dominant logic. *Journal of Retailing, 83*(1), 5–18.

Lyons, K., & Tracy, S. (2013). Characterizing organizations as service systems. *Human Factors and Ergonomics in Manufacturing & Service Industries, 23*(1), 19–27.

Maglio, P. P. (2014). Editorial Column—Smart Service Systems. *Service Science, 6*(1), i–ii.

Maglio, P. P. (2015). Editorial—Smart service systems, human-centered service systems, and the mission of service science. *Service Science, 7*(2), ii–iii.

Maglio, P. P., & Breidbach, C. F. (2014). Service science: toward systematic service system innovation. In *Bridging Data and Decisions* (pp. 161-170). Catonsville, USA: INFORMS.

Maglio, P. P., Kwan, S. K., & Spohrer, J. (2015). Toward a Research Agenda for Human-Centered Service System Innovation. *Service Science, 7*(1), 1–10.

Maglio, P. P., & Lim, C.-H. (2016). Innovation and Big Data in Smart Service Systems. *Journal of Innovation Management, 4*(1), 11–21.

Maglio, P. P., & Spohrer, J. (2008). Fundamentals of service science. *Journal of the Academy of Marketing Science, 36*(1), 18–20.

Maglio, P. P., & Spohrer, J. (2013). A service science perspective on business model innovation. *Industrial Marketing Management, 42*(5), 665–670.

Maglio, P. P., Srinivasan, S., Kreulen, J. T., & Spohrer, J. (2006). Service systems, service scientists, SSME, and innovation. *Communications of the ACM, 49*(7), 81–85.

Maglio, P. P., Vargo, S. L., Caswell, N., & Spohrer, J. (2009). The service system is the basic abstraction of service science. *Information Systems and e-business*

Management, 7(4), 395–406.

Matt, C., Hess, T., & Benlian, A. (2015). Digital transformation strategies. *Business & Information Systems Engineering*, 57(5), 339–343.

Mayring, P. (2015). Qualitative Content Analysis: Theoretical Background and Procedures. In *Approaches to qualitative research in mathematics education* (pp. 365–380). Dordrecht, Netherlands: Springer.

Medina-Borja, A. (2015). Editorial Column — Smart Things as Service Providers: A Call for Convergence of Disciplines to Build a Research Agenda for the Service Systems of the Future. *Service Science*, 7(1), ii–v.

Miles, I. (2007). Research and development (R&D) beyond manufacturing: the strange case of services R&D. *R&D Management*, 37(3), 249–268.

Miles, M. B., & Huberman, A. M. (1994). *Qualitative data analysis : an expanded sourcebook*. Thousand Oaks, California, USA: Sage Publications Ltd.

Miles, M. B., Huberman, A. M., & Saldaña, J. (2013). *Qualitative data analysis : a methods sourcebook*. Thousand Oaks, California, USA: Sage Publications Ltd.

Moeller, S. (2010). Characteristics of services - a new approach uncovers their value. *Journal of Services Marketing*, 24(5), 359–368.

Moore, G. A. (2006). *Crossing the Chasm: Marketing and Selling High-Tech Products to Mainstream Customers*. New York, USA: HarperBusiness.

Nambisan, S. (2013). Information Technology and Product/Service Innovation: A Brief Assessment and Some Suggestions for Future Research. *Journal of the Association for Information Systems*, 14(4), 215–226.

National Research Council (US) (1987). *Management of Technology – The Hidden Competitive Advantage*. National Academy Press, Washington.

National Science Foundation. (2014). *Partnerships for Innovation: Building Innovation Capacity (PFI: BIC) Program solicitation NSF*, 14–610.

NCR. (1987). *Management of Technology: The Hidden Competitive Advantage*. Washington, USA: National Academy Press.

Nölte, U. (2009). Determinanten des Informationsgehalts von Managementprognosen – eine empirische Untersuchung anhand der DAX und MDAX-Unternehmen. *Zeitschrift Für Betriebswirtschaft*, 79(11), 1229–1257.

Oesterreich, T. D., & Teuteberg, F. (2016). Understanding the implications of digitisation and automation in the context of Industry 4.0: A triangulation approach and elements of a research agenda for the construction industry. *Computers in Industry, 83,* 121–139.

Ordanini, A., & Parasuraman, A. (2011). Service Innovation Viewed Through a Service-Dominant Logic Lens: A Conceptual Framework and Empirical Analysis. *Journal of Service Research, 14*(1), 3–23.

Osterwalder, A., Pigneur, Y., Bernarda, G., & Smith, A. (2014). *Value Proposition Design: How to Create Products and Services Customers Want.* New Jersey, USA: John Wiley & Sons.

Ostrom, A. L., Bitner, M. J., Brown, S. W., Burkhard, K. A., Goul, M., Smith-Daniels, V., Demirkan, H. & Rabinovich, E. (2010). Moving Forward and Making a Difference: Research Priorities for the Science of Service. *Journal of Service Research, 13*(1), 4–36.

Ostrom, A. L., Parasuraman, A., Bowen, D. E., Patricio, L., & Voss, C. A. (2015). Service Research Priorities in a Rapidly Changing Context. *Journal of Service Research, 18*(2), 127–159.

Paluch, S. (2017). Smart Services – Analyse von strategischen und operativen Auswirkungen. In *Dienstleistungen 4.0* (pp. 161–182). Wiesbaden, Germany: Springer Fachmedien.

Parker, L. D. (2012). Qualitative management accounting research: Assessing deliverables and relevance. *Critical Perspectives on Accounting, 23*(1), 54–70.

Patrício, L., Fisk, R. P., e Cunha, J. F., & Constantine, L. (2011). Multilevel service design: From customer value constellation to service experience blueprinting. *Journal of Service Research, 14*(2), 180–200.

Patton, M. Q. (2002). *Qualitative research and evaluation methods.* Thousand Oaks, California, USA: Sage Publications Ltd.

Pawar, K. S., Beltagui, A., & Riedel, J. C. K. H. (2009). The PSO triangle: designing product, service and organisation to create value. *International Journal of Operations & Production Management, 29*(5), 468–493.

Payne, A., & Frow, P. (2013). Deconstructing the value proposition of an innovation exemplar. *European Journal of Marketing, 48*(1), 237–270.

Payne, A., Frow, P., & Eggert, A. (2017). The customer value proposition: evolution, development, and application in marketing. *Journal of the Academy of Marketing Science, 45*(4), 467–489.

Peffers, K., Tuunanen, T., Rothenberger, M. A., & Chatterjee, S. (2007). A design science research methodology for information systems research. *Journal of Management Information Systems, 24*(3), 45–77.

Perks, H., Gruber, T., & Edvardsson, B. (2012). Co-creation in radical service innovation: a systematic analysis of microlevel processes. *Journal of Product Innovation Management, 29*(6), 935–951.

Peters, C., Maglio, P. P., Badinelli, R., Harmon, R. R., Maull, R., Damsgaard, J., … Cousins, K. (2016). Emerging Digital Frontiers for Service Innovation. *Communications of the Association for Information Systems, 39*(2), 107–118.

Phaal, R., Probert, D. R., & Farrukh, C. J. P. (2004). A framework for supporting the management of technological knowledge. *International Journal of Technology Management, 27*(1), 1–15.

Polese, F., Russo, G., Carrubbo, L. (2009). Service Logic, value co-creation and networks: three dimensions fostering inter-organisational relationships: competitiveness in the boating industry. In *QMOD and Toulon-Verona Conference 2009 Proceedings*, 1–25.

Polese, F., Tommasetti, A., Vesci, M., Carrubbo, L., & Troisi, O. (2016). *Decision-making in smart service systems: A viable systems approach contribution to Service science advances*. In: *International Conference on Exploring Services Science* (pp. 3–14). Cham, Switzerland: Springer.

Priem, R. L., Wenzel, M., & Koch, J. (2018). Demand-side strategy and business models: Putting value creation for consumers center stage. *Long Range Planning, 51*(1), 22–31.

Pruitt, J., & Adlin, T. (2006). Persona Conception and Gestation. In *The Persona Lifecycle* (pp. 162–271). Burlington, USA: Morgan Kaufmann Publishers.

Reymen, I., Berends, H., Oudehand, R., & Stultiëns, R. (2017). Decision making for business model development: a process study of effectuation and causation in new technology-based ventures. *R&D Management, 47*(4), 595–606.

Roberts, E. B. (1988). Managing invention and innovation. *Research Technology Management, 31*(1), 11–29.

Rosemann, M., & vom Brocke, J. (2015). The Six Core Elements of Business Process Management. In *Handbook on Business Process Management 1* (pp. 105–122). Berlin and Heidelberg, Germany: Springer Berlin Heidelberg.

Ross, J. W., Sebastian, I. M., & Beath, C. M. (2017). How to Develop a Great Digital Strategy. *MIT Sloan Management Review, 58*(2), 7–9.

Roth, A., Höckmayr, B., & Möslein, K. (2017). Digitalisierung als Treiber für faktenbasiertes Service-Systems-Engineering. In *Dienstleistungen 4.0* (pp. 185–203). Wiesbaden, Germany: Springer Fachmedien.

Roth, A., & Möslein, K. M. (2014). Produzenten als Dienstleister: Auf dem Weg zu interaktiven hybriden Wertschöpfungssystemen. In *Enterprise -Integration* (pp. 139–151). Berlin and Heidelberg, Germany: Springer.

Rush, H., Bessant, J., & Hobday, M. (2007). Assessing the technological capabilities of firms: Developing a policy tool. *R and D Management, 37*(3), 221–236.

Saam, M., Viet, S., & Schiel, S. (2016). Digitalisierung im Mittelstand: Status Quo, aktuelle Entwicklungen und Herausforderungen. *ZEW - Zentrum Für Europäische Wirtschaftsforschung GmbH*. Received from: https://www.kfw.de/PDF/Download-Center/Konzernthemen/Research/PDF-Dokumente-Studien-und-Materialien/Digitalisierung-im-Mittelstand.pdf.

Sampson, S. E., & Froehle, C. M. (2009). Foundations and Implications of a Proposed Unified Services Theory. *Production and Operations Management, 15*(2), 329–343.

Schüritz, R., Seebacher, S., & Dorner, R. (2017). Capturing Value from Data : Revenue Models for Data-Driven Services. In *50th Hawaii International Conference on System Sciences (HICSS) 2017 Proceedings*, 5348–5357.

Schuh, G., Klappert, S., & Moll, T. (2011). Ordnungsrahmen Technologiemanagement. In *Technologiemanagement* (pp. 11–31). Berlin, Germany: Springer.

Siltaloppi, J., & Vargo, S. L. (2014). Reconciling Resource Integration and Value Propositions -- The Dynamics of Value Co-creation. In *Hawaii International Conference on System Sciences (HICSS) 2014 Proceedings*, 1278–1284.

Skaalsvik, H., & Johannessen, J. A. (2014). Service innovation: Suggesting a typology of service innovation. *Problems and Perspectives in Management, 12*(3), 38–45.

Skålén, P., Gummerus, J., von Koskull, C., & Magnusson, P. R. (2015). Exploring value propositions and service innovation: a service-dominant logic study. *Journal of the Academy of Marketing Science, 43*(2), 137–158.

Spohrer, J. (2017). IBM's service journey: A summary sketch. *Industrial Marketing Management, 60*, 167–172.

Spohrer, J., Maglio, P. P. (2005) Emergence of service science: Services sciences, management, engineering (SSME) as the next frontier in innovation. Presentation, Nordic Service Innovation Workshop, October 25, Oslo, Norway.

Spohrer, J., & Maglio, P. P. (2008). The Emergence of Service Science: Toward

Systematic Service Innovations to Accelerate Co-Creation of Value. *Production and Operations Management, 17*(3), 238–246.

Spohrer, J., Maglio, P. P., Bailey, J., & Gruhl, D. (2007). Steps toward a science of service systems. *Computer, 40*(1), 71–77.

Spohrer, J., Siddike, M. A. K., & Kohda, Y. (2017). Rebuilding Evolution: A Service Science Perspective. In *Hawaii International Conference on System Sciences (HICSS) 2017 Proceedings*, 1663–1672.

Spohrer, J., Vargo, S. L., Caswell, N., & Maglio, P. P. (2008). The Service System is the Basic Abstraction of Service Science. In *Hawaii International Conference on System Sciences (HICSS) 2008 Proceedings*, 1–10.

Spur, G. (1998). Technologie und Management: Zum Selbstverständnis der Technikwissenschaft. München, Germany: Hauser.

Strebel, H. (2007). *Innovations- und Technologiemanagement*, 2.Aufl. Wien, Austria: WUV.

Trigueros-Preciado, S., Pérez-González, D., & Solana-González, P. (2013). Cloud computing in industrial SMEs: Identification of the barriers to its adoption and effects of its application. *Electronic Markets, 23*(2), 105–114.

Tschirky, H., Koruna, S. (1998). *Technologiemanagement – Idee und Praxis*. Zürich, Switzerland: Orell Füssli.

Vajjhala, N. R., & Ramollari, E. (2016). Big Data using Cloud Computing - Opportunities for Small and Medium-sized Enterprises. *European Journal of Economics and Business Studies, 4*(1), 129–137.

Vandermerwe, S., & Rada, J. (1988). Servitization of business: Adding value by adding services. *European Management Journal, 6*(4), 314–324.

Vargo, S. L., & Akaka, M. A. (2009). Service-Dominant Logic as a Foundation for Service Science: Clarifications. *Service Science, 1*(1), 32–41.

Vargo, S. L., & Lusch, R. F. (2004). Evolving to a New Dominant Logic for Marketing. *Journal of Marketing, 68*(1), 1–17.

Vargo, S. L., & Lusch, R. F. (2008a). Service-dominant logic: Continuing the evolution. *Journal of the Academy of Marketing Science, 36*(1), 1–10.

Vargo, S. L., & Lusch, R. F. (2008b). Why "service"? *Journal of the Academy of Marketing Science, 36*(1), 25–38.

Vargo, S. L., & Lusch, R. F. (2011). It's all B2B...and beyond: Toward a systems perspective of the market. *Industrial Marketing Management, 40*(2), 181–187.

Vargo, S. L., & Lusch, R. F. (2017). Service-dominant logic 2025. *International Journal of Research in Marketing, 34*(1), 46–67.

Vargo, S. L., Maglio, P. P., & Akaka, M. A. (2008). On value and value co-creation: A service systems and service logic perspective. *European Management Journal, 26*(3), 145–152.

Vargo, S. L., Wieland, H., & Akaka, M. A. (2015). Innovation through institutionalization: A service ecosystems perspective. *Industrial Marketing Management, 44*, 63–72.

Velu, C., & Jacob, A. (2016). Business model innovation and owner-managers: the moderating role of competition. *R&D Management, 46*(3), 451–463.

Walls, J. G. (2013). Building an Information System Design Theory for Vigilant EIS. *Information Systems Research, 3*(1), 36–59.

Wellensiek, M., Schuh, G., Hacker, P. A., & Saxler, J. (2011). Technologiemanagement. In *Vorschau und Technologiemanagement* (pp. 89–169). Berlin and Heidelberg, Germany: Springer.

Witte, E. (1968). Phasen-Theorem und Organisation komplexer Entscheidungsverläufe. *Zeitschrift für betriebswirtschaftliche Forschung, 20*(10), 625–647.

Wlodarczyk, T. W., Rong, C., & Thorsen, K. A. H. (2009). Industrial Cloud: Toward Inter-enterprise Integration. In *IEEE International Conference on Cloud Computing* (pp. 460–471). Berlin and Heidelberg, Germany: Springer.

Wrona, T. (2006). Fortschritts- und Gütekriterien im Rahmen qualitativer Sozialforschung. In *Fortschritt in den Wirtschafts-wissenschaften. Wissenschaftstheoretische Grundlagen und exemplarische Anwendungen* (pp. 189–216). Wiesbaden, Germany: Gabler.

Wrona, T., & Gunnesch, M. (2016). The one who sees more is more right: how theory enhances the 'repertoire to interpret'in qualitative case study research. *Journal of Business Economics, 86*(7), 723–749.

Yin, R. K. (2009). *Case study research: design and methods* (4. ed.). Thousand Oaks, California, USA: Sage Publications Ltd.

Yin, R. K. (2014). *Case study research: design and methods* (5. ed.). Thousand Oaks, California, USA: Sage Publications Ltd.

Yin, R. K. (2018). *Case study research and applications: design and methods* (6. ed.). Thousand Oaks, California, USA: Sage Publications Ltd.

Yoo, Y., Boland, R. J., Lyytinen, K., & Majchrzak, A. (2012). Organizing for Innovation in the Digitized World. *Organization Science, 23*(5), 1398–1408.

Yoo, Y., Henfridsson, O., & Lyytinen, K. (2010). The New Organizing Logic of Digital Innovation: An Agenda for Information Systems Research. *Information Systems Research, 21*(4), 724–735.

Zahn, E. (1995). *Handbuch Technologiemanagement.* Stuttgart, Germany: Schäffer-Poeschel.

Zolnowski, A., Christiansen, T., & Gudat, J. (2016). Business model transformation patterns of data-driven innovations. In *European Conference on Information Systems (ECIS) 2016 Proceedings*, 1–16.

Zolnowski, A., Weiß, C., & Böhmann, T. (2014). Representing service business models with the service business model canvas - The case of a mobile payment service in the retail industry. In *Proceedings of the Annual Hawaii International Conference on System Sciences (HICSS) 2014 Proceedings*, 718–727.

Annexes

© Springer Fachmedien Wiesbaden GmbH, part of Springer Nature 2020
S. M. Genennig, *Realizing Digitization-Enabled Innovation*, Markt- und
Unternehmensentwicklung Markets and Organisations,
https://doi.org/10.1007/978-3-658-28719-1

Annex A: Related Publications

The research presented in this dissertation was developed over three and a half years and profited from the close collaboration with co-authors and colleagues in the national and international research communities at seminars and conferences. As some parts of this book build unchanged and verbatim on earlier research, this section clarifies sources and outlets.

For two parts of this research, earlier versions have already been published in co-authorship and as earlier versions in a scientific journal (Part VI) and at an international conference (Part IV). In these parts, the findings in this research remained largely unchanged from the previous publications:

Genennig, S. M., Roth A., Jonas J. M., & Möslein K. M. (2018). Value Propositions in Service Systems Enabled by Digital Technology: a Field Based Design Science Approach. *SMR Journal of Service Management Research, 2*(4), 6–21.

Genennig, S. M., Roth A., & Möslein K. M. (2017). The integration of digital technologies into service systems. *RADMA R&D Management Conference*, Leuven, Belgium.

Other parts of this research have been presented in co-authorship and as previous versions at international conferences and profited highly from presentation and discussion. The dissertation builds upon and extends these contributions. This applies for the following articles:

Genennig, S. M., Jonas J. M., & Möslein K. M. (2017). The integration of digital resources into service systems: drivers and challenges. *SOMF 9th Service Operations Management Forum*, Copenhagen, Denmark.

Genennig, S. M., Pauli T., Roth A., & Möslein K. M. (2018). Digitization-Enabled Innovation in Service Systems: An Empirical Analysis of the German MDAX Companies. *EURAM European Academy of Management Annual Conference*, Reykjavik, Iceland.

Genennig, S. M., & Roth A. (2018a). How Digitization is Changing Technology Management for Service Innovation – an Integrated Method. *RESER Annual Conference of the European Association for Research on Service,* Gothenburg, Sweden.

In all cases, the articles co-authored by Kathrin M. Möslein, Angela Roth, Julia M. Jonas and Tobias Pauli are mainly conceptualized by the first author. Also data collection, the analysis of the data, and the interpretation of the results are primarily attributable to the author of this book. However, the co-authors supported through their theoretical and structural guidance and support, as well as through feedback and minor operational activities and played an important role for the quality of the contributions.

Moreover, earlier stages of this research have been presented and discussed in the following doctoral colloquia for external feedback and discussion:

Genennig, S. M. (2018a). Service Systems Management: Realizing Digitization-enabled Innovation. *EURAM European Academy of Management Annual Conference Doctoral Colloquium,* Reykjavik, Iceland. Jun 18-19, 2018.

Genennig, S. M., & Roth A. (2018b). Technology Management for Digitization-Enabled Service Innovation – An Integrated Method. *13th Research colloquium "Innovation & Value Creation",* Chemnitz, Germany. Nov 30 – Dec 1, 2018.

Genennig, S. M. (2017). Forming a tool for structured development of digital-technology-enabled value propositions in service systems management. *12th Research colloquium "Innovation & Value Creation",* Hamburg, Germany. Dec 01-02, 2017.

Genennig, S. M. (2016). Service Systems Management – A Digital-Technology Management Framework. *11th Research colloquium "Innovation & Value Creation",* Linz, Austria. Nov 25-26, 2016.

Genennig, S. M., Jonas, J. M., & Möslein, K. M. (2015). Value Creation in Service Systems. *10th Research colloquium "Innovation & Value Creation",* Leipzig, Germany. Nov 27-28, 2015.

Annex B: Companies Listed in the MDAX Index in 2016

	Company	Sector
1	Aareal Bank AG	Banking
2	Airbus SE (former EADS)	Aerospace Manufacturer and Defense
3	Alstria office REIT-AG	Real Estate
4	Aurubis AG	Commodities (Copper)
5	Axel Springer SE	Media
6	Brenntag AG	Trading (Chemicals)
7	Ceconomy	Wholesale and Retail
8	Covestro AG	Chemicals
9	CTS Eventim	Trading
10	Deutsche EuroShop AG	Shopping Centers
11	Deutsche Pfandbriefbank AG	Banking
12	Deutsche Wohnen AG	Real Estate
13	Dürr AG	Automotive
14	Evonik Industries	Chemicals
15	Fielmann	Trading (Ophthalmic optics)
16	Fraport	Airports
17	Fuchs Petrolub SE	Chemicals
18	GEA Group	Machine Building
19	Gerresheimer	Packaging of Medicaments
20	Grand City Properties *(new 2017 / not considered)*	Construction
21	Hannover Rück SE	Insurance
22	Hella KGaA Hueck & Co.	Automotive
23	Hochtief	Construction
24	Hugo Boss	Textiles
25	Innogy SE	Energy
26	Jungheinrich	Machine Building
27	K+S AG	Mining
28	KION Group	Utility Vehicles
29	Krones	Machine Building
30	Lanxess AG	Chemicals
31	LEG Immobilien	Real Estate
32	Leoni	Automotive
33	Metro AG	Wholesale and Retail
34	MTU	Aircraft Engine Manufacturer
35	Norma Group	Joining Techniques
36	Osram	Lighting Technology
37	Rheinmetall	Automotive and Defense
38	RTL Group	Media
39	Salzgitter AG	Steel
40	Schaeffler Technologies AG & Co. KG	Mechanical Engineering
41	Stada Arzneimittel	Pharmaceuticals
42	Steinhoff International Holdings	Furniture
43	Ströer SE & Co. KGaA	Advertising
44	Südzucker	Food Processing and Sugar
45	Symrise	Producer of Flavors and Fragrances
46	TAG	Real Estate
47	Talanx AG	Insurance
48	Uniper SE	Energy
49	Wacker Chemie	Chemicals
50	Zalando SE	E-Commerce
-	*Bilfinger SE *(left in 2017 / part of sample)*	Construction
-	*Rational AG *(left in 2017 / part of sample)*	Kitchen Appliances

Annex C: Screenshots of the MAXQDA File for Document Analysis in Part III

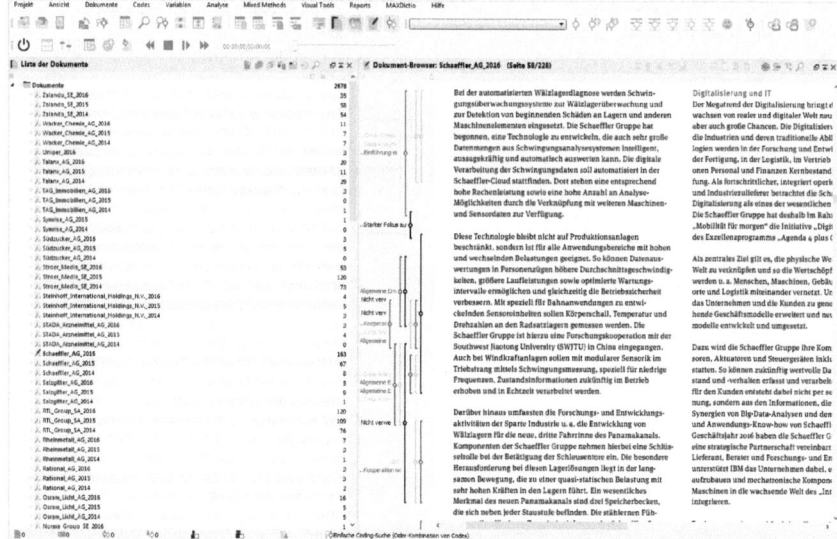

Figure: Example screenshot of the complete file

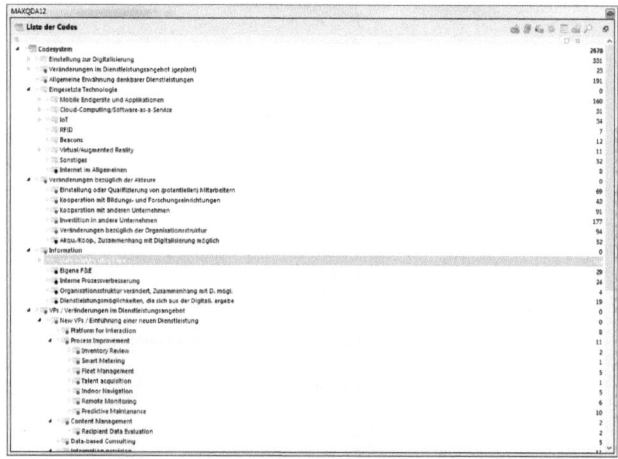

Figure: Example screenshot of the list of codes

Annex D: Mentions per Third Order Category of the Study in Part III

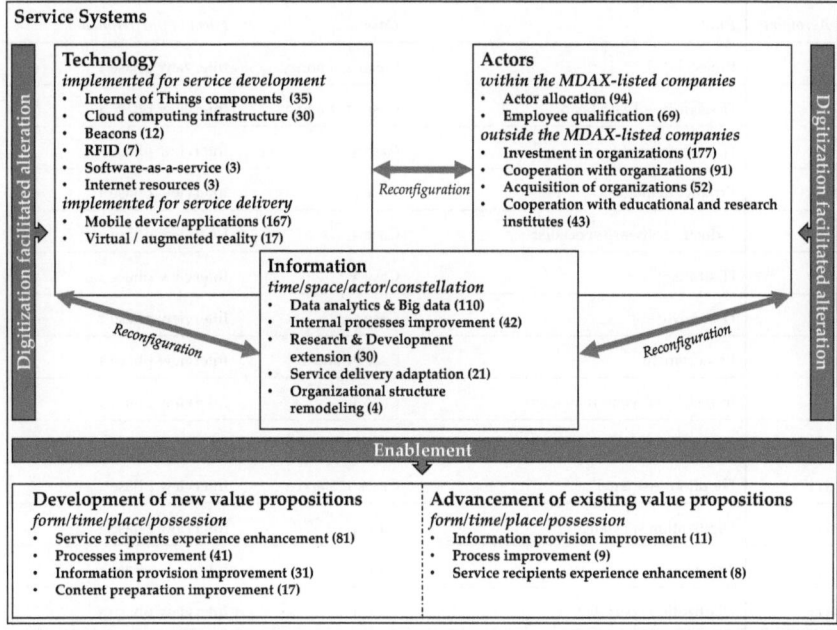

Figure: Digitization related alterations and digitization-enabled innovation in service systems with the number of mentions per third order category (own illustration)

Annex E: Participants of Interviews and Group Discussions Part V

Acronym	Role	Case	Form of participation
i01	Project head	Cases 1, 2 and 3	Interview phase 1
i02	IT security – Team head	Cases 1, 2 and 3	Interview phase 1
i03	IT procurement	Case 3	Interview phase 1
i04	Product manager	Case 3	Interview phase 1
i05	Industry software specialist	Case 3	Interview phase 1
i06	IT strategy	Case 3	Interview phase 1
i07	IT security	Case 3	Interview phase 1
i08	Procurement	Cases 1 and 2	Interview phase 1
i09	Industrial services manager	Case 3	Interview phase 1
i10	Project head	Cases 1, 2 and 3	Interview phase 1
i11	Shopfloor manager	Cases 1, 2 and 3	Interview phase 1
i12	Digitization specialist	Case 4	Interview phase 2
i13	Team head	Case 4	Interview phase 2
i14	Digitization specialist	Case 4	Interview phase 3
i15	Digitization specialist	Case 4	Interview phase 3
d01	Digital officer	Case 4	Group discussion phase 2
d02	Digital officer	Case 4	Group discussion phase 2
d03	Production planning specialist	Case 4	Group discussion phase 2
d04	Specialist manufacturing training	Case 4	Group discussion phase 2
d05	Digitization specialist	Case 4	Group discussion phase 2
d06	Service engineering researcher	Case 4	Group discussion phase 2
d07	Digitization specialist	Case 4	Group discussion phase 3
d08	Digitization specialist	Case 4	Group discussion phase 3
d09	Team head	Case 4	Group discussion phase 3
d10	Digital officer	Case 4	Group discussion phase 3
d11	Service engineering researcher	Case 4	Group discussion phase 3

Annex F: Template for the DIGITALISS Method in German Language

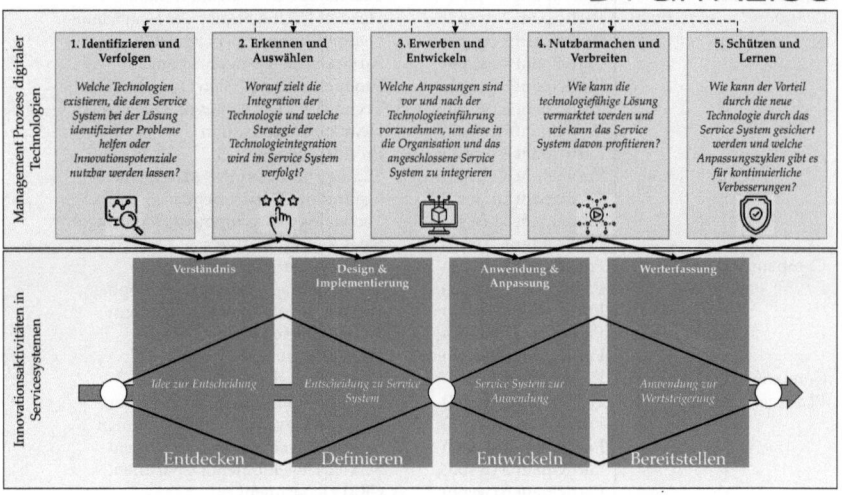

Annex G: Workshop Participants Part VI

Company	Workshop participant	Professional role
Company 1 (c1)	Participant 1 (wsp1)	Technology & Innovation Manager
Component manufacturer	Participant 2 (wsp2)	Head of Digital Strategy & Management
	Participant 3 (wsp3)	Digital Products Department
	Participant 4 (wsp4)	Service Strategy Department
	Participant 5 (wsp5)	Production Innovation Department
	Participant 6 (wsp6)	Technology Development Department
	Participant 7 (wsp7)	Head of IT-Innovation
	Participant 8 (wsp8)	Product Manager
	Participant 9 (wsp9)	Strategy and Business Management
	Participant 10 (wsp10)	Controlling Department
	Participant 11 (wsp11)	Technology Development Department
	Participant 12 (wsp12)	Sales Representative
Company 2 (c2)	Participant 1 (wsp1)	Head of Spare Parts Logistics
System manufacturer	Participant 2 (wsp2)	Senior Manager Service Development
	Participant 3 (wsp3)	Service Development Department
	Participant 4 (wsp4)	Sales Representative
	Participant 5 (wsp5)	CRM Department
Company 3 (c3)	Participant 1 (wsp1)	Head of Service Development
Plant manufacturer	Participant 2 (wsp2)	Head of Maintenance & Spare Parts
	Participant 3 (wsp3)	Business Development Department
	Participant 4 (wsp4)	Service Development Department
	Participant 5 (wsp5)	Service Development Department
	Participant 6 (wsp6)	CRM Department

Annex H: Screenshots of the V^{di}P Application

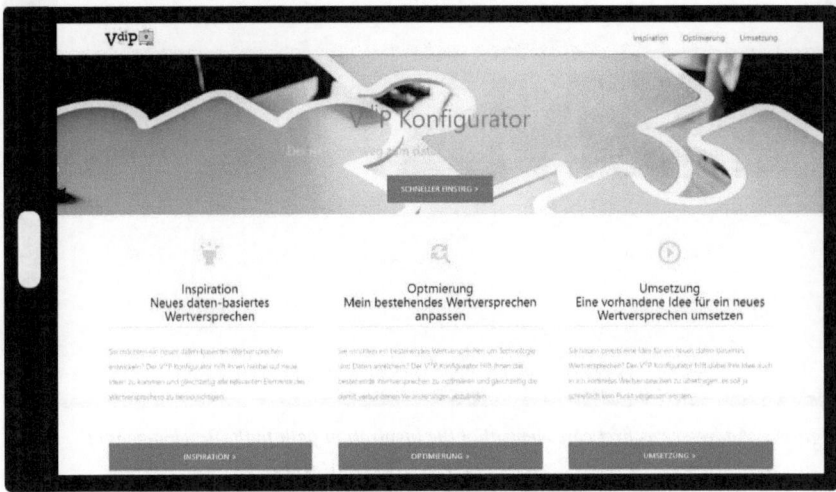

Figure 1: Detail of the landing page of the VdiP Application

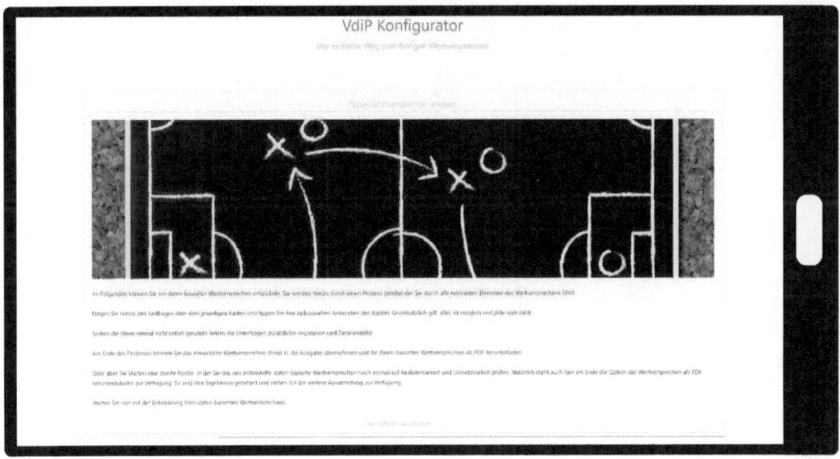

Figure 2: Start page with explanation of the chosen path "Inspiration"

Figure 3: Addressee as first core element of the inspiration path to the development of digitization-enabled value proposition and its design in the VdiP Application

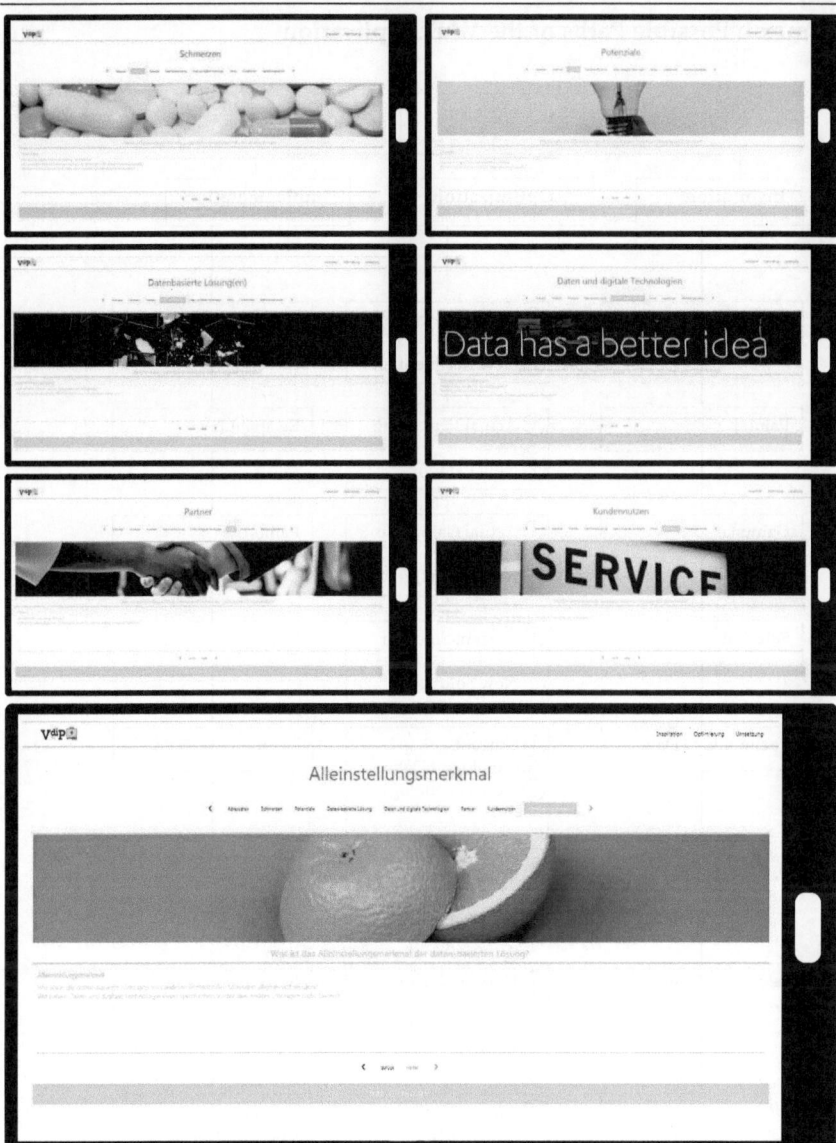

Figure 4: Exemplary selection of steps through the core elements of value propositions in the VdiP Application

Annex I: Possible Paths of the V^{di}P Application

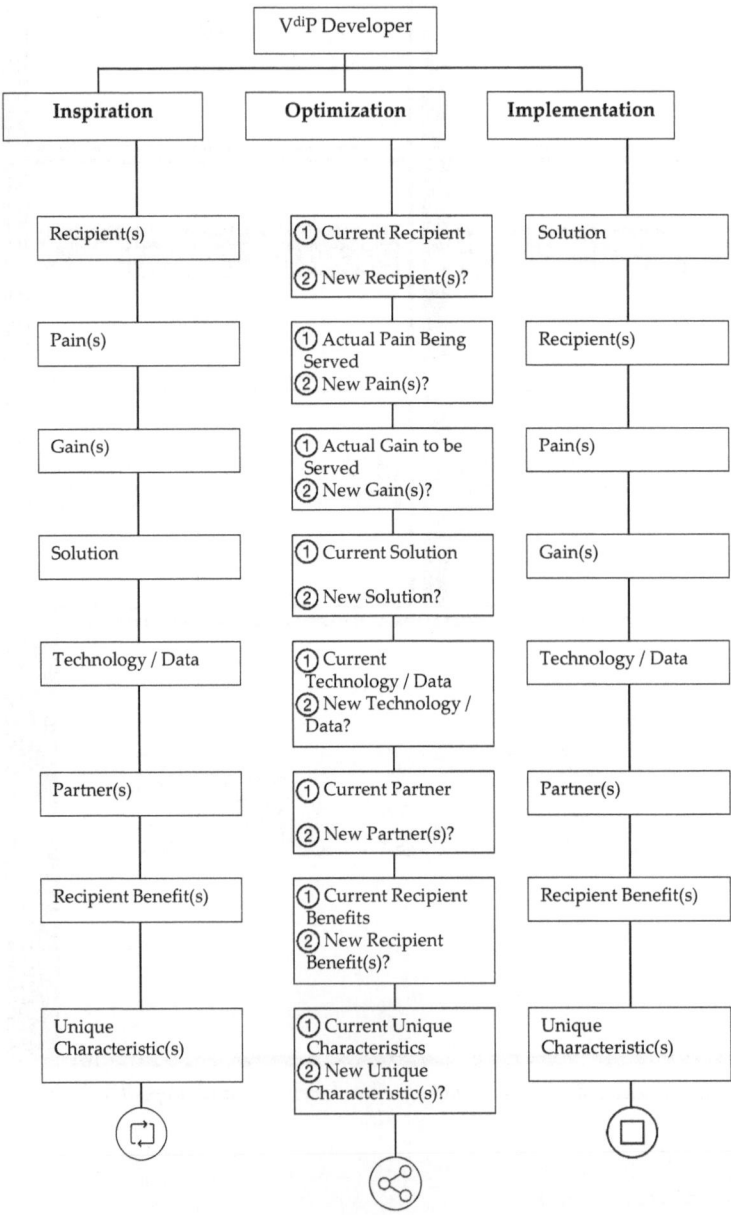

Annex J: Characteristics of the V^diP-Developer

Frameworks	Service orientation	Customer / Recipient focus	Network reflection	Service Systems reflection	Technology reflection	Data reflection	Supports VP development
Buyer Utility Map (Kim & Mauborgne, 2005)	+	++					+
Customer Fulfillment Lifecycle (Hamilton, 2013)	+	++					+
Deconstructing the Value Proposition (Payne & Frow, 2014)	+	++	+	+	+		+
Design Space for Value Facilitation (Alter, 2013)	+	++					+
Needmining (Kuehl, 2016)	++	++				+	+
Value Blueprint (Alter, 2013)	++	++	++	++			++
Valueprop Checklist (Horton, n.d.)	+	++					+
Value-Focused Enterprise Model (Barnes, Blake & Pinder, 2009)	+	++	+				++
Value Map (Osterwalder et al., 2014)	+	++	+	+			+
Value Proposition Builder (Barnes, Blake & Pinder, 2009)	+	++					++
Value Proposition Canvas (Osterwalder et al., 2014)	+	++					++
Value Proposition Framework (Kambil, Ginsberg & Bloch, 1996)	+	++	++				+
Value Stream Discovery (Cooper, Vlaskovits & Ries, 2013)	+	++					+
Value Stream Loop (Rother & Shook, 1999)	++	++					+
Value Stream Mapping (Rother & Shook, 1999)	+	++	++	+	+		+
V^diP-Developer	++	++	++	++	++	++	++

Explanation of the table:

++ fully represented; + partially represented; "*empty*" no consideration.